GENERAL VALLEJO
AND THE ADVENT OF THE AMERICANS

General Vallejo

and the Advent of the Americans

A BIOGRAPHY

Alan Rosenus

Heyday Books / Urion Press

HEYDAY BOOKS
URION PRESS
© 1995, 1999 BY ALAN ROSENUS

Library of Congress Cataloging-in-Publication Data

ROSENUS, ALAN, 1940 –
    [GENERAL M.G. VALLEJO AND THE ADVENT OF THE AMERICANS]
    GENERAL VALLEJO AND THE ADVENT OF THE AMERICANS / ALAN ROSENUS.
        P.   CM.
    ORIGINALLY PUBLISHED: GENERAL M.G. VALLEJO AND THE ADVENT OF THE AMERICANS.
ALBUQUERQUE : UNIVERSITY OF NEW MEXICO PRESS, C1995.
    INCLUDES BIBLIOGRAPHICAL REFERENCES (P.   ) AND INDEX.
    CONTENTS: THE GIFTS OF FORTUNE–THE PIVOTAL YEAR: 1841–THE ADVENT OF THE AMERICANS–A NEW GOVERNOR BRINGS CRISIS–A SMALL WAR HEATS UP–"OJALÁ QUE LO TOMEN LOS AMERICANOS" ("I HOPE THE AMERICANS TAKE IT")–PRELUDE TO REVOLT–"MEN WITH NOTHING TO LOSE"–THE REVOLT BEGINS– ORDEAL ON THE SACRAMENTO–MURDER AND MISDIRECTION–WHAT FRIEND LARKIN WILL DO–A CHANGED MAN–THE CALIFORNIANS RETAKE THE SOUTH–THE SLIP AND SLIDE TRANSITION– CONSEQUENCES.
    ISBN 1-890771-21-X
    1. VALLEJO, MARIANO GUADALUPE, 1807–1890. 2. PIONEERS–CALIFORNIA BIOGRAPHY. 3. MILITARY GOVERNORS—CALIFORNIA BIOGRAPHY. 4. MEXICANS–CALIFORNIA BIOGRAPHY. 5. FRONTIER AND PIONEER LIFE–CALIFORNIA. 6. CALIFORNIA–BIOGRAPHY. I. TITLE.
F864.V2R67 1999
979.4'04'092—DC21
[B]   99-27932
                                                                         CIP
COVER PHOTO: CALIFORNIA STATE LIBRARY, SACRAMENTO, CA
COVER ART: "KORTUM CANYON" BY JOSHUA ADAM, COURTESY OF THE GALLERY ON MAIN STREET, ST. HELENA, CA
COVER DESIGN: REBECCA LEGATES
PRINTING AND BINDING: THOMSON-SHORE, INC., DEXTER, MI

ORDERS, INQUIRIES, AND CORRESPONDENCE SHOULD BE ADDRESSED TO :
HEYDAY BOOKS
P.O. BOX 9145
BERKELEY, CA 94709
(510) 549-3564, FAX (510) 549-1889
HEYDAY@HEYDAYBOOKS.COM
PRINTED IN THE UNITED STATES OF AMERICA
10 9 8 7 6 5 4 3 2

Acknowledgment is made to the following publishers and holders of copyright:

John Woolfenden and Amelie Elkinton, *Cooper.* Copyright 1983 the Boxwood Press. Excerpts reprinted with permission of the publisher.

Thanks to Mr. Robert Minge Brown, son of Madie Brown Emparan, and the conservators of the Estate of Madie Brown Emparan for permission to quote from Madie Brown Emparan's *The Vallejos of California.* Copyright 1968 by Madie Brown Emparan.

In memory of my father and mother

Contents

Illustrations

Acknowledgments

A project that spans the better part of a decade naturally accumulates worthy benefactors to whom a special debt of gratitude is owed. In the early stages of my research, Clyde Arbuckle, Ferol Egan, Colonel Milton F. Hawlsey, Barbara Warner, Tom Lucy, and George Kobayashi made suggestions that later proved to be helpful.

For editorial assistance with the manuscript, I am grateful for the insightful criticisms of Larry Durwood Ball, who reviewed the manuscript for the University of New Mexico Press and provided much-needed direction. Thanks are also due to Louise Shannon, Jan Bellard, Lois Hicks, Richard von Busack, Peter Jodaitis, Ellen Walker, Sam Hernandez, Lou Wynne, Lois Langland, Susan Denison, and Karen Dunn-Haley who provided comments and editorial assistance.

Help with translations was supplied by Margarita Guy, Carol Hanson-Daniels, José Colchado, and Rafael Riquelme.

Numerous institutions afforded invaluable aid, especially the Bancroft Library, where Richard Ogar supplied microfilms and photocopies with unfailing courtesy. My thanks also go to the California State Library, Sacramento; the San Jose Public Library, San Jose; the Huntington Library, San Marino; and the Green Library, Stanford University. Members of the Sonoma Valley Historical Society shared information and provided encouragement, especially James "Beach" Alexander, Betty Stevens, James Vanderbilt, and General Vallejo's great-great-granddaughter, Martha Ann McGettigan. My thanks also go to Zella Pitts, Bob Cannard, and the late Brad Champlin. Of great assistance as well were Eleanor Baker and Toby Bloxam of the Sonoma League for Historic Preservation.

For help with obtaining photographs, duplications, and permissions, I'd like to express my appreciation to the staff of the Department of Parks and Recreation, Sacramento; Betty Stevens of the Sonoma Valley Historical Society; Stanleigh Bry and Gretchen Schneider of the Society of California Pioneers, San Francisco; the staff of the California Room, California State Library, Sacramento; the staff of the Bancroft Library, Berkeley; and James Kern of the Vallejo Naval and Historical Museum, Vallejo.

For patience and persistence extraordinary, my thanks to Carol Minikus, who helped with word processing.

Preface

Popular mythology provides a handful of images to portray California's early past: Father Serra scans heaven for approval while directing the work of dutiful (albeit dispossessed) Indians. James Marshall whoops lustily at the shining nuggets in his gold pan. For General Mariano Guadalupe Vallejo — commandant general of California and director of colonization of the northern frontier — there are few convenient legends to distract us. Definitely a one-of-a-kind individual, he was viewed in his own time as a man "fifty years in advance of his countrymen in intelligence and enterprise" — a leader who possessed "a degree of . . . steadiness almost unknown" in the remote coastal province.[1] In our own century, social historian Bernard DeVoto summed him up as "the most considerable citizen in California," and Richard Dillon noticed that the General's forecasts seemed to reveal a "20/20 vision of the future."[2]

Vallejo's unique qualities were obvious. While most rancheros of the period were tentative entrepreneurs at best — leaving construction and farming jobs to the Indians — he took an active part in improving his wheat fields and vineyards. Vallejo's attitude toward the Indians was also unusual for the time. It is well known that he and his brother Don Salvador Vallejo played a major role in subjugating the Native Americans north of San Francisco Bay and often wreaked havoc in their lives. But Vallejo did not dismiss the Indians as *gandules* (subhuman clowns) as did the majority of his compatriots. Whenever possible he resolved conflicts with them by treaty rather than by war, and the Indian way of life held a permanent fascination for him. He was a close friend of the Suisun Chief Solano and the Miwok Chief Camilo Ynita, often receiving the former at his home as a guest and looking out for Solano's widow long after the chief's death. His respect for formal learning, and his insistence on acquiring reliable information, also set Vallejo apart from most Californians. Hardly a one-dimensional model of virtue, he was rather an alloy of the good and bad. He could be egotistical, vain, and at times autocratic. In the present biography, I make no attempt to sidestep unflattering conclusions about him when events seem to justify such remarks, nor do I inflate his virtues. The fact remains, however, that the American and Mexican frontiers boasted few men who were as articulate, far-seeing, and reasonable as Vallejo. In most cases, he had the instincts to do the right thing at the right time (even if he did not always do it), and his life gave ample proof of his courage.

An inheritor of the Romantic aesthetic, he was not yet in his teens when Spain's colonial empire was being swept from the New World. Political ideas traceable to the Enlightenment and the American Revolution were helping to speed the process, and Latin American nations looked up to the United States as a positive revolutionary example. At the time Mariano Vallejo was born, America's founding fathers were already famous men in California. If Vallejo's countrymen had not actually read the Declaration of Independence, they were aware of the significance of George Washington and Thomas Jefferson, and had more than a vague notion of the political ideals that had brought the American republic into being. When Mexico broke away from Spain, her leaders identified with the U.S. system, and one of the earliest ceremonies of the Mexican constitutional congress was to place a portrait of George Washington in its gallery of heroes.[3] By virtue of circumstances, training, and personal philosophy, Vallejo was extremely partial to American political thought. He was also impressed by the talented, sometimes unpredictable American immigrants — all of whom were trying to get a "leg up" in the province. From the early 1840s on, his desire to make California a part of the United States became his most urgent political goal.

By 1843 it was already obvious that one of the great maritime powers — France, the United States, or England — would eventually make California a protectorate. California's strategic location, its proximity to the Far East, and its *defenselessness* made this outcome a near certainty. Vallejo believed that a tie with the United States would offer California the best opportunities for cultural and economic development. His desire for American annexation came to be his school, his credo, and finally his secret enemy. Prior to the war of conquest, he was a futurist whose herds and lands increased almost exponentially while he imagined ways to bring innovation to the province. After California became a part of the Union, and even after most of the General's property had been transferred into the hands of American mortgage holders, he could still declare that "American Democracy is the Best Democracy." Nevertheless, he knew that no single designation — American, Spaniard, or Californian — adequately characterized him as an individual. But after his misfortunes drew him into a vortex of pain, he became less of a futurist and more of a traditionalist, spending time remembering and valuing the heritage upon which he based his honor as a Hispanic and paterfamilias. "The Wheel of Fortune is very fickle," the impoverished Vallejo would muse, and — referring to his vanished affluence — he would add, "It hit me among the first."[4]

Though I give a somewhat detailed summary of the General's early career in chapter 1, and I later follow the downward trajectory of his fortunes, this book is primarily concerned with the Vallejo of the middle years, who admitted the first wagon train of American immigrants, discouraged California's civil conflicts, found himself at odds with Governor Alvarado, John Sutter, and Captain John Charles Frémont, and who successfully fostered ties with the United States. This was a period during which the allegiances of Americans and Californians underwent constant change. Sometimes it seemed as though not only the players, but the checkers and even the squares on the board were moving. The era saw the influence of Americans increase dramatically — going from negligible to predominant.

A complete study of Vallejo's life would require a two-thousand page book, since from the 1820s on, he affected every California institution, secular and military, political and economic. Therefore, some aspects of his life's story will receive minimal treatment here. For instance, wine-loving residents of the Sonoma and Napa valleys will note the lack of detail regarding Vallejo's career as California's first commercial wine-grower. It is fortunate that his skill was passed in a direct line to Charles Krug, and Vallejo's friendly rivalry with Agoston Haraszthy resulted in many improvements in the quality and technology of California viticulture.[5] A somewhat more complete picture will be given of the mature Vallejo, who almost alone among his generation believed in the conscious creation of culture as a basis for education and growth. His tireless efforts to help Hubert Howe Bancroft preserve both the positive and negative aspects of California's past represented an undertaking to which Sutter, Frémont, Larkin, or even Juan B. Alvarado would have devoted little energy. Despite the limitation of time and space, the reader will see California in the 1840s through Vallejo's eyes, and will become more intimately acquainted with the General than has been possible in previous books.[6]

It should be mentioned that the highest military rank Vallejo attained was that of colonel in the Mexican army. However, after he became Commandant General Vallejo in 1836, he was always referred to by scholars, diplomats, and his compatriots as "the General." I follow this tradition.

General Vallejo
and the Advent of the Americans

THE SCENE OF GENERAL VALLEJO'S ACTIVITIES IN NORTHERN CALIFORNIA FROM 1807–1890

1

The Gifts of Fortune

When God gives, fill your hands.
—Spanish proverb

I

*M*onterey in 1807 was not always an easy place to spot from the sea, mainly because of the tawny embankment of sand that fronted the harbor and stretched for twelve miles toward the Salinas River. Fog and low-hanging clouds often obscured all signs of the tenacious Spaniards' activities, but a half-mile back from the embarcadero, like a human exclamation point, rose the bell tower of the Royal Chapel, a building which still stands today. This was the church in which Mariano Guadalupe Vallejo was baptized on July 5, 1807, one day after his birth. An 11-foot wall surrounded not only the chapel, but the crowded presidio itself, which included the soldiers' barracks, priests' quarters, and workshops. The entire settlement covered an area approximately 330 by 250 feet, and its total population was hardly grand — some 300 people.[1]

Despite the protective coastal rocks that extended toward Pacific Grove, almost all of the shoreline was vulnerable to attack. A low white fort, called the *castillo,* was perched a long stone's throw from the water, housing guns that had less than a third the firing power of a single American frigate. If an emergency required the use of the fort's eight cannons, one of the men likely to be called to duty in 1807 would have been the father of Mariano Vallejo, Sergeant Ignacio Ferrer Vallejo. This impatient soldier had arrived in San Diego in 1774, a full generation before his son's birth, with an expedition captained by Fernando Moncada.[2] Later described by his illustrious son as a man of "brilliant spirit, with an unequaled propensity for taking part in wars, intrigues and amusements,"[3] Ignacio Vallejo had begun his training for the priesthood in Jalisco, New Spain, but had soon abandoned it, leaving behind possessions he would never reclaim. As a Spanish soldier, he served as an escort to Father Junípero Serra at the founding of the San Francisco presidio in 1776, and was with Serra again a month later at the establishment of Mission Dolores on a hill above San Francisco Bay. Of course, when Ignacio Vallejo arrived in California, there were no Americans to confront, or with whom to exchange timely news: the United States (and Mexico) did not yet exist. The billowing white sails of the first American ships did not appear off the California shoreline until 1787, signaling the beginning of the China trade. By 1801, however, more than fourteen American vessels might be seen along California's coast during a single season.[4]

Ignacio Vallejo and his countrymen tolerated the American ships as a practical necessity — even though, according to Spanish law, all U.S. trade with California was illegal. The Boston skippers used old ploys learned during America's Revolutionary War to hone their California smuggling skills. As a result the Spanish soldiers and missionaries received an ample supply of New England tools and manufactured goods. Signal fires were lit, gifts were exchanged, and one shrewd padre sent a little pig to American Captain George Eayrs to soften him up prior to their bargaining.[5] What did the American skippers need so badly on the isolated coast? Furs, primarily, since a single sea otter pelt in the Orient might bring as much as $120 — worth approximately $1,560 in 1990 dollars.[6]*

Vallejo's father worked primarily as an engineer on irrigation projects, and it is doubtful that he ever took a direct part in the smuggling operations. He was a trusted administrator and Indian-fighter, but he never advanced above the rank of "distinguished sergeant." The problem may have been an excess of libido. Spanish soldiers like Vallejo's father wrongly assumed that the exploitation of Indian women was a right of conquest. According to Alberto Hurtado, "sexual philandering [by the Spanish soldiers] was a part of daily life." After being appointed alcalde of San Jose (in hopes that he would instill more upright habits in the community), Ignacio Vallejo received a scathing letter from the governor, accusing him of setting a bad example by his promiscuity.[7] His reputation definitely suffered. But other soldiers received promotions readily enough and their conduct was no better. General Vallejo later gave two reasons for his father's low rank. First, according to a royal military decree, men born in New Spain instead

---

* Until 1846, the U.S. dollar and Mexican peso were close equivalents,
and throughout this book their values will be used interchangeably.

of in Europe "could not be promoted to the rank of officers without previously having climbed every rung of the military ladder."[8] More to the point, perhaps, the sergeant's belligerence created friction not only with his military superiors but with California's governors. Mariano Vallejo remembered one incident involving his father and Governor Sola, which could have ended in family disaster. The pre-teenage Mariano and his father were out in the field with Sola one day when the governor asked Don Ignacio to bring him a light for his cigar. The sergeant sent young Mariano with the light instead. When the governor demanded an explanation, Sergeant Vallejo replied, "Since your Excellency came out without your orderly, Dolores Mesa, you should have provided yourself with what is necessary for getting a light, for the soldiers of the king cannot engage in servile occupations." Sola was the sort of governor who would not hesitate to punish a soldier himself if the wrongdoer enraged him. But in this case, his face flushed red and he controlled his temper. Using a tone that was more charitable than angry, he muttered, "You doubtless forgot, Don Ignacio, that I was addressing a friend, the father of that child, whom I love as a son, and not Distinguished Sergeant Ignacio Vallejo."

To make things right, Don Ignacio later sent the governor a large bouquet of flowers, delivered by Mariano. Had he wanted to, of course, Sola could have destroyed Don Ignacio's career and with it the reputation of the Vallejo family.[9]

Many years before the above incident took place, Ignacio Vallejo had shown remarkable foresight when it came to providing himself with a wife. He was visiting a friend named Francisco Lugo in San Luis Obispo when Lugo's wife went into labor. The medical training Don Ignacio had received while studying for the priesthood enabled him to act as medical attendant during the birth. Having successfully performed the service, he could expect a fee. In payment, he asked for the hand of the newborn infant in marriage — after, of course, she had come of age. Fourteen years later at Mission Santa Barbara, the outstanding debt was paid. His union with María Antonia Lugo lasted more than forty years, produced thirteen children, and was said to be a successful one.[10]

By the time the sergeant's eighth child and third son, Mariano Guadalupe Vallejo, was born on July 4, 1807, Don Ignacio and most of the people of Monterey had begun to realize that for all intents and purposes, they were independent not only of Europe but of New Spain to the south as well. The burdens the mother country placed on the colony were light, and supply ships arrived infrequently. Finances were handled from afar, and the higher courts were also vast distances away, in Sonora and Sinaloa. This meant the Californians lived largely undisturbed and could pursue their favorite occupations: gambling, horse racing, fandangos, and church pageants. Young Mariano learned to perform "the mysteries of the rosary," which were sung every Sunday in a procession on the sandy plaza.[11] The boy did not have to travel very far to encounter the awesome natural environment Americans would later describe as "God's country": cougar, bear, and antelope could be seen from the presidio walls. Migrating birds were so abundant they literally darkened the skies for hours on end. The skeletons of whales and remnants of shellfish and other ocean dwellers were piled up on the beaches in enormous shell middens — some 270 feet long by 90 feet wide — indicating the presence of the Costanoan Indians along the shoreline for thousands of years.[12]

Had the Rumsen and Esselen tribes of Costanoans been more stubborn in their resistance to the Spanish soldiery, it probably would have done them little good. Technically speaking, the Indians were free men (according to Spanish law). But their labor could be required by force, if necessary, by the soldiers, missionaries, and rancheros. Spanish institutions like the *encomienda* and *repartimiento* legalized the exploitation of Indian labor in the New World, and as a result the Californian Indians were always kept in servitude and/or debt. By the time Mariano was born, the Indians were doing much of the gardening and housework for the Spaniards.[13]

For the Monterey colonists, there was one drawback to the absence of close Spanish control: the Californians lacked a navy and were poor shipbuilders. Their coast was practically defenseless, and no Spanish flotillas were on hand to help in case of trouble. In 1818 Mariano's first lesson in the meaning of the word "revolution" came from the Pacific. A warning had been forwarded to the governor that an audacious rebel — Hippolyte Bouchard — was on his way to convince Californians to join in a revolt against Spain. Bouchard commanded two Argentine ships, and his men were well armed. Their method of persuasion would be violence.

Vallejo's future mentor, Governor Pablo Vicente de Sola, had no intention of surrendering Monterey to Spain's enemies. Despite shortages of clothing and gunpowder, California was enjoying relative contentment under his rule.[14] He did not know exactly how many guns the rebel ships were carrying, but he placed Monterey's eight cannons in readiness.

Valuable ornaments from the Royal Chapel were sent inland to Mission Soledad. Mothers were told that if the rebels succeeded in landing, the children would have to be taken inland across the Salinas River to Mission Soledad, or to Mission San Antonio at the southern end of the Salinas Valley. Sergeant Ignacio Vallejo and his eldest son, twenty-year-old José de Jesús remained behind with 38 men to defend the capital. To overwhelm this small force of Californians, the Argentine invaders had 285 sailors and 66 guns.[15] During the cannonading, José de Jesús earned fame for the accuracy of his artillery fire, which succeeded in disabling the smaller ship's masts, and hit the frigate repeatedly above the waterline. Nevertheless, the rebels' numbers soon prevailed. The Argentines were able to make a surprise landing from the north. The defenders were pushed from the fort and presidio, and all of Monterey had to be abandoned to the invaders.

Eleven-year-old Mariano Vallejo, along with his brothers and sisters, fled along the main road that led across the sandy fords of the Salinas River. "Six blankets obtained from Padre Florencio at Soledad were our only bedclothes," Vallejo remembered. He also recalled the rickety carreta, with its cowhide roof, and the children "sitting or lying, weeping and shivering, cared for by my poor mother with inimitable patience."[16]

The rebels remained in control of Monterey for almost a week. Houses were looted, and both the fort and presidio were set ablaze before Bouchard's men headed south.

After the rebels had gone, the Montereyans recrossed the Salinas River to their homes. Everything of value had been taken or destroyed. For months the charred beams reminded them of the incident, for the rainy season had set in, and it was some time before repairs could be made.[17]

Years later, as commandant general of California, Vallejo urgently advised the strengthening of the coastal forts. When he did so, of course, the memory of the Bouchard attack was in the back of his mind.

To Vallejo and the other children of the town, Governor Sola seemed protective, both more imposing and communicative than the presidio soldiers. The young people trusted him.[18] He selected three boys for special attention: Mariano Vallejo, Juan Bautista Alvarado (a future governor), and José Castro (a future commandant general). All three were quick-witted. Sola gave them government reports and newspapers from New Spain to read, as well as copies of the classics, like *Don Quixote*. The tall Mariano had a bright, clear mind; but of the three,

Alvarado was probably the shrewdest. The hawk-eyed Castro — future foil of John Charles Frémont — was the most volatile.

Alvarado's mother happened to be Vallejo's older sister, María Josefa. Born in February of 1809 Alvarado was only a year-and-a-half younger than his playmate-uncle Mariano. María Josefa's husband had died when Alvarado was still an infant, so mother and child came to live in Sergeant Vallejo's house. The boys, Mariano and Juan, grew up as virtual siblings, and the basis for future rivalries may have been established when they were living under the same roof. It has been said that for minor infractions, Don Ignacio Vallejo would make Alvarado go to a corner and kneel in front of a stool to eat his dinner. There is little reason to doubt that Mariano, at times, received similar punishments.[19]

Though less abrasive and prickly than Don Ignacio, Governor Sola was not an easy mentor to emulate.[20] Official visitors from New Spain who proved unsympathetic to California's needs might receive a cool tongue-lashing from him, or a disobedient presidial soldier could find himself being pummeled by the fists of the governor himself. Just the same, with his powerful physique and affection for Monterey's youth, the influence of such a man on Vallejo and Alvarado was bound to be crucial. Under Sola's guidance they became observant and studious — later they were commanding. From him, they received their first dose of liberalism — not the violent Mexican variety, but the Spanish type that sought peaceful change under the monarchy.[21] And it was probably from him that the two boys got their first impression of the Americans who frequented the coast — and also of the Yankees' land-based rivals in California, the Russians. In 1812 the Russian-American Fur Company had arrived without invitation and had built a stockade at Fort Ross, located approximately eighty-five miles north of the San Francisco presidio. The intruders had soon dropped their defiant posture, becoming diplomats instead, because without the wheat they bought from the Californians, the Russian colonies in Alaska would have been "threatened with starvation."[22] Sola resented their presence in California, and for a time he stopped trade with them altogether. They were so eager to change his mind they sent him expensive presents, including a handsome carriage. Finally, he relented, but trade was allowed only by his "special permission." He also made them pay a "delivery tax" on cargo brought to California ports.[23] This personal style of doing business would reappear in the practices of future Commandant General Vallejo and his astute nephew, future Governor Juan B. Alvarado.

Undoubtedly because of Sola, young Vallejo and Alvarado acquired a sophisticated outlook. Vallejo's skills were also accelerated by the tutoring he received from William Hartnell. An Englishman with a scholarly turn of mind, he was nicknamed "white eyelashes" by his students.[24] Hartnell's mastery of Latin impressed the mission fathers, which helped him corner the hide-and-tallow market for the British-owned firm of John Begg & Co. Noticing Mariano's unusual quickness, Hartnell taught him English, French, and Latin, and during this same period, Vallejo worked for Hartnell as clerk and bookkeeper. Vallejo was later hired by David Spence, a resourceful Scot, to do similar work.

Keeping accounts for the foreigners schooled Vallejo in the formalities of making out invoices, handling bills of exchange, and entering credit — crucial aspects of California's commercial life. No less important, the youngster learned the intellectual and social habits of men of European background.

After Governor Sola returned to Mexico in 1822 to serve in the legislature, Vallejo became personal secretary to his successor, Governor Luis Argüello. Then fifteen years old, Vallejo was on hand when California received news that Mexico was independent of Spain. Not having a large enough population to qualify as a state, California, like Texas, was classed as a Mexican department. Its vast boundaries extended across present-day Utah to the Rocky Mountains. The flag of the Spanish monarchy fluttered to the ground for the last time and was replaced by the green, white, and red tricolor of the Mexican Republic.[25] California's official acknowledgment of the transfer of allegiance from Spain to Mexico, it has been said, was drawn up in the graceful script of Argüello's somewhat amorous secretary, Mariano G. Vallejo.[26] (Young Mariano already had several *novias* [sweethearts], but in his relations with the opposite sex he was considerably more discreet than his father. For one thing, he was never reprimanded for sexual misconduct.)

With breathtaking speed, Spain's commercial laws were tossed aside. Now American and Russian ships could legally use California's vulnerable ports for trade. Other important changes took place almost as fast. Under Mexican rule, many provincial soldiers, including Vallejo's father, were able to receive land grants. This meant that after being confined to the presidios for fifty years, the chrysalid soldiers now emerged as transformed individuals: rancheros. Vallejo's father was granted the fertile Rancho Bolsa de San Cayetano, an 8,881-acre parcel approximately twenty-three miles north of Monterey. Only about thirty grants had been made prior to 1822, but in the next decade that number doubled.[27] As the rancheros prospered, the mission padres fell from power, losing their monopoly on farming and stock raising.[28] Eleven years after Don Ignacio's retirement, Mariano Vallejo would be raising cattle and wheat himself.

Early in 1824 Governor Argüello tried to check the impetuous habits of his young secretary by enrolling Vallejo in the Monterey company as a cadet. Mariano quickly obtained practical military experience and was promoted to corporal. Then at age nineteen he became a member of the territorial legislature, the *diputación,* which met in Monterey.

By this time, America's desire to make the Pacific Ocean its western boundary had been voiced by more than one president, but the Californians were not yet seriously alarmed, for the practical means of bringing this change about had not yet surfaced.

Seagoing Americans continued to drop in at the tiny port of Monterey, sometimes becoming highly-prized men in California. In 1827 the Vallejo family acquired a flawed gem when they gained an American in-law, Captain John B. R. Cooper, an unusual blend of breezy seadog and irascible businessman, who married Encarnacíon Vallejo, one of Mariano's sisters. Judged by his exterior alone, Cooper had enough quirks to please Charles Dickens. A wound had damaged the nerves in his left hand, and whenever angered, he would "take a cruel nip at the member," after which he was able to control his temper.[29] He was a generous, high-spirited man, who at one point was not too proud to admit that a pair of his pants had "more than four patches in the arse."[30] A native of the Alderney Islands of England, he had arrived in Boston as a child in the company of his widowed mother. He was only ten when she married her second husband, Thomas Oliver Larkin Sr., whose name, through their son Thomas Oliver Larkin Jr., would become famous in California. Larkin would join his half-brother John Cooper in Monterey in 1832.[31] Four years before his marriage to Encarnación Vallejo, Cooper had sailed into the California port as master of the *Rover.* He was lucky to find a niche for himself in California's staple trade, hide-and-tallow gathering. In December of the same year, 1823, Governor Argüello demonstrated his appreciation for the American's talents: he bought Cooper's ship and retained him as captain. Cooper then provided an important source of income for California by sailing to China with 303 otter skins and 1,310 seal skins. He brought back salable merchandise: carved chairs, rosewood tables, carpets, and other household luxuries.[32] In this way, Argüello hoped to support the local troops. The soldiers were so impoverished by then that they were going around dressed in "trousers made from blankets."[33] (Mexico's neglect of these men, along with an annoying system of taxation, was serving to increase the Californians' resentment of Mexico.)

About a year after the China venture, Cooper began to lodge at the Monterey home of Don Ignacio Vallejo. He later referred to Mariano's sister, Encarnación, as a "Long-spliced girl . . . got to like her and married her . . . I put it down as one thing done right in my life."[34] The increasingly busy Mariano Vallejo was impressed by Cooper and — like most people — amused by him. Anyone who traveled around the country with the Yankee got used to the ornate style in which he damned fleas, addressing each one individually. Cooper used the same explosive language to damn the local customs duties which, in time, came to support California's government. As he saw it, the high tariffs made everything so expensive that the economy was chronically stifled. Cooper's brother-in-law, Mariano Vallejo, thought otherwise, believing that local industries had to be encouraged to produce necessities like boots, clothing, and wine; therefore, even higher tariffs ought to be used to keep these items out.[35]

The same year Cooper married Vallejo's sister, he served as bondsman for a more threatening sort of American visitor, a blue-eyed trapper named Jedediah Smith. Cooper pledged "by all that he possessed" that Smith would leave Mexican territory and end his hunting operations. Smith's sudden arrival had irked Governor Echeandía, who feared Anglo immigration.[36] California might need sea captains, but trappers merely depleted resources. Smith didn't leave by the route agreed upon, which could have hurt Cooper's bond, but the skipper never regretted having stuck out his neck for him. In the future, Cooper encouraged Americans of all sorts to come to the province.

Two years after Cooper married Encarnación Vallejo, the twenty-two-year-old Mariano Vallejo began to establish his military reputation. He had already been promoted to the rank of *alférez* (second lieutenant), and in 1829 he defeated a sizable force of Miwok Indians, who were led by Estanislao, a gifted ex-mission neophyte. Earlier attempts to frustrate the Indian leader had failed. Estanislao's celebrated *machismo* was so pronounced that on one occasion he was observed tossing his hat in the air, taunting his enemies in Spanish, while firing at them with his carbine. His tactics and marksmanship made him more than a match for the Californian soldiers who were cursed with clumsy tower muskets. Estanislao had no fear of his enemies and little affection for the director of mission affairs, Padre Durán.

Vallejo battled Estanislao for three days, trying to overcome the Miwoks' defenses, which included a series of trenches, stockades, and European-style breastworks. At this time, Vallejo was not lacking in *machismo* himself. He liked his uniforms to be spotless, and knew that a theatrical entrance accompanied by drum roll could add to a commander's effectiveness. Capable of a warmly expansive, if formal, friendliness, he was also admired for his aggressive persistence. His army of some 150 men finally overcame the Indians' breastworks by setting the surrounding thickets on fire, forcing the defenders to retreat.

Following the three-day battle with Vallejo, Estanislao escaped to Mission San José, where he found refuge with his former accuser, Father Durán. This was the closest Durán had come to settling accounts with the rebel, and the padre suspected that the best way to put down widespread Indian revolts would be to pardon the Indians' most effective leader. Durán complained to Governor Echeandía that the Miwoks had been mistreated at the hands of Vallejo's army and accused Vallejo himself of ordering the execution of at least three, and perhaps as many as five, Indians after the battle. Vallejo had been exhorted to "retaliate in full for all damage inflicted," and there can be no doubt that some of the captured Indians were killed. But according to Corporal Joaquín Piña's account, Vallejo, besides approving the execution of several captives, prevented his soldiers from killing three women, including a neophyte, Agustina. After hearing the testimony of eyewitnesses and noting the wide discrepancies in their reports, the *fiscal* who acted as judge in the case concluded that two Indians had been unjustly killed and one soldier, Joaquin Alvarado, was guilty. A neat balance was struck: Estanislao was pardoned and Vallejo was exonerated. Second Lieutenant Mariano Vallejo may, in fact, have been involved in wrongdoing; but the extent of his guilt will never be known.

None of the Indian wars were very humane, and Vallejo took a grim attitude toward carrying out his campaigns — for these forays always had unpleasant consequences. But, unlike his brother Don Salvador, he did not relish battling the Native Americans. Within eight years, he would attempt to weave a protective net of treaties among the tribes north of San Francisco Bay, thus reducing the need for conflict.[37]

At age twenty-two, Vallejo had numerous irons in the fire; and he was a precocious political leader who had achieved some impressive military victories. This was something his nephew Alvarado had not yet accomplished. Both uncle and nephew were becoming familiar with the Mexican strain of liberalism. Under the tutelage of José María Padres — whose radical objectives aimed at reducing Church power, expanding education, and spreading wealth to small property owners — Vallejo and Alvarado began to picture a utopian destiny for California. And like prominent liberals in Mexico, Vallejo thought of the United States as a model to be emulated.

But Vallejo was also a discouraged citizen, deeply unhappy with California's malfunctioning political system. He and his friends had often spoken of the idea of a free and independent California. Had he been born in Mexico instead of California, his dreams might have been more exotic — certainly more bloody. In Mexico, leaders of the ruling class sought to become military dictators (*caudillos*). Because other strong-men already held power, it was necessary to get rid of the incumbents by force. Cities were invaded and sacked, and the bodies of dead soldiers blackened the Mexican plazas. To be a violent warlord of this kind had never captured the imaginations of the Californians. As will be seen shortly, Vallejo usually had to be lured or pushed into positions of power. However, for now, he was looking for ways to improve California's disjointed administration. Rivalries between Monterey, Los Angeles, and San Diego caused some of the worst problems, and regional politics were largely a matter of family politics. The picture did not improve, even after a governor with smiling eyes and coercive habits, Manuel Victoria, was shipped back to Mexico in 1831 for trying to rule "without legal formalities." Victoria's excesses piqued Vallejo into political activism, and the rebellious Mariano took part in installing the governor's emergency replacement, Pío Pico.[38]

Mariano's bitter feelings were greatly eased by Victoria's official successor, José Figueroa, a prime-mover in California history and a man who attached wings to Vallejo's career. Figueroa, who was part-Indian, had already served as commandant general of Sonora and Sinaloa, and he arrived in California in 1833 with clear instructions from Mexico City regarding his authority.[39] Upon meeting Vallejo, he immediately took a liking to him.

By this time Vallejo was married to a frank, beautiful young woman, who was also quite a good shot with firearms — Francisca Benicia Carrillo. That spring of 1833, a year after their wedding, the seventeen-year-old Francisca was nursing their first son, Andronico, and the new family was living in the whitewashed headquarters at the San Francisco presidio, where Vallejo was serving as military commandant. From the casement windows of the *comandancia,* the second lieutenant could see the vast stretch of water known as the Bahia de San Francisco. About three miles to the east was an inlet called Yerba Buena — a smooth sandy beach with steep rocks on one side. Behind it rose the future site of San Francisco, a *tabula rasa* of sand hills, chapparel, and roaming cattle.[40]

In mid-April, Figueroa sent the young officer a set of orders which prepared the way for Vallejo's virtual autonomy in northern California and also helped to establish the foundation of his personal wealth. Vallejo was to lead a military escort on an eighty-five-mile trek to Fort Ross. After reconnoitering the area, he was to find a good location for a presidio north of San Francisco Bay.[41]

Months later, after considering the most likely alternatives, Figueroa authorized Vallejo to establish a military post at Sonoma, about forty miles northeast of the San Francisco presidio. It was probably no accident that the location of the new headquarters was also the site of Mission San Francisco de Solano — or that the choice was made on the eve of the secularization of the missions.

Clearly, this mission was too important a windfall to be overlooked. In addition, Vallejo would soon receive a sizable parcel of his own. To help him colonize the Sonoma region and to create a buffer zone between the Russians and the Californians, Figueroa gave Don Mariano title to a ten-league grant known as the Rancho Petaluma, a parcel eventually enlarged to include some 66,000 acres. It embraced most of the country between the Petaluma River and Sonoma Creek. Dividing the grant was the Sonoma Mountain Range. On one side was the Sonoma Valley; on the other were undulating grasslands that descended toward the Petaluma River. The missionaries tried to block the grant, but since the legislature in Monterey approved it and secularization was inevitable, the padres stepped aside.

This land was Vallejo's to dispose of as he wished — the beginning of his personal empire. Excellent for agricultural pursuits of all kinds, the Rancho Petaluma contained some of the best wine country in the world and had direct access to San Pablo Bay. All this would have been enough. But the golden note of good fortune which had sounded for Vallejo in 1833 was sustained well into the following year when secularization became a fact, and he was appointed *comisionado* (administrator) of Mission San Francisco de Solano.[42] It was by no means a distressed property, and Vallejo was able to enlarge upon the advantages his recent good luck had brought him. The mission boasted 6,000 cattle, 6,000 sheep, an orchard of more than 3,000 trees, a carpenter's shop, vineyard, tannery, granary, and all the tools and supplies necessary to maintain it. As *comisionado* Vallejo was instructed to use half the mission's assets for the benefit of the Sonoma pueblo. The other half was to go to the Indians.[43]

The period 1833–34 was an eventful one for Vallejo: he had to defuse a revolt against Governor Figueroa, deal with the death of his first son, and make up for the perennial shortages of food suffered by his men at the San Francisco presidio. On the plus side, he had ample resources at Sonoma with which to create a prosperous center that would attract colonists. In June of 1835 Vallejo became director of colonization of the northern frontier as well as military commandant, with authority over the unspoiled dominion north of the bay. Henceforth, he was "the only one empowered by the Supreme Government to grant land in the Frontier. . . ."[44] In giving him these expanded powers, Governor Figueroa felt

> satisfactorily convinced that you are the only officer to whom so great an enterprise can be trusted. . . . [which is] warranted by the prudence, patriotism and good faith of which you have given so many proofs. . . .[45]

Figueroa had already gained a clear idea of Vallejo's positive traits. Notwithstanding the deep respect he had for him, he realized that two of Vallejo's shortcomings were ambition and vanity. "This government trusts," he wrote, that ". . . you will not let escape an opportunity to deserve the premium to which all men aspire — POSTHUMOUS FAME. . . ."[46] His words were not wasted.

From the mid-1830s on, Vallejo "had full control in Sonoma, his will was law and no one dared gainsay it."[47] In spite of his being fair-minded, with a many-layered sense of humor, he soon acquired a reputation for being a leader who rode around the countryside with a large military escort and expected the boring formalities of military protocol to be honored. Though not yet thirty, he could also be condescending when annoyed, and if he sensed defiance, he wouldn't hesitate to let an acquaintance — friend or foe — spend a few days in jail to think things over. In the future, he would employ a punishment which, for Californians at least, was mildly sadistic. As a people, they hated the ocean, and a good pair of sea legs was practically unknown in the country. Notified that a schooner was about to sail, Vallejo might send a wrong-doer out to spend a few days on rough seas to let his attitude do somersaults on the brine.

Vallejo brought his cavalrymen north from the San Francisco presidio and garrisoned them in the sunny spot known as Sonoma. Called the Valley of the Moon, the Sonoma Valley was actually shaped more like an oblong bowl with the south side broken away. To the east and north, it was encircled by the rugged Mayacamas Range, and on the west by the Sonoma Mountains. For the first time since his birth in Monterey, Vallejo was able to live at a comfortable distance from the cold sea wind, and he could plan a private residence. The two-story

adobe he built on the north side of the Sonoma plaza did not lack
grandeur. A spacious breezeway led from the street to the rear court, and
behind the house was an orchard with a well near its center. The adobe
walls were almost four feet thick; wide second-story balconies extended
from the front and rear of the house, protecting the walls from rain and
creating shade.[48] It was the sort of hacienda which any Mexican official
(such as Governor Manuel Micheltorena) would have been proud to
occupy — a fitting center from which to administer the North Bay
empire.

II

So far, Vallejo's career had been based on an abundance of natural
gifts, his excellent connections, and a great deal more uphill toil and
sweat than have been chronicled here. Rewards for his services had been
handed out quickly, almost too fast for him to absorb. Although his
personal empire placed him far from Monterey, which was the locus of
political power, his ego did not really hunger for much more than
dominion over his sprawling Sonoma ranchlands.

Then, without warning, in September of 1835, Governor Figueroa
died. After the governor's death, "it seemed that a pall of sadness was
spread over California," Vallejo remembered.[49] From 1835 on, the era
of good feeling that had existed between Mexico and California came to
an end. The dynamic Figueroa was the last Mexican governor the Californians were willing to tolerate.

Though Vallejo was not ambitious for high political office, one of
the most important posts in the country suddenly sped toward him as
though shot from a cannon. All he had to do was say yes. As these events
took shape, American frontiersmen became involved, and his nephew
Alvarado orchestrated the whole thing.

For decades Americans had been straggling into the country singly
or a few at a time, as trappers, deserters from whalers, mountain men,
and ships' captains. Vallejo was by no means the only Californian
who had acquired Anglo in-laws. Most of the provincial leaders (the
Picos, Bandinis, Carrillos, and De la Guerras) possessed similar ties.
This was because the Yankees' commercial talents were so desperately
needed. Only skippers like John B. R. Cooper, Alfred Robinson, and
William Heath Davis were capable of sailing cargoes to Boston and
the Orient and back, while performing all the necessary commercial

steps in between. Cattle ranchers like the Vallejos had no interest in sailing, or in storekeeping for that matter. Thomas Larkin in Monterey bought and sold trade goods, stored inventory, occasionally loaned money, and in some instances, acted as a banker. Without his services, the doors of commerce would have frozen shut. The Californians were willing to trust a man like Larkin. Both he and "Horsefaced" Abel Stearns were held in greater esteem than the Mexican governors. Stearns eventually married Arcadia Bandini, a woman of the country, which is more than the Mexican governors did. They flaunted local custom by arriving with mistresses. Governor Nicolás Gutiérrez kept an assortment of prostitutes on hand, which scandalized the Californians. His disregard for the political and social institutions of the place gave Vallejo's ambitious nephew, Juan B. Alvarado, good reason to believe that Gutiérrez could be overpowered and replaced with an honorable Californian (like himself). Alvarado also guessed that an American frontiersman named Isaac Graham might be useful to him in such a revolt. Though there were fewer than 350 foreigners of all nationalities in California, the Tennessean Graham was perhaps the most infamous of the group. He was said to have entered the country sometime between 1833 and 1835.

For all that, Graham did not have the earmarks of an unusual man. He was a glib hunter who had an impulsive way of doing things, a prodigal disregard for the law, and when he broke it, a flair for getting caught. Obviously, he was not the sort of American the Californians prized. He distilled liquor, which he sold to friends and patrons at a grog shop a few miles north of present-day Salinas, close to the San Juan Grade Road which, then as now, led over the Gabilan Range to the interior headquarters of San Juan Bautista.[50] As far as his political philosophy went, Graham was impressed by Sam Houston's successes in Texas, and he thought California politics should proceed along similar lines. A crack shot, within four years he would give his name to the Graham Affair — the most damaging international incident to befall California prior to U.S. annexation. Not too surprisingly, he and his shaggy-haired friends were not appreciated by upstanding citizens like Larkin and Cooper. Graham was overly aggressive and self-confident, and his being an American gave him a sense of moral superiority. He viewed Californians through the wrong end of a telescope, mistakenly picturing liberals like Alvarado and Vallejo as agents of bloody tyranny, scions of the defunct Spanish monarchy, or worse. Alvarado should have given Graham a wide berth — but he didn't.

Juan B. Alvarado was an extremely popular man with the people and owed his appeal "more to his eloquence and boldness" than to anything else, Vallejo remembered.[51] Alvarado also understood the craft of political intrigue better than his uncle. When he tried to get the thoughtful Vallejo to cooperate in a revolt, Don Mariano advised a wait-and-see policy, for he did not think Gutiérrez's actions had been brazen enough to justify an overthrow. The political betrayals that had followed Governor Victoria's ouster had made Vallejo doubt that revolutions did any good.

But waiting did not suit the local daredevils. Opposition to Gutiérrez grew, and Alvarado was sure he could manage to bring off the uprising with the help already on hand. As he surged ahead in his bid for power, he gathered into his following twenty-five or thirty Americans under Isaac Graham. Muscular frontiersmen from the United States, acting as a group, now made their colorful, unscheduled, and perhaps inevitable entrance into California politics. They could never again be dismissed as trivial factors in the department's affairs.

In keeping with California's time-honored military strategy (and to make a shooting war unnecessary), Alvarado wanted to create the impression that Gutiérrez's fifty soldiers would be inundated by the rebels. The maneuver worked, so we will never know if Graham's men were superfluous. José Castro, leading the Californian army and supplemented by Graham's *rifleros americanos,* surrounded the Monterey presidio. As soon as the first cannonball was fired through the roof of the governor's house, frantic talks began. There never was a battle. On November 5, 1836, Gutiérrez surrendered.[52] Two days later, Alvarado sent a somewhat bold-faced confession to his uncle, admitting that he had told everyone that Vallejo would cooperate. "We have said that you were the chief mover of this although your signature is not present." He begged Vallejo to come to Monterey and take a hand in the government. "The welfare of the country depends upon your coming and you ought not to allow any sacrifice, however great, to interfere since all await you as the man who is to create the prosperity of the country."[53]

Vallejo left his building projects at Sonoma and hurried to Monterey where he was received as a hero. According to his later recollection, when he reached the capital, he found that Isaac Graham and his riflemen were ready to kill all the Mexican nationals in the town. Vallejo warned Graham's men that there "was a great difference between liberty and license," and he urged them to respect California's laws.[54] On November 29, 1836, the Monterey *diputación* promoted Vallejo from the rank of second lieutenant (*alférez*) to colonel of cavalry, and on that same day, over the heads of forty men who were of higher rank, he became Commandant General M. G. Vallejo, military governor of the "Free State of Alta California." Now the uncle and nephew, both in their late twenties, controlled California.

From that time until the American takeover, the province enjoyed varying degrees of self-rule. One more Mexican governor, Manuel Micheltorena, would arrive from the south, but he too would be expelled. Ironically, the supreme government would later confirm Vallejo's post as commandant general and Alvarado's civil governorship, both men receiving further promotions and thanks for their patriotism.[55]

Approximately four years later, Governor Alvarado would be forced to realize that he had acquired a political millstone in the form of Isaac Graham. There had been no bloodshed and only a modicum of glory during the 1836 revolt, but some Americans believed they had played a vital role in the takeover, and they wanted more rewards than they had received. Alvarado found it either impossible or inexpedient to compensate men who had become social undesirables. Groups of Americans clustered around his residence in Monterey, making demands. Sometimes there was a threat behind their familiarity, a suggestion that violent consequences would result if things were not done their way.

Alvarado complained to his friend Alfred Robinson, "I was insulted at every turn by the drunken followers of Graham; and when walking in the garden, they would come to its walls and call to me in terms of the greatest familiarity: 'Ho! Bautista, come here, I want to speak to you'; Bautista here, Bautista there, Bautista everywhere."[56]

The taunting Graham spoke a good deal about his fondness for a Texas-style takeover, but it is impossible to say how prepared he was to start a revolt. Physically powerful and fearless, he and his associates could turn a simple civic duty like an arbitration hearing into an event requiring a judge and undertaker. In 1838 he was sentenced to eight months on a chain gang for killing cattle on Joaquín Gómez's rancho south of San Juan Bautista.[57]

In the early months of 1840, a naturalized Englishman and a padre warned Alvarado that Graham's followers were about to overthrow the government and take control of California.[58] The governor must have thought the 1836 revolt was sitting up in its coffin. Alvarado knew that men like John B. R. Cooper and his half-brother, Thomas O. Larkin, had even less liking for the unruly Americans than the Californians did.[59] Certainly, the governor was tired of the frontiersmen's threats about making California into another Texas. Hoping to rid the political system of his erstwhile allies, Alvarado touched off the infamous Graham Affair, thus triggering the first prolonged controversy between Americans and Californians. On April 5, 1840, he told Commandant General Vallejo that the time had come to expel the would-be revolutionaries. Anyone who had entered the country illegally was to be deported — except men known to be married and of good character. The policy was to be carried out in both northern and southern California.

Acting with more zeal than good judgment, Californian officers in the north arrested approximately one hundred Americans and Englishmen. Some law-abiding citizens like Dr. John Marsh and William Heath Davis were included in the roundup. They were soon released, along with approximately forty-one others.[60] Though no proof of conspiracy had been found, the emergency at the time seemed real enough to Vallejo.[61] He responded to his nephew's appeal, sending arms, men, and all possible help before going to Monterey himself to assist with the deportation.

Vallejo had developed a positive attitude toward American immigrants which, in the case of the violent Graham and his friends, he was willing to ignore. He ordered wealthy trader José Aguirre to prepare the *Joven Guipuzcoana* for departure to San Blas. While the ship was being stocked with provisions, the American and English captives spent an uncomfortable two weeks in a reeking Monterey jail. The first two or three days were especially trying. The men were crammed into a room approximately 18 by 20 feet. The prisoners' food was scarce, but on the third day, Thomas Larkin took it upon himself to furnish the prisoners with meat, bread, beans, and tea on a daily basis.

From then on, exaggerated stories about abuses committed on both sides made the rounds. Graham gained the sympathies of a footloose attorney named Thomas Farnham, who subsequently wrote a book that credited all of Graham's complaints and greatly exaggerated the Californians' cruelty. His volume, *Travels in the Californias and Scenes in the Pacific Ocean* (published in New York, in 1844), later gave many would-be California immigrants second thoughts about trying their luck in the province. Like Graham, Farnham thought California should be in American hands; his patriotism was of the fiery kind that compounded threats of violence with hatred of the Spaniards. Skillful at propagandizing, he used a thick brush to paint the Californians blacker than Goya ever painted the Duchess of Alba's gown. If the undeserving military bureaucrats were greedy and unjust, they might rightfully be turned out of their country — so ran his logic.

In his book Farnham recalled that he had been kept awake at night in Monterey by the piteous appeals of the prisoners; more than once, he had gone close enough to Graham's cell "to hear the lion-hearted old man roar out his indignation," and had listened while "dying Americans ... unconquerable sons of the republic," sang "Hail Columbia" and the Britons had answered with "Rule Britannia."

According to Farnham, the prisoners endured nothing less than "suffocation, the pangs of death, one at a time coming slowly by day and among the sleepless moments of the long and hot night — life pendent on the mercy of the Californian Spaniard." In reality, however, no Americans died.[62]

Graham's own version was less inflammatory. He admitted that Larkin "assisted us not only in food" but with other necessities. "Some of us were taken out of prison from time to time and released by the intercession of friends or through sickness."[63]

On April 24, 1840, José Castro and fifteen or twenty soldiers boarded the *Joven Guipuzcoana* to accompany the forty-seven foreigners on the voyage to San Blas. When British and American diplomats in Mexico protested the deportations, President Bustamente chose not to complicate his country's problems by antagonizing two of the world's greatest maritime powers. Mexico was already a debtor nation — owing England some fifty million pesos — and the supreme government was morbidly sensitive to British opinion. Not too surprisingly, then, the burden of guilt shifted to the Californian officials who had to endure a lengthy ordeal of shame. Governor Alvarado received criticism for not having sent proofs of conspiracy, and José Castro and his escort were placed under arrest. British and American ministers pressed charges against Castro, and his court martial dragged on for five months. Manuel Micheltorena, California's future governor, served as his defense attorney. The court finally absolved Castro of all blame and permitted him to return home.[64]

But Graham and nearly twenty of his associates were judged innocent of the charges brought against them. Not only did they receive compensation for damages,[65] but Graham and some eighteen of his companions were allowed to return to California. When the troublemakers arrived aboard the *Bolina,* passports in hand, in 1841, their presence was like salt to the Californians' wounded pride.[66]

Vallejo's aggressive younger brother, Don Salvador Vallejo, was infuriated by Isaac Graham's return. From 1841 on, it seemed that the Californians' hands were going to be tied by "international considerations." And this was taking place at a time when the Californians

needed all of their perogatives. A new chapter was opening in their relations with visitors to their rugged, unglamorized coast.

Readers impatient to trace the course of hostilities between belligerent Americans and native Californians can pick up the thread of the
conflict in chapter 5. But a few important matters need to be described
first in order to illustrate why California in the early 1840s was a place
that was bound to slip out of Vallejo's and Alvarado's hands.

2

The Pivotal Year: 1841

*F*or more reasons than one, the year following the Graham Affair, 1841, deserves to be called California's Pivotal Year. During this period Commandant General Vallejo demonstrated the approach he was going to take toward American immigrants. The Russians had decided to sell out and leave the coast, which was a positive omen from the Californians' point of view. Other incidents, however, created feelings of disquiet: a sizable American fleet under Lieutenant Charles Wilkes reached San Francisco Bay, and a few weeks after it disappeared downwind, Vallejo set his famous precedent when he welcomed the first company of U.S. immigrants, the Bidwell–Bartleson party.

Gatelike, the year 1841 swung outward, allowing the Russian colonists to make their exit; then inward, permitting new groups to enter and establish roots. Not only were the Russians going to clear out of California, they were going to sell strategic Fort Ross. The events that led to its purchase by a political wild card in the California deck, a Swiss immigrant named John A. Sutter, brought all of the country's defects into relief and showed why California would have new rulers within less than seven years.

On New Year's Day, 1841, Vallejo wrote the Mexican minister of war, telling him that the Russians wanted to sell Fort Ross to a European and that he hoped the deal would not go through. California's interests would best be served, he thought, if a company of married cavalrymen were garrisoned on the northern coast to help settle the region and create a barrier against hostile tribes.

Before long, Vallejo received a letter from the manager in charge of Fort Ross, Peter Kostromitinov, who did not mention John Sutter by name but asked permission to sell the property to a private individual. Vallejo's own desire to buy the fort may have been simmering by then.

He dutifully answered, however, that "the Government of the Nation has the first right," meaning of course, the Mexican nation.[1] When Kostromitinov later asked Vallejo directly if he wanted to buy the fort himself, including livestock and machinery, for $30,000, half of which could be paid in "products of the country" (wheat, hides, wine, etc.), Vallejo, having made Mexico City's approval a prior condition, jumped at the chance, even agreeing to some of the terms.[2]

Nothing further could be done until consent came from Mexico. Meanwhile, Vallejo continued to add refinements to the Casa Grande and carried out his plan to erect a barracks for his frontier garrison. In late spring, dressed in work clothes, he was helping his men with a project on the Sonoma plaza when a stranger arrived, who looked like he had been transplanted from the court at Versailles. This was Duflot de Mofras, rumored (incorrectly) to be a bastard son of the French king. Mofras had been serving as a member of the French legation in Mexico City and was traveling, it was said, on a "scientific mission." He longed to secure California for France.

Mofras's bad reputation preceded him. His tasteless amours had caused gossip in the northern part of the province, and he had been arrested for the mistreatment of Indian muleteers. Vallejo later mused that Mofras did not seem to care if he was with "the elite of California society or in a corral surrounded by Esselen Indian women."[3]

When the two men sat down to talk in the General's headquarters, Mofras ruined things for himself by dropping hints that were extremely nettling to Don Mariano. "My friend, look closely at the clause of my passport which says that all necessary assistance shall be extended me." After glancing at it, the General pointed to another place which explained that Mofras would pay for such aid at a just price. The visitor made some unflattering references to the Graham Affair, which caused Vallejo to think he was being threatened.[4] Tiring of the Frenchman's airs, Vallejo sent him off to Fort Ross with an escort of ten soldiers.

Subsequently, there was no story so bad about Mofras that Vallejo would not willingly believe it — including an anecdote told about the Frenchman's arrival at the home of Vallejo's former Latin tutor, William Hartnell. It may have been embellished in the retelling, but it proves that Vallejo loved savory gossip.

Having arrived at the Hartnell rancho unannounced (as was his custom), Mofras found Hartnell's fertile wife, Doña Teresa de la Guerra Hartnell, managing alone. Mofras made his introductions, saying that the master himself had invited him to spend as much time as he liked.

The Frenchman turned out to be a very difficult man to embarrass. He searched behind the books in Hartnell's library until Doña Teresa caught him at it. Even then, he did not seem ashamed of his bad manners. Some of Hartnell's best wine was stored in the guestroom where Mofras was staying. One morning, when he did not make his appearance at break- fast, Doña Teresa sent a servant to call him. No answer came from be- hind the doors, so she ordered her men to force their entrance. "And there," she later reported,

> stretched upon the floor my Frenchman lay dead drunk, bed- ding in a filthy state and many gallons of the wine missing from the barrel. A spell of sickness overtook the drunkard; during days I watched over him with the care of a mother; at last he got stronger. . . .
>
> One day, however, he suddenly left taking along with him a new suit of black clothes belonging to Mr. Hartnell. . . .[5]

When the time came for Mofras to write his diplomatic reports, he recommended that France should try to snare California, for the province would serve as a useful link between Canada and the French markets across the Pacific. And how could this provincial bonbon be grabbed? Mofras boasted that California might "belong to whatever nation chooses to send there a man-of-war and 200 men. . . ."[6] The French navy was actively shopping for colonies at the time, treating the Pacific Ocean as a convenient emporium. Within little more than a year, Rear Admiral Du Petit Thouars would take control of the Marquesas Islands and would add Tahiti and the Society Islands to his nation's possessions.[7] In the course of his travels, Mofras had taken care to make a good friend of John Sutter, and as more information filtered in about this connection, Vallejo assumed that France "was intriguing to become mistress of California."[8]

Not long after Mofras left Sonoma, Vallejo was seriously injured while roping cattle. He was still troubled by a dislocated hip when the Russian manager, Peter Kostromitinov, left the rocky coast at Fort Ross and traveled to Sonoma, bringing a contract ready for Vallejo's signa- ture. The papers stated that "His Majesty the Emperor of all the Russias, cedes its rights to Mr. M. G. Vallejo over all settlements and farms on the coast of New Albion at the Port of Bodega, and . . . at the presidio of Ross."[9] Besides the written contract, Kostromitinov brought along a catalog of four other properties that would be included in the purchase price of thirty thousand dollars. In all, there were many hundreds of acres of farmland, orchards, vineyards, three thousand head of livestock, and much machinery besides.

Though unable to get out of bed, Vallejo made sure the Russian manager was comfortable and received the best care possible. Vallejo was glad to note that a launch he had asked for, plus three smaller boats, were included in the sales price. He sent off a letter to his nephew Alvarado, saying that Kostromitinov's visit was "more efficacious . . . than the science of Aesculapius." The happy uncle was now able to stand up and take walks around his room.[10]

Bad news from Mexico City reached Alvarado in late June and was forwarded to Sonoma. Ignoring the facts of the situation, President Bustamente instructed Alvarado to appoint a prefect and subprefect at Ross. Clearly, Mexico was not going to exercise her "first right" to buy the fort. Might Vallejo purchase it himself? Nothing was said about that. President Bustamente assumed the Russians would leave Ross intact, like an empty stage-set, to be occupied by the Californians.[11] The Russian-American Company, meanwhile, had other ideas. Its managers were careful businessmen who wanted to recover as much of their losses as possible by liquidating livestock, machinery, and improvements.

Vallejo encouraged Alvarado to ignore Bustamente's lack of realism. A bureaucratic formula existed, which consisted of just five words: *recibidas, obedecidas, y no cumplidas* ("received, obeyed, and never carried out").[12] For instance, in this case, a proclamation should be posted with all proper ceremony, announcing the arrival of President Bustamente's orders. At the same time, Vallejo should buy Ross. With the Russian properties under Vallejo's control, the amount of coastline actually occupied by Californians would increase by eighty-five miles. Vallejo therefore urged his nephew to cooperate with him in the venture so that the two of them might "unite in giving these neighbors of ours *bon voyage.*"[13]

Unfortunately for California's future, Alvarado feared that his uncle's aim of building up California's defenses concealed a tyrannical motive and, what's more, that Vallejo would reduce the civil budget in favor of the military. Since the two leaders had assumed control of the country, they had disagreed on almost everything. Alvarado, in poor health and suspicious of everyone, had let his mistrust of his uncle reach a climax in 1840 when he convened the Monterey legislature in order to accuse "certain men" (Vallejo among them) of plotting his overthrow.[14] The charges against Vallejo were untrue, but in the sum-

mer of 1841, Alvarado had no need to think about how to reply to
Vallejo's urgings about the Russian fort. Alvarado's none-too-apolo-
getic dispatch referred to Ross as "such an interesting part of the country," and he practically yawned between sentences as he told his Uncle
Mariano that the fort could not be bought "on account of the government." It would therefore not be "proper for you or me (in my opinion) to take this step, that is, speaking of our private interests." He
referred to Bustamente's letter, which assumed that the fate of Ross
would remain up in the air until the Russians "abandon it." To make
his refusal slightly more polite, Alvarado asked Vallejo to join Captain John B. R. Cooper, Vallejo's older brother José de Jesús Vallejo,
and himself in the purchase of an American brigantine for the purpose
of setting up a trading company — an irrelevant proposal which Vallejo
could not have found very consoling.[15]

Stung by Alvarado's opposition to the Ross deal, Peter Kostromitinov went to Monterey, hoping to change the governor's mind. When
he asked Alvarado about the "acts from the Mexican government" which
prevented the sale of Ross to Vallejo, the governor made his uncle look
like a fool by saying "he had never received such acts."[16]

Alvarado's hostility toward Vallejo would soon have a telling effect
on the growth of the foreign element's influence in northern California,
for the next step in the Ross saga brought the princely manipulator John
A. Sutter into the picture.

Today, Sutter's name is more famous in California than Vallejo's.
The exuberant Swiss had arrived in 1839, emerging from a background
that was truly mysterious. Vallejo had been skeptical about the rover's
intentions from the start. Vallejo's touchy sister, Rosalía, thought that
Sutter should marry a Spanish-Californian woman and settle down. But
for some reason, Alvarado encouraged the newcomer to establish himself in the country, even though Sutter defied local custom by living with
Hawaiian concubines. Vallejo's outspoken sibling Rosalia (who had
brought another Anglo-American into the family by marrying trapper
Jacob Leese "on the sly" in 1837), would eventually come to hate Sutter.

Like many nineteenth-century wanderers attracted to the region,
Sutter deserved to be called a man on the run. After going bankrupt in
Switzerland, he had deserted his wife and five children, and his creditors
in Berne had asked the police to issue a warrant for his arrest.[17] Arriving
in the United States in 1834, he had tried his luck at trading in Missouri
and New Mexico, leaving behind a string of fleeced victims who had
loaned him money. A cagey man, he was gifted with a benign air that

made people trust him. Even after Sutter defaulted on a note, a lender might feel almost shamefaced to realize that he had been taken in by such an exemplary gentleman. In 1835 Sutter pushed off from New Mexico for the West Coast, crossing the frozen Cascades to Fort Vancouver. Here, one of the chief factors in the Hudson's Bay Company, James Douglas, was told that Sutter had formerly held the commission of captain in the French army, and had "left Europe with a respectable fortune."[18] Not easily fooled, Douglas nevertheless took the traveler at his word.

The tireless Sutter finally reached California on July 1, 1839, bearing a letter of introduction addressed to no less a personage than General Vallejo himself from John Coffin Jones, the U.S. consul in Honolulu. Sutter had brought along a handful of Hawaiians who had signed on with him for three years at ten dollars per month. There were several women in the group, and one of them, Manuiki, became his particular favorite. In Monterey, he made an excellent impression on Governor Alvarado, then announced his desire to establish a colony on the Sacramento River. Sutter had learned that a fortune might be made there in furs. Since the Great Valley had always needed a colonist to govern the Indian tribes, Alvarado favored the idea, though he could not guarantee that Sutter would survive the ordeal. Nor was Alvarado thinking very far ahead, for he assumed that a rival for his uncle was just what was needed north of the bay. He warned the European that Vallejo would probably want him to settle near Sonoma; that temptation should be avoided.[19]

Accompanied by Doña Francisca Vallejo's brother-in-law, Benito Wilson, Sutter headed for the Valley of the Moon. Vallejo recognized trouble when he saw it, and he never had reason to change his mind. As predicted, the General urged Sutter to buy land nearby, where his actions could be watched. Wilson offered Sutter a cattle ranch at a bargain price. When the European refused, Wilson blurted, "Well, I'd like to know what you really want!" At critical times like this, just when his real motives were about to be unmasked, or punishment seemed ready to descend on his worthy head, Sutter had a talent for coming up with the right answer. Since a simple explanation was called for, he announced with a smile, "I prefer to be on a navigable river." For the time being at least, the answer was satisfactory.

Sutter's credit (established by his letters of introduction) enabled him to stow tools, seeds, provisions, and weapons aboard three boats. To increase his manpower, he signed up some drifters who had jumped ship, and the adventurers then headed toward the confluence of the American and Sacramento Rivers. As months passed, Sutter succeeded in creating the cozy settlement known as New Helvetia (Sutter's Fort).

Vallejo's desire to buy Fort Ross had blocked Sutter's attempts to gain some of the Russians' assets. But when Governor Alvarado scotched Vallejo's bid later in the year, Sutter moved in. The third week in September he nabbed the property.[20] He was now in a position to become almost as permanent a fixture in California as Vallejo himself.[21]

Vallejo's protective instincts toward California had been aroused, and he was deeply troubled by Alvarado's approval of the transaction. He wrote Minister of War Almonte to explain just how poor — from the supreme government's point of view — the Ross deal might turn out to be. Until Sutter paid off his debts, the Russians would hold mortgages on New Helvetia and the coastal properties. Should Sutter default (and his performance to date suggested he well might), the Russian-American Company would not only acquire a new foothold at the confluence of the American and Sacramento Rivers but would regain all their former properties at Ross.[22]

While Vallejo was doctoring his pride over this territorial letdown, the American presence in California increased dramatically. The U.S. sloop-of-war *Vincennes* arrived under the command of Lieutenant Cadawalader Ringgold. He had come in advance of a naval expedition, totaling six ships and six hundred men, sent to the Pacific under Lieutenant Charles Wilkes. It was the largest U.S. expedition of its kind to date, and no less a literary figure than Nathaniel Hawthorne had applied for the post of cruise historian.[23] One important task of the expedition was to chart the West Coast, especially San Francisco Bay. The flotilla had scientific objectives that were better documented than similar claims by other visitors during the year: its experts included three naturalists, a miner- logist, a botanist, and a philologist.[24]

Ultimately, the negative opinions of Lieutenant Charles Wilkes should have tarnished Vallejo's reputation in the eyes of the U.S. naval personnel, but they didn't. Lieutentant Ringgold was courteous enough, and Vallejo remembered that the American seemed "so pleased with the hospitality I was able to extend him, he sent me . . . cases of good whiskey, tobacco, and cigars." Ringgold urged Vallejo to bring Doña Francisca and the family to inspect the *Vincennes,* but the General's hip had become so painful again that he sent his brother Don Salvador in his place.[25]

The high-strung Commander Wilkes himself had remained anchored in rainy Oregon Territory and did not come south until October 19. While still in Oregon, he let the British Hudson's Bay Company know that he would "brook no interference" with his mapping operations, and he predicted that Oregon would soon be a part of the United States.[26]

Once anchored at San Francisco Bay, Wilkes stayed close to his ship. He never met Vallejo or visited Sonoma, but when it came time for Wilkes to record his impressions of Vallejo's role in California, his tone vibrated with scorn. He seemed to be echoing Mofras when he announced that California would one day "control the destinies of the Pacific" and "must be" possessed by the United States.[27] He also directed potshots at the General, claiming that the residents of Sonoma lacked virtue and were "wretched under their present rulers."[28] His accusations characterized Vallejo as a leader who had complete "disregard for the lives as well as the property and liberty of the Indians and *gente de razón* — "people of reason" (i.e., the Californians). Added to this was a claim that ships arriving at San Francisco Bay were subject to the whims of the tyrant Vallejo, who might levy "an indefinite amount of duties." Overall, Wilkes' approach was quite similar to that of anti-Californian propagandist Thomas Farnham. Both men represented the California leaders as corrupt "usurpers" who had come to power through revolution and who could be removed without apology. Oddly, neither traveler noticed that some of the Californians — notably Vallejo — had pro-American sympathies, or that the province might become a U.S. possession *with* the Californians' help.

Wilkes would achieve his greatest notoriety when he arrested Confederate diplomats Mason and Slidell during the American Civil War. But his California observations were better known for their oddness than for their accuracy. For instance, he compared San Francisco's climate to that of Cape Horn, and he dismissed the Sacramento Valley as being useless for agriculture.[29] Interestingly enough, even at this early date, General Mariano G. Vallejo was singled out as a political target — despite Richard Henry Dana's having called him "the most popular among the Americans and English, of any man in California."[30]

Wilkes helped accomplish one thing for Vallejo: the American ships — impressive machines of war — combined grimness with beauty. Their presence convinced Governor Alvarado that the United States possessed sufficient naval power to pose a serious threat to California's autonomy. For a while, Monterey officials, who usually gave little consideration to Vallejo's suggestions, were willing to listen more carefully to the General's plans for the common defense.[31]

The year 1841 gave the California leaders little time to relax. As the Pacific door swung wide, allowing the American fleet to exit, the barrier which until then had been thought to be insurmountable — the high wall of the Sierras — was crossed by a tired group of U.S. immigrants. The American travelers were members of the Bidwell–Bartleson party, and in November 1841, it was up to Commandant General Vallejo to decide what to do with them.

3

The Advent of the Americans

I

One of General Vallejo's most important roles in northern California was to colonize the thousands of square miles of potentially fertile land; and strange as it may seem today, he had a difficult time finding enough qualified people who wanted to settle in the temperate paradise — the wealth of which had not even been scratched. Instructions from Mexico City required that Russians, Americans, and other foreign colonists be kept in a minority, which was easy enough.[1] But where was Vallejo to find sufficient numbers of talented Mexicans to occupy land grants? People in Mexico pictured Alta California with dread, as "a region of exile and penalty," likening the province to "the ends of the earth."[2] Since Vallejo's main objectives were to improve agriculture, increase capital, and foster "enlightenment," the pardoned convicts the government sent north were hardly in keeping with his ideals.

Mexico had enough land of her own during this period and was noticeably underpopulated. Her main cities sheltered a highly stratified society still living in Spain's cultural shadow. More than once her national congress had debated tolerating Protestantism but had rejected the idea. Sad to say, dozens of catchwords were used to classify the country's different racial mixtures, and at the very top of the social pyramid were families thought to be of pure Spanish blood. The abuses of the military leaders were felt in painful ways. For instance, it was not uncommon for the victor of a successful revolt to butcher the soldiers of the opposing army. Such things were unknown in California, where bloodless warfare was an art, and the wounding of three or four men in a civil conflict was considered to be a major disaster. Nevertheless, the Mexicans were not envious of Californians and looked down on the northerners as poorly educated inferiors.

If the Californians had a brutal side (which was apparent in their exploitation of Indian labor), their prejudices had limits. One of the country's most popular political leaders, Pío Pico, was a mulatto, and he suffered no discrimination because of it. California's military bureaucrats (including Vallejo, Alvarado, and José Castro) had peaceful rather than bloody dreams. They merely wanted to collect their share of the customs duties, own victorious racehorses, and watch their herds multiply. Mexicans saw no reason to gravitate north. Why should they envy such an unambitious people?

In November 1841 a worried General Vallejo had much more than social prejudices (or the shortage of needed colonists) to worry about as he rode south toward Mission San José to keep an appointment with his boyhood friend, Lieutenant Colonel José Castro. This was California's pivotal year, and Don Mariano already suspected that permanent changes might be in store: the Fort Ross fiasco would certainly help no one but Sutter. Also, one of the worst droughts in recent memory was destroying California's crops. The General skirted herds of gaunt cattle, noticing the parched streambeds and the absence of game. (It had been the seared appearance of these hills that had caused Lieutenant Wilkes to draw some very wrong conclusions about California's agricultural potential.) Hostile feelings between Vallejo and Alvarado had not softened, and when the two leaders needed to discuss government affairs, they sometimes used an intermediary. Their mutual friend, José Castro, had arranged to meet the General at Mission San José — a convenient midpoint between Sonoma and the capital.[3]

During the second week in November, while Vallejo and Castro were still having their talks, the gossipy subprefect, Antonio Suñol, hurried into Vallejo's mission headquarters to inform him that thirty-one Americans had found refuge at John Marsh's rancho northeast of Mt. Diablo. About half of them had made their way to the pueblo of San Jose and were being held in jail. What did Vallejo want to do with them?

The sudden arrival of so many unexpected newcomers would have been understandable if Lieutenant Wilkes' ships had returned to San Francisco, or if a band of trappers had traveled south from Oregon Territory. But the members of this party were a different breed altogether. With considerable luck, they had found a more direct route to California's Great Valley, abandoning wagons and much equipment as they crossed first the Rockies and then the Sierras.

General Vallejo summoned the prisoners to his headquarters at Mission San José. When they arrived, he was impressed by their appearance.

Usually, mountain men from the United States liked to let their hair grow until it reached their knees and were happy if someone shouted at them, "I took ye for an injin."[4] But these American overlanders had shaved their faces and had cut their hair; they definitely looked like they had known a settled way of life. Vallejo was told that one member of the company, Benjamin Kelsey, had brought a wife and child.[5]

Official word from Mexico City had already spelled out the supreme government's attitude toward incoming Americans. The most recent orders said that unless U.S. residents arrived with passports and consular permission in hand, they were to be sent out of the country.[6] Events in Texas had inspired the new orders. Though almost half a continent away, the Texas Republic was turbulent enough to create a strong political undertow in California. By 1841 more than twenty thousand Anglo-Americans were living in Texas, mainly in the river valleys that stretched in an arc from Nacogdoches to the site of present-day San Antonio, and they outnumbered Hispanic residents five to one.[7] The oldest American settlements were the creations of Stephen Austin. But by 1832 (three years before Vallejo would become director of colonization of the northern frontier in California), Austin's role as colonizer in Texas was coming to an end. Austin had wanted Texas to become a state within the Mexican federal system, a political entity like Jalisco or Guerrero. Being singularly free of prejudice, he had hoped the new society would be nourished by two cultural springs, Anglo and Hispanic, and would pass legislation guaranteeing religious freedom to Protestants and Catholics alike. In 1833, he discovered that some of his objectives were not acceptable to the Mexican government. For one thing, the institution of slavery (dear to the Texans) was expressly forbidden by Mexican law. Austin spent more than a year in prison while Mexican officials tried to find flaws or signs of treason in his plans for Texas statehood. The supreme government had already forbidden further Anglo immigration into Texas, and eventually, Austin gave up his faith in Mexico.

Then, anti-Mexican Texan leaders emerged, the most important of whom was Sam Houston. He favored statehood under the Stars and Stripes instead of under the Mexican banner.[8] In 1836 Houston won the Battle of San Jacinto, but the United States failed to annex Texas. Now, five years later, the Lone Star Republic's troubles were still far from over: Mexico did not recognize Texan independence, and the United States was under no obligation to defend it.

In California the population figures were all slanted the other way. There were between 6,500 and 7,000 Hispanics and fewer than 400 foreigners of all nationalities there in 1841.[9] Spanish-Californians outnumbered Anglos by more than sixteen to one. True, a handful of immigrants like Isaac Graham and his followers had turned out to be unsavory. But there were also valuable citizens like Thomas Oliver Larkin, Jacob Leese, John B. R. Cooper, and George Yount. As Vallejo tried to decide what to do with the wayfaring Yankees at Mission San José, he, like many of his countrymen, believed that Alta California was perilously underpopulated.

One of the American newcomers, John Bidwell, was only twenty-two years old at the time of his arrival in California, and he was probably the most wildly optimistic member of the much larger party that had left Sapling Grove, Kansas, in May of 1841. He had been lured to California by some of the same guesswork, fears, and personal misfortunes that would bring thousands of future pioneers. Wanderlust and malaria had figured in the equation. Known as "the shakes" or ague, malaria was rampant throughout the Midwest. Armed with a pocket-knife and carrying his worldly possessions on his back, Bidwell had first tried to take up one of the 160-acre parcels that were being handed out to homesteaders in Iowa Territory. An epidemic of malaria, however, had driven him to Platte County, Missouri, where he taught school and pieced together a fair-sized claim.[10] Returning from an excursion along the Missouri River, he discovered that his land had been occupied by a claim jumper who had murdered a man in an earlier run-in. Bidwell, barely out of his teens, decided that a showdown might not be worth the risk. His neighbors tried to intervene, but because he had not built a house on his claim, had not reached his majority, and had no family, the law gave him no protection.

Soon enough, Bidwell heard of a place called California from a Santa Fe trader named Roubidoux. The Frenchman touted the region as a land of perennial spring. His other claims have been repeated so often in travel brochures that only a few need be mentioned: Oranges grew there in winter, and people never got sick. Once, in Monterey, a man fell ill, and this was considered to be such a phenomenon that people traveled "eighteen miles into the country to see him shake."[11] Thousands of wild horses and cattle roamed the territory free for the taking. All the Mexican officials were friendly. Implausible as these stories might sound, the malaria-haunted Midwesterners were ready to believe them. Letters and maps penned by Vallejo's near neighbor, Dr. John Marsh, reinforced the tales.

Young Bidwell had helped organize a group of pioneers called the "Western Emigration Society," which soon totaled five hundred subscribers, all prepared for a long journey to the Pacific. Membership plummeted to one, however, after it was learned that Isaac Graham and his followers had been arrested and shipped off to a Mexican prison. Thomas Farnham's exaggerated accounts, republished from New York newspapers, had frightened off everyone except the determined ex-school teacher. Bidwell scraped together the means to buy a wagon, a gun, and provisions, for he still intended to go.[12]

As Bidwell made his way toward Sapling Grove, Kansas, other pioneers were yielding to the same temptation. The Mexican government — even before the advent of large-scale immigration — was trying to divert the tide of travelers. Notices were sent to New Orleans, Boston, and other cities explaining that passports and consular permission would be required before Americans could enter the department. Even settlers who had been in California for years, the government warned, could be deported unless they obtained the proper *cartas de seguridad*.[13] Travelers who disobeyed the regulations would be entering the country at their own risk, and the Mexican government would assume no responsibility for their safety. Vallejo and Alvarado received their orders from Minister of War Almonte on May 18, 1841 — exactly one day before Bidwell and his countrymen headed toward California's healing sunshine.

With some sixty-eight companions, Bidwell started west under the leadership of Captain Thomas Fitzpatrick, who had previously guided trapping parties into the Rocky Mountains.[14] Herds of buffalo covered the plains "as far as the eye could reach," sometimes forcing the travelers to take defensive measures to avoid being trampled. An approaching tornado "seemed to draw its water from the Platte River," and the entire array of wild clouds passed within a quarter of a mile of the emigrants: the wind gusted so strongly the men had to brace themselves against their wagons "to keep them from being overturned."[15]

East of Salt Lake, Captain Fitzpatrick swung north toward Oregon Territory with about half of the group. But approximately thirty-one individuals, led by Bidwell and John Bartleson, took the fork to California. By late fall they had trudged through alkali country and had crossed a high tier of mountains. Ahead, they saw what looked like desert. Food and water had been painfully scarce, but at the base of the nearby slopes they found a stream and an abundance of antelope. They jerked the meat and prepared for a march of five hundred miles. Although they did not know it, they were already in the Sacramento Valley, "almost down to tidewater." Before long, an Indian guided them to Dr. Marsh's rancho.[16]

Being something of a misanthrope, Dr. Marsh (who had arrived in California from Santa Fe in 1836) had not written his promotional letters to American newspapers because he longed for more company. In simple terms, he was a real estate speculator. But this did not mean he was run-of-the mill. While in the Midwest, he had compiled a dictionary of the Sioux language and had organized one of Minnesota's first schools. True, his Bachelor of Arts degree from Harvard did not entitle him to be called "doctor," but he practiced his limited skills as a physician anyway and did not hesitate to charge a fee of fifty cows if he had to stay at a rancho overnight. The letters he had published in Missouri newspapers had dismissed most of the difficulties of coming to California as "imaginary." His Mt. Diablo homestead looked downright scruffy to the travelers. They had expected to find fenced lands and carefully tended farms, but most of the dwellings resembled "sun-burned brick kilns." Windows were opened and closed with shutters instead of glass, and floors were made from hard-packed dirt.[17] The effects of the drought were obvious: wheat, beans, everything had failed. Nevertheless, the Americans were glad to meet the quirky doctor. He slaughtered a couple of pigs for their supper, and to show their gratitude, some of the overlanders gave him their most valued possessions: a cheap but serviceable set of surgical instruments, a butcher knife, and other useful items.[18] Probably the only thing that reminded the pioneers of the prosperous farmlands they had left behind was the corn whiskey they swallowed to wash down their dinner of pork and tortillas.[19]

Dr. Marsh had been very liberal with his ink, but he turned out to be, in Bidwell's words, "one of the most selfish of mortals." During the night some of the travelers slaughtered two of his best oxen without his permission, and the next day Marsh complained that the "company has already been over a hundred dollars' expense to me, and God knows whether I will ever get a *real* of it or not."[20]

Once the Americans learned that they needed passports, about half of them headed toward San Jose to obtain papers. They had excellent luck finding accommodations along the way. At the rancho of José Higuera, they attended a fandango and learned dance steps like the *jota* and *jarabe* while appreciating the unaffected beauty of the women. Even in hard times, the Californians were hospitable and knew how to enjoy themselves.

Following this productive visit, the Americans continued toward the pueblo of San Jose, about fourteen miles distant. The road took them toward a high, pommel-like mountain called Loma Prieta. But before they reached the pueblo, they found themselves surrounded by a squadron of cavalry; courteously enough, the immigrants were placed under arrest. A few days later, they were led into the long, white mission building that still stands today a little east of Fremont, where General Vallejo was awaiting them.

Vallejo, at thirty-four, had come to realize that he had some personal shortcomings, having stubbed his toes on more than one political rival. If someone under his authority seemed helplessly in the grip of a ruling vice (but was not all bad), a friendly glint might come into the General's eye. People's faults amused him; it pained him to recognize his own. The General was known throughout California as the "Lion of the North," probably owing to his successful Indian campaigns rather than to the daunting cordiality he sometimes used to subdue political adversaries. For a Californian, he was slow to anger and was known to be a careful reasoner, which meant he could state warmly and clearly why he was right and could convince others to believe it. On the other hand, it wasn't always easy to strike up a friendship with him since he did not take an immediate liking to everyone; but he admired hard-working settlers and individuals with talent.

One gaunt member of this fortunate Bidwell party, Joseph Chiles, had met and befriended Vallejo on an earlier trip to California. Chiles now got the impression that the General did not really like the formal role he had to play.[21] Vallejo and Chiles had a mutual friend, George Yount, a hunter from North Carolina whose land grant in the Napa Valley had been approved by Vallejo in 1836.[22] Yount had surprised the General by showing him something new: when lined up and made to overlap, thin slabs of wood (called shingles) made a fine roof.

Vallejo reminded the hopeful Americans that their presence in California was illegal: by law, passports were required. Several of the weary men feared they would now have to start back across the Sierras at a time when snow was already beginning to fall in the Rockies. The travelers probably suspected that they posed no actual threat to the Californian authorities. In the past, Yankees who wanted to settle in the province had learned the Spanish language, professed the Catholic faith, married local women, and eventually applied for naturalization papers. Perhaps, the new arrivals reasoned, they would be able to do the same. Also in the Americans' favor was the fact that Vallejo and Alvarado were fed up with the supreme government in Mexico City. Mexico's leaders, having repudiated the liberal constitution of 1824, were reviving a harsh form of centralism. In 1840 Vallejo and Alvarado had been censured for expelling Isaac Graham and his followers. Who was to say that the Californians would not be criticized again if the thirty-one American travelers were forced to return to the United States?

Discovering that John Marsh's letters had nerved the Americans to make their long journey, Vallejo ordered the doctor to come to San Jose "with the greatest possible promptness."[23] Marsh arrived in an irritable mood and did not deny writing the letters that had whetted the Americans' appetite for California's teeming resources. Faced with a remote government that tended to give mixed signals, the guilty Marsh, and thirty-one reasonably civilized Americans, Vallejo decided to let the travelers stay. Very sensitive to his need for qualified colonists, he issued passports and told the newcomers to legalize their residence as soon as possible. Marsh was asked to serve as bondsman for about fifteen of the party. Other long-term residents, including John Sutter, assumed responsibility for the rest.[24]

On November 17, Vallejo sent a letter to Sonoma, telling one of his stewards that five travelers would soon be arriving; they were to be fed and given rooms while they made a study of the surrounding countryside.[25]

The gloomy Dr. Marsh was handed documents for the men still at his rancho in the north. Though the passports had cost him nothing, he tried to recoup his losses by charging his guests five dollars apiece. Since the men had no money, he took notes or goods in barter.[26] He had been hoping John Bidwell would "stay at his ranch and make a useful hand to work," so he did not offer him papers. But Bidwell scorned the doctor and went south to get his own passport, arriving at Mission San José just as the dry ground was receiving its first dose of rain. When Vallejo learned of Bidwell's predicament, he immediately had his secretary, Victor Prudon, make out a passport for him and signed it himself. Now Bidwell was free; no charge was made for the papers, and Bidwell felt a twinge of satisfaction, knowing Marsh had been denied a small profit.[27]

Vallejo's confidence in Bidwell and Chiles proved to be well founded. After Bidwell became a significant agricultural entrepreneur, he and Vallejo would write laws together for California's state legislature, and Bidwell later served in the U.S. Congress. He and Chiles also turned out to be Vallejo's staunch friends during the Bear Flag Revolt.

Vallejo's obliging welcome for this first group of overland settlers emerged not only from his needs as colonizer but also from his cosmopolitan attitude, which had its origins in the early influence of Governor Sola and William Hartnell. His actions certainly reinforced the impression Richard Henry Dana had received in 1835, when he noted that

Vallejo was "favourably inclined to foreigners."[28] The General's establishing a precedent of tolerance would carry over into the distant future. It is not too far-fetched to suggest that Americans of diverse backgrounds today still feel some of that sense of accommodating broadmindedness in California. If he was not actually the founder of California's diversity, Vallejo was certainly one of its chief architects. In 1841 the province could not boast an affluent society, but Vallejo helped to make it a place of refuge. Obviously the General did not object to sharing California with Americans (or Europeans) — offering them opportunities that his Native American neighbors were seldom asked to enjoy.

There was also a practical side to Vallejo's generosity. The newcomers had skills, which made them too valuable to send away. Years later, he put it bluntly:

> The arrival of so many people from the outside world was highly satisfying to us "arribeños" [northern Californians] who were ... gratified to see numerous parties of industrious individuals come and settle among us permanently. Although they were not possessed of wealth, due to their goodly share of enlightenment, they could give a powerful stimulus to our agriculture which, unfortunately, was still in a state of inactivity, owing to the lack of strong and intelligent workers. . . .[29]

Here, Vallejo was pointing obliquely to a major flaw in California's labor system, which stemmed, in turn, from the Californians' abuse of the Indian workers. As mentioned earlier, the Native Americans performed most of the unskilled and semiskilled jobs in the province, but most Indians would have preferred to live on their tribal lands. Given food and clothing but paid no money, they were unable to enter the marketplace as equals, so they balked at the work ethic. This did not mean they weren't useful. Vallejo, who benefited from (and also abused) Indian labor as much as any ranchero, willingly credited them with having fashioned the province with their own hands. But since there were practically no avenues of advancement for the Indians, they had no reason to improve their skills for their oppressors. They also had not picked up the sort of technical knowledge (possessed by a man like Chiles) which would have enabled them to construct mills.[30]

The General presented a very different picture when he explained his hospitality to the supreme government. He claimed that the Americans had been allowed to stay in California as "the only means to recon-

cile justice with the present circumstances" because "we cannot prevent
them from entering, and all because we lack troops."[31]

But this was literally not the case. If the California authorities in 1840
were able to round up one hundred of the most belligerent men in the province (including Isaac Graham), Bidwell's party of thirty-one travelers could
not have posed an insurmountable threat only one year later.

Vallejo realized, however, that it would only be a matter of time
before military problems arose. In his letters to Mexico, he continued to
stress California's defensive needs. He told Minister of War Almonte
that the port of San Francisco "deserves to rank among the principal
ones of the world"; yet, in spite of the province's ideal geographical
location and mild climate, California lacked enough population to defend itself. The Russians and the Hudson's Bay Company had been able
to hunt out two species of fur-bearing animals, Indian tribes virtually
controlled the interior, and "we have to endure all those ills because we
cannot prevent them, since we have no troops."[32] Vallejo admitted that
"the danger seems closer than the help," and he made several suggestions. Most important, a new governor should be appointed who would
unite civil and military authority. The official should have no ties of
kinship to California's leading families. A large colony of Mexicans,
mainly artisans and farmers, should be sent to California with a military
force "of at least two hundred men, all secure in their salaries." Finally,
not only should the decrepit fortification at the mouth of San Francisco
Bay be repaired, but a wharf, barracks, and customs house should be
built at San Francisco. [33]

Governor Alvarado's outlook on immigration was very much like
Vallejo's. He accepted the General's decision regarding the Americans,
though in his official letters to Mexico City Alvarado excused himself
for having done nothing to stop the Bidwell party's entry by claiming he
had not wanted to create a dispute with his dictatorial uncle.[34]

The same could not be said of Don Mariano's older brother, Don
José de Jesús Vallejo, who, along with a few other prominent citizens,
had difficulty accepting the presence of the Americans. The General's
brother asked him to create a "Committee of Public Safety," with headquarters at San Jose and branch offices in all the towns of the department; but Don Mariano did not favor such a plan, believing that troops,
money, and Mexican colonists in sufficient numbers were needed to
counterbalance the overland immigration, since the influx was going to
be a long-term problem.[35]

The members of the Bidwell group were not the last arrivals of

1841. As the year drew to a close, a ship fleeing from a series of storms sailed through the narrow waterway the Indians called Yulupa (later known as the Golden Gate). Among the passengers was the powerful governor general of the Hudson's Bay Company, Sir George Simpson.[36]

II

Balding, portly, and fastidious — a man who had risen by his own efforts from illegitimate birth to knighthood — Sir George Simpson was not as careless with his barbed judgments of the Californians as Lieutenant Charles Wilkes had been, nor did he possess the annoying affectations of the Count Duflot de Mofras. As governor general of the Hudson's Bay Company, he was an expert at sizing up opportunities for trade and at getting local moguls to cooperate with the Company's hunting operations. The English presence in California was not negligible, and Simpson had tremendous leverage. He had met Lieutenant Wilkes at Fort Vancouver, where the American had made caustic remarks about the Hudson Bay Company's overwhelming presence there. In fact, the Company had been in Oregon Territory so long that its initials, H.B.C., were sometimes jokingly interpreted to mean "Here Before Christ."[37]

Because General Vallejo had jurisdiction over trapping operations north of San Pablo Bay, Simpson hoped that a friendly meeting would lead to an extension of the Company's privileges. Two days after New Year's, with eight or nine traveling companions, Simpson headed for Sonoma to pay the General a visit. A dense fog made landmarks invisible, and the travelers were drenched by a January rain. Showers were still falling when they reached Sonoma Creek. The colors of the Mexican flag — accompanied by an official salute from brass cannon — greeted the Britishers as they entered the spacious pueblo. Vallejo had laid out Sonoma on a grand scale, making the lots unusually large — 300 feet square. The impressive southern approach, the Calle Principal, was a boulevard 110 feet wide, known today as Broadway. At the center of the promising settlement, Vallejo had created the largest plaza in California, each side measuring 222 yards and affording future Sonomans an area the size of a small college campus in which to spend their leisure time.[38]

The evening of Simpson's arrival, Vallejo — who had been bedridden all day — came to dinner wrapped in a cloak. His troublesome hip was worse now, mainly because a British physician, Dr. Edward Turner Bale, had sent him a "blister of cantharides" instead of a healing plaster.

The mistake may have been deliberate. Bale resented the punishments he had received from Vallejo after the doctor touched off a dispute with landlord Thomas Oliver Larkin. During the course of the legal battle, Bale had shown little respect for the wishes of Monterey officials, and Vallejo had ordered him locked up for eight days.[39]

Simpson was quite impressed with Don Mariano's appearance:

> General Vallejo is a good-looking man of about 45 [sic], who has risen in the world by his own talent and energy. His father died about ten years ago, leaving to a large family of sons and daughters little other inheritance than a degree of intelligence and steadiness almost unknown in the country.[40]

Simpson was an extremely persuasive spokesman for the British Crown, but that did not mean that the pro-American Vallejo was eager to embrace the sons of Albion. And for the immediate present, Simpson had definite reservations about the Californian's cuisine. He recalled that the evening meal was a superabundant affair (though poisoned "with the everlasting compound of pepper and garlick"). He noticed that Vallejo's floor lacked a carpet and that the chairs were "gaudy" (a word applied to cheap products made in the Hawaiian Islands). There were some twenty people at the table, including Vallejo's mother, Doña Antonia Lugo de Vallejo. She added a certain spice to the conversation, and Simpson could not help envying the luxury of her being surrounded by so many of her offspring, several of whom had already distinguished themselves in the country.[41]

After dinner, the women went to the sala and the men took a stroll outside. Perhaps at this time, Vallejo and the governor general compared notes on the Wilkes Expedition. If California was to become a protectorate of a leading maritime nation, Simpson was sure that England would provide greater benefits than any other country. British sympathizers like Pío Pico or Raymundo Carrillo in southern California would have welcomed Simpson's suggestions with encouraging nods. But Vallejo was already under the spell of the American continent and its awesome prospects; he preferred closer ties with the U.S. government. He had nothing against Simpson or the British. He merely felt that the United States was more inclined than England to try out new ideas, and he liked the fact that America had no titled nobility, was a republic, and shared the same land mass with California. Social and economic progress would evolve naturally from American institutions.[42]

Simpson was able to relax so completely with the Vallejos that he felt he might have been in the north of Scotland observing "Auld

Yule."[43] After he left Sonoma, his writings showed that the Californians had successfully challenged some of his prejudices. He candidly admitted that Vallejo's compatriots were far happier than the general run of Englishmen. Though indignant about the way Indian laborers were fed from a common trough — not only at Sonoma but elsewhere in California — he was nevertheless amazed to see people from all social strata, of both sexes, mingling "as members of one and the same harmonious family" at public events.[44] Such social democracy was unknown in his country.

England might easily take control of California, he thought, without resorting "to force or fraud." He knew of one treaty that gave England the right to "colonize a considerable portion of the upper province" of California to within "range of the settlement of San Francisco."[45] There was also the matter of the fifty million pesos Mexico owed Britain. It had already occurred to Vallejo that the supreme government might have to give up whole sections of California in order to meet the debt.[46]

Like Vallejo, Simpson found John Sutter's presence repellent. Simpson gave warning that New Helvetia was positioned at the intersection of two important immigration routes from Oregon and Missouri, thus virtually barring the native Californians from "the best parts of their own country." Sutter certainly might stir up trouble for the Hudson's Bay Company, as well as for the Californians.[47]

Simpson's fears were confirmed soon after he left the Vallejos in Sonoma. Sutter was feeling pinched for cash, and he planned to raise money by taking beaver pelts. He did not want the Hudson's Bay Company anywhere near his eleven-league land grant (a holding almost sixty miles long which Alvarado had approved the previous June). Californians had already seen John Sutter as the merry, well-dressed, energetic colonizer; they had heard the promises of the graceful borrower. Now another aspect of his character was about to be revealed: the agitator. No troops had attacked New Helvetia and none were planning to; but Sutter found it hard to believe that Vallejo, Alvarado, and Castro would actually allow him to establish a nearly impregnable fortress on the Sacramento River. Surely, the Californians would try to destroy the fort before he could finish its construction. He had other illusions. Having enjoyed friendly talks with Duflot de Mofras, he flattered himself with the heady dream that French gunboats would sail up the Sacramento River to defend New Helvetia against the Californians' attack.

Unable to enjoy being California's luckiest man, Sutter wanted to see himself as a conqueror. He wrote a frenzied letter of warning to

Jacob Leese. (Leese, the reader will recall, was Vallejo's second American brother-in-law — a smooth-faced, smiling trapper from Ohio who had married the General's sister Rosalia. Since Leese lived on the southwest corner of the Sonoma plaza and saw Vallejo on a daily basis, many people in California, including Larkin and Sutter, knew that writing to him was practically tantamount to writing to Vallejo himself.)

After reading the letter — and especially after reconsidering it — Vallejo mused that Sutter was acting a little like the knight from La Mancha, who after "earnestly fighting some windmills ... went to the alcalde of Valladolid ... to collect a large amount of money for his efforts on behalf of that town." It seemed to him that the European must be involved in a personal charade, and was merely pretending "to have received word that [José] Castro was going to come and expel him from New Helvetia." Moreover, the General resented Sutter's inventing "wrongs for which he declares he will make [the Californians] pay through the intervention of French warships."[48]

Taken by itself, Sutter's letter was a raspingly intense piece of ill humor:

> ...when this Rascle of Castro should come here a very warm and harty welcome is prepared for him. ... I have ... about fifty faithful Indians which sho[o]t their musquet very quik. ... the first french fregate who came here will do me justice. ... It is to[o] late now to drive me out the country.[49]

Sutter swore that if the Californians tried to move against his fort, he would issue "a declaration of Independence and proclaim California for a Republique independent of Mexico." Among his allies he listed "60 or 70" Hudson's Bay Company trappers, Indian scouts, and men from Oregon. Then he made an astounding suggestion: he would like General Vallejo to "join us in such a case."[50]

The letter may have been a poor attempt to forestall attack; but even imagining an alliance between himself and General Vallejo required a brand of starch never before seen in the country. Vallejo sent the original of the letter to Governor Alvarado, listing Sutter's offenses, which included waging war on the Indians, providing refuge for foreigners, making treasonous threats, and assuming dictatorial powers. Not surprisingly — in view of the Fort Ross fiasco — Alvarado dismissed the whole thing as bluster.[51]

Sir George Simpson was quick to affirm his support of California's laws and sent Vallejo a letter which denied any connection between his men and the eccentric European.[52]

Vallejo told his Mexican superiors that there were probably enough soldiers on hand to destroy Sutter's Fort, but that New Helvetia was now serving as a useful buffer between the coastal settlements and the chronically angered Indian tribes; a prosperous colony had always been needed on the Sacramento River.[53] Vallejo's ambivalence toward Sutter has subsequently led historians to conclude that the Sutter-Vallejo rivalry was more like a duel between puff adders than rattlers.

Governor Alvarado, however, thought it would be in his interest to *increase* Sutter's powers, never guessing what Sutter's expanded political influence might mean in the future.

4

A New Governor Brings Crisis

I

$\mathcal{T}$he Mexican supreme government usually ignored Vallejo's requests, which may have been a blessing in disguise. But in one instance, his appeals were answered. A replacement for Vallejo and Alvarado was sent from Mexico to serve as California's new governor. The appointee, General Manuel Micheltorena, was a friend of the tyrannical Santa Anna and was bringing an army of three hundred men.[1] As it turned out, the troops were not trained regulars; they were "chiefly criminals without military discipline." When the ragged soldiers landed at San Diego in August of 1842, Micheltorena had to be saluted with Yankee gunpowder because the Californians had exhausted their own supply.[2] The new governor did not trust his men enough to give them weapons, so no muskets were issued; but almost as soon as the ex-convicts landed, they began to plunder the local kitchens and henhouses for food. It was a cruel mockery of Vallejo's high expectations.[3] Fortunately, Alvarado's friend José Castro continued to show gratitude for Micheltorena's help during the Graham Affair; otherwise, there might have been political fireworks from the very start, because Alvarado did not want to recognize the Mexican appointee.

Micheltorena — far from being a dictator at heart — was easily intimidated. This became obvious within a matter of weeks. Since he planned to assume his post of leadership at the old capital, Micheltorena slowly led his troops toward Monterey. But word reached him that the northern port had been seized by two American warships. It was true. On October 20, 1842, the American flag was snapping in the breeze over Vallejo's birthplace. Though Micheltorena's troops outnumbered the 150 U.S. sailors and marines who had taken the port, the Mexican governor quickly did an about-face and marched back to Los Angeles. It would be another ten months before he saw the sparkling waters of Monterey Bay.

But why had the capital been seized? The American skipper responsible for the coup, Captain Thomas ap Catesby Jones, had read some
newspaper articles which reported that "a conditional" state of war existed between Mexico and the United States. (Supposedly the war had
been touched off by the Texas dispute.) Another news item claimed that
California had been ceded to England for $7 million; if true, this was a
violation of the Monroe Doctrine. Captain Jones had immediately left
his Pacific Squadron station at Callao, Peru, setting course for California. His hope was to prevent Admiral Thomas of Great Britain from
reaching the province first.

Jones's flagship, the *United States*, was one of the fastest ships in the
water, but it would be remembered long after for another reason. Within
a matter of months, Herman Melville would step aboard as an ordinary
seaman. His voyage would lead to the publication of a scathing indict-
ment of naval discipline on American men-of-war, *The White Jacket*.[4]

On October 19, the cusp of Monterey's harbor came into view. Captain Jones placed his two ships, the *United States* and *Cyane*, in battle-
readiness and demanded the capital's surrender. His proclamation proved
that his doubts could easily be submerged in bombast. "It is against the
armed enemies of my country, banded and arrayed under the flag of
Mexico, that war and its dread consequences will be enforced."[5]

Monterey's defenses were still "good for nothing"; the low fort
protecting the harbor had not yet been repaired, and its eleven guns
were useless. Acting-Governor Alvarado, wearing a solemn expression
(but perhaps inwardly gloating over the plight of his successor,
Micheltorena), signed the articles of capitulation at Monterey, claiming
he was doing so "from motives of humanity." Then he left for his rancho
across the Salinas River.[6]

Gladly abandoning the confines of their warships, the plucky American sailors occupied the town. Monterey was thus overwhelmed far more
easily in 1842 than it had been in 1818 by Hippolyte Bouchard.

The night of the occupation, David Spence wrote General Vallejo,
"All is tranquil; and the town is almost deserted, for many of the
officials have fled the country."[7] At this point, the good judgment of
Thomas Oliver Larkin served Californians and Americans alike. He had
been in the country for slightly more than ten years now, finding in
California the prosperity and marital happiness that had eluded him in
North Carolina. Though he had acquired a plantation in the South and
had served as postmaster there, he had also gone bankrupt while owning
slaves. Married now to Rachel Holmes — an American he had met en

route to Honolulu — the wiry, slightly deaf Larkin was a civic-minded
sort of man who one day would arrange to have more than three hundred Montereyans vaccinated at his own expense during a smallpox epidemic.[8] One of Monterey's most respected citizens, he was also unaffected
by most forms of political hysteria, and he tried to convince Captain
Jones that the navy was making a blunder. The next day, he showed the
officer Mexican newspapers and commercial letters from Mazatlan which
made it seem unlikely that a state of war existed between the two countries. The Mexican documents were far more recent than the news Jones
had read in Callao. The captain had been in the service for thirty years
and had a long record to protect. Once he realized his mistake, the U.S.
flag was hauled down, the Mexican banner was hoisted in its place, and
the embarrassed sailors were hustled back to their ships. Then Jones
honored the Mexican pennant with a full salvo from American guns. He
also repaid the Californians for all the gunpowder he had used in salut-
ing the Stars and Stripes.[9]

This double-quick repair of the diplomatic breach was carried out
so handily that normal life in Monterey was calmly resumed. International repercussions, however, would drag on for months. News of the
fiasco broke up trilateral talks between Mexico, the United States, and
Britain about California's boundaries.

Jones sailed to southern California to reassure Governor Micheltorena that no harm had been meant. Feeling he was entitled to
damages, the timorous governor sensed his advantage and tried to force
Jones's hand. As compensation for the boo-boo, he demanded fifteen
thousand dollars, along with 1,500 military uniforms, and a complete
set of musical instruments.[10] A man Vallejo called the "Mirabeau of
California," José Antonio Carrillo was on hand during the talks. When
Jones treated the governor's requests as a joke, Carrillo hastily led
the American out of the meeting place before either officer could take
offense.[11]

From the willful, brandy-loving Carrillo, Vallejo received unflattering appraisals of the new governor, including the suggestion that too
much "cogitation" had blunted the force of Micheltorena's brain. Carrillo
also faulted the governor's fondness for platitudes and mentioned a few:
"True force and well being lie in good understanding between states. . . .
Fortunate is the politician . . . who is humane toward strangers. . . . [W]ars
destroy republics and exhaust treasuries. . . ." After having corresponded
with the governor and having seen some of his state papers, Vallejo agreed
with Carrillo's appraisal.[12]

Even before Vallejo actually met the aristocratic Micheltorena, he was able to form his own opinion of the American Captain Jones. Their introduction took place in late 1842, just a few days before Christmas. Vallejo had promised Jones a friendly greeting, but the expectations of both men were disappointed on the very first day. As ordered by the General, a welcoming party carefully monitored a wide stretch of water in anticipation of Jones's arrival, but the Yankee and his sailors approached via a different estuary several miles to the east. Having made their landing, they were suddenly arrested by a detail of cavalrymen under the command of Doña Francisca's brother, Ramón Carrillo. The capture took place on the Huichica Rancho, where some 1,400 of Chief Solano's Suisun tribesmen were training for battle. (Since 1835 an alliance with the six-foot, seven-inch Chief Solano had enabled Vallejo to enforce treaties with the numerous Indian tribes in the area.)

Jones was fascinated by what he saw of the maneuvers, but he wasn't allowed to watch for long. Captain Salvador Vallejo took Jones and his men across grazing land dotted with helmet-shaped boulders that were so abundant it seemed as though an invading army had already been routed. Upon reaching Sonoma late that night, the Americans were locked up in the flag room in the barracks.

Don Salvador's patience with armed foreigners was wearing thin, and he took a perverse delight in the way the tables had been turned on Jones. During the skipper's visit, he continued to hang around like a gloomy cloud, for he knew Jones had been instructed to collect additional claims for damages resulting from the Graham Affair. To many people, Salvador Vallejo must have seemed like a cross between a Cossack and a wolverine. His relentless style of Indian warfare had made him a feared man in northern California, and his aggressiveness had never been tempered by Governor Sola's guidance.[13] He was certainly glad to learn, months later, that because of Jones's illegal seizure of Monterey, Mexico had rejected U.S. attempts to buy California. A three-way arrangement between England, Mexico, and the United States had been in the works whereby the United States would have accepted the settlement of the Oregon border at the Columbia River; Mexico would have recognized Texan independence; and the United States would have paid several million dollars for Alta California. But these talks were broken off, and as a diplomatic gesture, Jones was recalled from duty.[14]

General Vallejo had more of a sense of humor about Monterey's capture than his brother. Sometime after midnight, he rescued Jones from the flag room and did his best to change the unfriendly mood Don Salvador had created.

The next morning a thirteen-gun salvo was fired on the Sonoma parade ground in Jones's honor. The skipper added another stroke to the ludicrous portrait of Micheltorena that had been forming in Vallejo's mind when he remarked that the governor would have fired a twenty-one-gun salute in honor of his visit, instead of the correct thirteen, just as though Jones were the president of the United States or some European dignitary.[15]

Feeling more at ease, the captain asked if he could return to the place where the Indians were training for war. Soon, the Californians and Americans were backtracking to the Huichica grant, where Chief Solano's maneuvers were still under way. General Vallejo thought that the chief's Suisun (Patwin) tribesmen were the finest developed people he had ever seen, and he was later heard to say that "any one of them might have served as a model for a sculptor."[16] Both sexes of the Suisuns were tall, but unlike Anglo-Americans, even the largest of them had small feet.[17] After Vallejo's son Platon had learned the Suisun language, he interpreted the word Patwin to mean "people of the open," and noted that in matters of war, ". . . the wives and children of the soldiers followed them in their campaigns. The women cooked, washed and served as nurses for the wounded, something on the Red Cross style."[18]

Captain Jones was surprised by the number of females present on the field. He asked if the wives ever took part in the fighting. Don Salvador hadn't cooled off yet and growled, "Those women do not fight against the Satiyomi Indians, but if it were a matter of fighting the Yankees, they would take part in the battle and would know how to give a good account of themselves."[19] Courtesy, especially toward guests, was a touchy point with General Vallejo; he thought Don Salvador's remarks uncivil and told him so.

While Jones was still in Sonoma, a three-day fiesta took place. Beef, chicken, and kid were cooked in open pits, and tortillas swelled on the soapstone griddles. Captain Jones sampled the General's wines and also his *aguardiente* — a flavorful brandy made from grapes — some 280 gallons of which had been produced that year in the winery.[20]

When an Indian runner received first prize for winning a race, Jones added a gold coin to his reward. He also gave his former captor, Ramón Carrillo, a gold pen case to prove there were no hard feelings for the surprise arrest.

Though in later years General Vallejo would sometimes grumble about the wasteful magnificence of women's clothes, which made it seem "that half the modern young ladies are born solely to cause the other half of them to die of envy,"[21] he had recently gone pretty far toward creating envy himself. That day, everyone was talking about Doña Francisca's tortoiseshell comb, for which, it was said, Vallejo had paid Captain Fitch some six hundred dollars.[22]

The American sailors could not hide their appreciation for the Indian women who, "clothed only in a short skirt that covered their waists and part way down their thighs," were dancing on the plaza. A few of the sailors wanted to go downstairs and move to the drumbeat with the dancers. When asked permission, the General answered that it would be unwise. Alcohol had "befuddled the brains" of the Indians, and Don Salvador's troopers were also intoxicated. The combination of jack tars, Californian troopers, and Indian women might create unfriendly results.[23]

Jones's stay ended peacefully enough. Not many days after the captain left Sonoma, Vallejo was rowed out to the *Cyane* at Sausalito. The steep limb of Mt. Tamalpais rose in the background at the northwest end of the bay; and as Vallejo reached the sloop-of-war, a thirteen-gun salute honored his arrival. The sound drifted above the low hills, which were still a parched brown from the previous summer's heat.

Jones's ships had again demonstrated that Monterey was incapable of defending itself. But as Vallejo knew, the biggest breach in California's defenses was located at the place the Indians called Yulupa, the mouth of San Francisco Bay. The now decrepit *Castillo de San Joaquín*, a fort shaped like a horseshoe, had been erected there in 1795 at a point directly under the first span of today's Golden Gate Bridge. At the time of Jones' visit, the *castillo* boasted some thirteen bronze cannons, most of which dated from the mid-seventeenth century. Few of the guns were in good working order, and they fronted the ocean swells from ruinous walls. When Vallejo inspected the deteriorating *castillo*, he could see the speed with which time was conquering the works of the Californians. During the seventy years of Hispanic colonization, institutions had toppled overnight. The twenty-one California missions already resembled remnants of another century, but only twenty years earlier they had been the economic and spiritual centers of California life. They could be seen now all along the Camino Real with bandaged-looking walls and broken bell towers, little more than ghosts.

A young American sailor saw Vallejo during this period and described him as "a very gentlemanly Mexican," a leader

> fifty years in advance of his countrymen in intelligence and enterprise and yet I do not believe he was appreciated by his Mexican associates. Perhaps it was because he saw their defects

and tried to remedy them, an impossibility at that time when there was no incentive to labor for great reforms and revolutions were the fashion. [Vallejo] was quite affable to us boys, often giving us a silver dollar for pulling him on board the ship and on shore. He spoke nice English and always had a pleasant word for us or a joke at our expense. Lewey [the sailor's companion] found out that he had several pretty daughters . . . and wanted to run away and go and have a peep at them, but I discouraged the idea and he finally abandoned it. The General was a frequent visitor when we were in port and everyone liked him.[24]

II

One reason an endless flow of American wagon trains had not materialized in 1842 and 1843 (as the Mexican government had feared) had been the publication of Thomas Farnham's account of the Graham Affair in U.S. newspapers. John Bidwell admitted there was no unanimous opinion among his former trailmates about California's desirability; the Americans either looked on the province "as the garden of the world or the most desolate place of creation."[25] Joseph Chiles, whose type of grim visage would later be immortalized in Grant Wood's paintings of Midwestern farmers, shook the dust of the Napa Valley from his feet and headed back to the United States — not to abandon California, but to bring back more settlers. John Marsh increased the flow of his promotional writing, and in February of 1843, Thomas Oliver Larkin began composing letters to the *New York Herald* that described the abundant virtues of the Pacific Coast.[26] At this point, California officials did not need another melodramatic incendiary like Thomas Farnham in their midst, but they got one in July of 1843 in the person of Lansford Hastings, who brought sixteen or seventeen armed men and a like number of women and children to Sutter's Fort.[27]

A month after the Hastings party, thirty-four strong, augmented the population at New Helvetia, Governor Micheltorena finally moved his troops to Monterey. He had already borrowed money from Vallejo on a couple of occasions, but more often from local financier Thomas Oliver Larkin. This was necessary because when Micheltorena reached California, the treasury contained a sorry greeting: "*Entradas, $000; salidas, $000; existencias, cuatro reales.*"[28] Larkin did not hold vast ranchos like Vallejo, but he had made definite strides as a merchant. Beginning with capital of five hundred dollars in 1832, his net worth ten years later had grown to $49,147 (approximately $638,911 in 1990 dollars).[29] In the loans he made to Micheltorena, however, Larkin's judgment seemed to go astray, for neither the governor nor the supreme government nor the administration that followed Micheltorena's wanted to make good on the debts.

Governor Micheltorena found Vallejo a lot harder to deal with than Larkin. But he did secure five thousand dollars from him for the support of the *batallón fijo* by granting Don Mariano an 80,000-acre land grant, which later came to be known as the Rancho Soscol, in a region adjacent to the Carquinez Straits. The grant was executed on March 15, 1843. A year later, Micheltorena actually deeded the land to Vallejo. In addition to the cash, the governor received $11,000 worth of agricultural products and supplies.[30]

Micheltorena soon struck up a friendship with John Sutter. This amity was odd, because Sutter treated California military authorities with defiance. John Sutter's praises continued to be sung by a multiplying chorus of Americans. Sutter lodged them at his fort, sent his employees into the mountains with provisions to help travelers find their way, and even sent promises of land to remote way stations on the Oregon Trail. Sutter's hostility toward California's military authorities made Americans feel safe behind his walls. Sutter's Fort had become, in fact, a flourishing American oasis — a sort of growth node that promised to produce a new slew of trouble in the Great Valley. This fact was emphasized in June of 1844 when the Kelsey party arrived. If there were Indians around and laws to be obeyed, the Kelseys were bound to wind up at odds with the authorities. Two of the Kelsey brothers, Andrew and Benjamin, had come to California in 1841 with Bidwell's group. In 1843 the hot-tempered Benjamin had gotten into a scrape of some kind with Don Salvador Vallejo, soon after which he and Andrew had departed for Oregon. When the Kelseys returned to California in 1844 with a party of approximately thirty-eight people, Samuel and David Kelsey accompanied them, and they brought their families.[31] Thanks to the Kelseys and some of Sutter's other fidgety guests, the summer of 1844 turned out to be an unpleasant one for the Vallejos. The new arrivals' tempers segued behind a feud that had been heating up for some time between Don Salvador Vallejo and the troublesome Doctor Edward Turner Bale, the man who had aggravated Don Mariano's injured hip several years before.

A chronic problem for the Californians, Dr. Bale had nevertheless been outwardly respectful of the department's laws — adopting the Catholic faith, marrying Salvador Vallejo's niece, Maria Soberanes, and obtaining all necessary papers. But he was unable, as it has been delicately put, to "understand the affectionate and demonstrative manner of the Spanish Californians in their family relations."[32]

Before he was well acquainted with Bale, General Vallejo had appointed him surgeon-in-chief to the provincial army. In 1844 Bale had resigned his post and had begun spreading rumors about Salvador Vallejo's integrity. This was provocative and it was also dangerous, because Don Salvador was a fighting man. When Bale challenged him to a duel, Salvador countered all of Bale's moves with ease, finishing the matter by using the flat of his sword to give the Englishman a whipping.[33] Bale, whose temper always seemed to be at half-cock, nursed his grudge for about four months, and in July of 1844 he persuaded a number of Americans to ride with him to Sonoma to even the score. One of his allies was Granville P. Swift, who had arrived at Sutter's Fort with the Kelseys and was said to be the fastest load-and-shoot man on the West Coast.[34] Bale's other helpers were thought to include Benjamin Kelsey (who had been at odds with Don Salvador before) and a hard-drinking hunter named Ezekiel Merritt. With some fourteen armed men in all, Bale rode into the pueblo just as Don Salvador Vallejo was strolling across the plaza with his friend Cayetano Juárez. The enraged doctor got to within point-blank range and fired twice. One of the shots grazed Don Salvador's chest and the wadding from the other shot hit Juárez in the jaw. Bystanders rushed Bale, who escaped across the plaza to the house of the friendly Jacob Leese (Vallejo's brother-in-law). Leese, who was then serving as Sonoma's alcalde, barred the doors and windows, but he couldn't save Bale from capture. Don Salvador's grim comrade-in-arms, Chief Solano, gathered about fifty men, broke into Leese's residence, and dragged Bale and his helpers from the house. A convenient lynching post called the *encina del castigo* (punishment tree) stood nearby. Had Don Mariano been at the Petaluma Rancho instead of in Sonoma that day, Bale's life would have expired at rope's end. But Bale's luck held out. When General Vallejo learned what was taking place, he collected an escort and prevented Solano from hanging the would-be murderer.[35] No one doubted Bale's guilt, but the General wanted a court to legalize the outcome. The doctor and his companions were thrown into jail, and Bale was fitted into a pair of leg irons.[36] The Californians felt no sympathy for Bale, so it was futile for him to offer his jailers a large sum of silver to permit his escape. Sergeant Berreyessa simply doubled the guard.[37]

On August 4 General Vallejo received a letter from his long-time friend William Richardson, which referred to a plan by Americans at Sutter's Fort to rescue Bale. Was an American revolt in the making?

Richardson didn't credit the rumors, but thought he should keep the General informed. Toward the end of the month, Alcalde William Hinckley of Yerba Buena was told that five of the Kelseys and Zeke Merritt had sworn to free Bale by force. In addition, some forty men on the Sacramento were ready to take up arms.[38]

Hot, dusty days seemed to be breeding revolutionary thoughts. Don Mariano ordered the Kelseys and Merritt questioned. The Americans denied all charges regarding a planned rescue, saying it was just talk. And, indeed, it was.

A trial was held in Sonoma in late September. The prosecutor was Vallejo's personal secretary, Victor Prudon, a Frenchman who had arrived in 1834 as a teacher. With so many eyewitnesses giving testimony, the verdict of guilty was inevitable. But the judgment had to be sent to Governor Micheltorena for confirmation. Though Monterey was thousands of miles from Mexico City, the governor acted as though the Graham Affair had taken place only months before. Seldom did the supreme government forget the fifty million pesos Mexico owed England. Anything having to do with English citizens was handled with special care, and Bale was a native of the British Isles.

Micheltorena wanted the case dropped immediately. Angered by his suggestion, Vallejo shot back a message saying that Bale had established his Mexican citizenship years earlier. A direct order arrived just as promptly from Micheltorena, demanding the doctor's release. This made Vallejo think that British partisans in Monterey, especially Micheltorena's friend, Dr. William H. McKee, had influenced the governor's decision.[39]

Vallejo asked Don Salvador to escort Bale from the pueblo. They traveled together as far as the Huichica Rancho. Before they parted, Don Salvador told Bale that, because of Micheltorena's order, his freedom was being granted. But Don Salvador also promised to get even for the Englishman's attempt on his life. Surprisingly, Bale knelt down and asked his enemy's forgiveness. The two men embraced and the incident was finally closed.[40]

For a while, Sonoma became known for its divided minds and quick tempers, and the year's violence wasn't over yet. By befriending Dr. Bale, Jacob Leese may have sacrificed some of the Vallejos' patronage. Leese was a cool, efficient, not very broad-minded man who could be counted on to carry through on ordinary business affairs; but a self-important streak lay beneath his smooth exterior. He hadn't liked being threatened by the gigantic Chief Solano. The truth was, Leese thought that *all* Indians should be made strictly subservient to the *gente de razón*.

While Victor Prudon and Leese were crossing the plaza one day, Prudon accused him of overstepping his bounds by intruding into military affairs in his role of alcalde. Leese took a poke at his critic. Not far from the spot where Bale had tried to kill Don Salvador, Prudon and Leese had a slug-fest. It is uncertain who won. Don Mariano decided that Leese needed time to cool off, and the American was relieved of his post as alcalde.[41] One thing was certain: it was becoming increasingly difficult to keep all factions at peace on the Sonoma frontier — where General Vallejo was still serving as "military commandant of the northern line."[42]

5

A Small War Heats Up

*D*espite the violent raid by Dr. Bale and his American friends (which had almost cost Don Salvador his life), General Vallejo had proven his willingness to protect the rights of Americans. Not only did he possess a degree of psychological steadiness rare on the frontier, his gaze was firmly fixed on the years ahead, and he knew that Americans were the people of the future. A few turbulent adventurers did not change that fact.

His overall strategy — to give newcomers land grants but not power — was designed to keep the political reins in the hands of either the Californians or naturalized citizens like Jacob Leese and Timothy Murphy. To use hostile Anglo-Americans as soldiers in civil conflicts would destroy the balance required to control the province. But as Alvarado and Micheltorena made preparations for civil war, they sought American allies and completely upset the equilibrium.

Although Vallejo had little faith in Governor Micheltorena's administrative abilities, he had no desire to take part in a war to get rid of him. And without the albatross of the hated convict-soldiers around his neck, the governor might have survived the intrigues of Juan B. Alvarado. Micheltorena was essentially a benevolent, sociable, comfort-loving man who had no inclination to limit the rancheros' power. But his lack of ties to any of the leading families may have kept him from attracting strong loyalties. Given his wayward sense of direction, he was never able to concoct measures that would place California's political system on a stable footing. It wasn't long before the currents of antagonism that ran through the country began to overwhelm him.

In 1844 Micheltorena strengthened his ties with Sutter. As a result, he eventually acquired the support of most of the American malcontents who had congregated at Sutter's Fort. Vallejo was no more able to control Micheltorena's actions than he had been Alvarado's. Small things revealed Don Mariano's feelings, however. When Micheltorena wanted to buy one hundred horses, Vallejo made the governor an easy mark. The usual price for a horse was between five and eight dollars, but Micheltorena agreed to pay fifty dollars apiece. The gouging may have been an ironic form of jest, because at the time the arrangement was made, Don Mariano had little reason to believe he would ever be paid. This did not mean he wanted to replace Micheltorena with a local leader. In fact, as Alvarado began to organize a revolt, Vallejo warned Micheltorena in advance — thus signifying that he had no intention of taking part in it.[1] During the coming months, Vallejo revealed his unique virtues as a patriot. He wanted something new to take hold in California, something that would work without everyone yielding to impulsive rivalries or war drums.

By fall of 1844 hatred of Micheltorena's Mexican troops had reached the point where Alvarado thought a takeover might succeed. Not only were the convict-soldiers raiding the Californians' pantries, but there were more serious complaints: a Frenchman was crippled for life when he refused to give the soldiers some of his brandy, and one of Larkin's servants was assaulted and robbed by a member of the *batallón fijo*.[2] Repeating a time-honored formula, Alvarado tried to get Vallejo to co-operate with his plans. When the General refused, it seemed like a bad omen, so Alvarado postponed his revolt. Some of his followers, however, were so angry with the governor's Mexican lieutenants, they could no longer be controlled. After rounding up Micheltorena's horses, the rebels drove them to the Salinas Valley. An army without mounts was crippled — an object of scorn. The rebel officers issued a *pronunciamiento*, rallied the people, and prepared to rid the country of the unwanted troops. Alvarado's doubts evaporated, and he assumed control of the uprising.[3]

Micheltorena did not like to get out of bed much before noon, but he suddenly adopted an energetic, tyrannical style, promising death to any immigrants who helped the Californians.[4] He knew he could count on Sutter's loyalty, and also on the allegiance of Larkin, who had loaned him money.[5] Naturally, Micheltorena's creditors did not want to see him tossed out of the country. But history had already shown that once the rancheros decided a Mexican governor had to go, it was only a matter of time before he was shipped off to Mexico. Real-estate promoter John Marsh had witnessed the eviction of two Mexican leaders, Governors Chico and Gutiérrez, in one year, and he assumed that any Americans who helped Micheltorena would be wasting their time.

A somewhat suspicious development was noted: the speed with which Micheltorena's friend, José Castro, took command of the rebel army. It was unlike Castro to oppose his *patrón* — especially since the elegant Micheltorena had recently promoted him.[6]

Vallejo believed that the two men had arranged a sham revolt in order to give the governor an honorable excuse to leave California.[7] It was reported that a letter had been captured in which Micheltorena explained the whole plan to Castro.

> My godson, a revolt has broken out . . . among some hot-headed young men. This suits me, but I do not wish for any personal persecution or vengeance. Put yourself at the head of this movement, and we shall come to an understanding.[8]

The original of this letter does not exist, but some of Vallejo's countrymen claimed to have seen it. If a compact of this sort had been arranged between the two "opponents," Vallejo assumed anyone who took part in the dispute would waste resources without gaining an advantage.

Alvarado and Micheltorena both tried to commandeer Vallejo's loyalty, but the General didn't like being saddled with other peoples' bad politics. He wrote to the governor on November 18, 1844, making two points: if the *batallón fijo* were sent out of the country, Alvarado's revolt would disintegrate by itself but as long as the thieving soldiers remained in the country, there could be no peace. The convicts had to go; with that resolved, Vallejo would continue to defend Micheltorena's authority.[9]

Micheltorena had the power, of course, *to order* Don Mariano to defend the government, and Vallejo's refusal might have been interpreted as insubordination. But would it have been conceivable for Vallejo to join the governor's defenders and fight against his own brother José de Jesús Vallejo or his nephew Alvarado?[10] His solution surprised everyone. Without a word of warning, on November 28, 1844, General Vallejo dismissed his Sonoma troops. The men he had outfitted and fed for a decade, often at his own expense, found themselves free to travel north or south. Vallejo hoped this move would resolve the dilemma of his remaining neutral during the coming war.

If Micheltorena's sense of humor was slumbering, it probably revived when he read Vallejo's reasons for disbanding the garrison: the General claimed that he was too poor to support the troops, mentioning that a crop failure had further reduced his resources.[11] Don Mariano's assets, however, were no secret to the governor. In the recent past, Vallejo had given Micheltorena $2,000 in gold, in return for which he had received five leagues in the upper Petaluma Valley. Vallejo also had

acquired the four-league Rancho Suisun. Not since Figueroa's administration had his holdings increased so dramatically.[12] William Heath Davis
estimated Vallejo's income from hides and tallow alone at $96,000 a
year.[13] Even if the estimate was too high, the General claimed income
from goods manufactured at the Rancho Petaluma, and from the sale of
wine, wheat, and other produce. From the Hudson's Bay Company, he
received fees for pelts taken north of San Pablo Bay. Sometimes when he
acted as middleman, he picked up commissions from wheat growers like
Camilo Ynita of Olompali. By the end of the following decade, his land
would encompass more than 175,000 acres, including the Rancho Yulupa,
the Agua Caliente grant, an eight-square-league rancho in Mendocino
County, the Rancho Temelec, the "Entre Napa," and other parcels. Several of his nearly contiguous grants would stretch all the way from
Mendocino County to the Carquinez Straits.[14] General Vallejo was indeed a considerable citizen.

Now he was claiming to be too poor to support the Sonoma garrison, which must have made the governor snigger. Still, whether or not
Vallejo could afford the soldiers, the fact remained that Sonoma was
virtually defenseless and would remain so until the end of Mexican rule.
The unemployed men either drifted south to San Jose, where they joined
Alvarado's rebels, or went northeast to Sutter's Fort, adding their strength
to the loyalist cavalry being organized there.[15]

At the end of November, during a steady rain, the first chapter began in one of California's only charming wars. Alvarado's followers,
some 220 strong, advanced on General Micheltorena's position south of
San Jose. Relying again on frontiersmen, Alvarado had gained the back-
ing of a band of Americans led by the energetic and unpredictable Prus-
sian, Charles Weber, a man who believed that as long as the *batallón fijo*
could march through rancho courtyards collecting utensils and chickens, no one's property was safe.

The Californians seldom lacked for colorful apparel. Rancheros without uniforms wore jackets trimmed in scarlet or silver, hats covered with
oilskin, their legs protected by embroidered deerskin leggings. Beauti-
fully equipped horses stormed from hill to hill in the drizzle, and enough
equestrian feats were performed to frighten off a horde of Cossacks. The
objective, however, was not a bloody victory, but arbitration. By December 2, the Treaty of Santa Teresa had been signed, and Micheltorena
had agreed to send his convict army back to Mexico. The rebels would
be granted complete amnesty and their expenses would be paid by the
public treasury.[16]

The generous spirit of the treaty seemed to confirm Vallejo's initial idea of the war as interesting theater. But the drama wasn't over. Governor Micheltorena reneged and asked Mexico to send reinforcements.

Castro and Alvarado began preparing for a real war and worked hard to secure Vallejo's allegiance. Having no affection for the convict soldiers, and unhappy with the tie between Sutter and Micheltorena, Vallejo was tempted to join his nephew. Once again, however, he saw a dangerous development in the participation of the foreigners. If the immigrants managed to gain the upper hand, it would be no easy task to dislodge them after the conflict was over. Obviously, the lessons of the Graham Affair had been forgotten.[17]

Sutter suddenly gained an edge in his recruiting efforts when the governor, by means of a general title, gave the colonist the power to grant lands to foreigners in Micheltorena's name. This meant that Sutter's powers now exceeded Vallejo's. The Americans in northern California flocked to the governor's cause, for it seemed obvious to them who was likely to win.[18]

Vallejo was understandably contemptuous of the fawning style the governor employed to flatter Sutter ("What you may do, I approve, what you promise, I will fulfil; what you spend, I will pay").[19] Don Mariano wrote Sutter in a much different vein:

Don Juan Vaca showed me a letter of yours in which you incite true patriots to join with you to march against the rebels and to aid the government. All the government being in full peace, I am obliged to suppose that the rebels only exist in your fevered imagination.[20]

The General enclosed a copy of the Treaty of Santa Teresa, reminding Sutter that the governor had promised to rid California of the hated convicts, so the Sacramento leader should stop organizing foreigners and respect the treaty as signed.

Few American players in this game could predict the real probabilities of the outcome. The conflict for many of them became like a jumping contest in which they dexterously zigzagged across ties of loyalty. As a good indication of how things were going, Isaac Graham — still nursing his old grudge against Castro, Alvarado, and Vallejo — intended to support the governor.[21]

Sutter resumed his pretense of companionability with Don Mariano, inviting him to help put down Alvarado's revolt. In fact, he thought Vallejo should ride at the head of the New Helvetia army to protect the governor. Meantime, there was a shortage of horses at New Helvetia. Sutter asked Don Mariano to send him a hundred head from the government herd pastured on the Rancho Soscol. In return, Vallejo could have the use of Sutter's schooner or the services of his employees anytime he liked.[22] Sutter also mentioned the arrival of a large party of Americans who had recently entered the Great Valley — taking care to exaggerate their numbers to suggest a burgeoning supply of allies.[23]

Vallejo's answer was somewhat prophetic: the final results of the military contest might be the reverse of what the adventurers expected. Vallejo stated he would never want a foreigner to help him against his own countrymen, and the immigrants really had no reason to complain: they had been well treated in California — far better than what the law prescribed. Why should they aid a doomed leader like Micheltorena or help him despoil the country?[24] So far, nothing had stopped Sutter, and he ignored the General's advice. He planned to give the Californians a lesson in military science. Nothing suggested that within eight weeks, his life would be hanging by a thread, subject to the whims of Castro and Alvarado.

Radiating an infectious gloom, John Marsh persisted in his efforts to discourage Americans from joining Sutter. So did Charles Weber, Alvarado's ally, who bravely set out from San Jose to New Helvetia to explain the flaws in Sutter's plan. In the long run, a return to Californian self-rule might be better for the Americans than a continued Mexican governorship. And why should American frontiersmen defend Micheltorena's Mexican soldiers? Many of the Americans listened to Weber and defected. Resentful of his intrusion, Sutter put Weber in jail where he could do no more harm.[25]

On December 22 Sutter sent a raiding party of twenty Americans to the Soscol Rancho, where the much-desired herd had been pastured. But the horses had been driven off a couple of days earlier by a Monterey officer named Francisco Rico. Vallejo's employees watched with shocked faces as the unexpected visitors cast about, looking for the vanished mounts. Were these Anglo-Americans scouts? Obviously, they were hungry, because they shot a cow and ate it. Their ear-bending brand of English was incomprehensible to the vaqueros. But their gestures were clear enough: the Americans offered the Californians a share in the feast of broiled steaks. After finishing a hasty meal, they identified themselves as having come from the east and pronounced the name Sutter. Since there was no herd to bag, they took the few horses in sight, along with some saddles, and rode off.[26]

The daring move completely surprised Vallejo. He now faced the dilemma of a leader who still has great prestige but must rely on passive strength to maintain his authority. The recent theft was the first price he had to pay for his neutrality.

Jacob Leese, once again serving as the pueblo's alcalde, claimed that no single individual could accomplish the job of recovering Vallejo's equipment and livestock. At a meeting held in Sonoma, he swore that even ten soldiers would be inadequate to the assignment of dealing with Sutter's well-armed troops.[27] The next day, however, he offered to take Vallejo's protest to New Helvetia with an inventory of the missing goods. Upon reaching the snug fort, he renewed contact with some of his American friends and received a cordial reception from Sutter.

Not too surprisingly, Leese came back from New Helvetia empty-handed.[28] Meanwhile, reports were filtering in from Vallejo's other ranchos that Sutter was stealing more horses and cattle. The extent of the European's exhilaration can be felt in a letter he wrote to William Hartnell: "Right here, I am still in a state of war. Every day, drilling is going on. I have a strong garrison, and several thousand Indians who . . . are ready for service in a moment."[29] When Sutter said he would not hesitate to use these Indians against the Californians, he made a serious propaganda error which would haunt him in later weeks. But for now, Micheltorena's forces outnumbered the rebel troops four to one. Sutter could boast, "The whole country stood in awe of me." He had put together one of the strongest armies ever assembled in California.[30]

On January 6, 1845, José Castro and Alvarado sprinted south to Los Angeles by way of the Salinas Valley. This was their "strategic withdrawal," and they did not have to look back. Governor Micheltorena, never a model of aggressiveness, was being troubled by an affliction that makes horseback riding a painful ordeal. Sutter rode alongside his hemorrhoidal chief, and the army made little forward progress.

Alvarado was clever enough to realize he stood little chance of succeeding in the pro-American north, so he placed the fulcrum of his revolution in Los Angeles, which drew Sutter away from the Sacramento Valley. This was a brilliant stroke, for the Los Angelenos already hated the *batallón fijo* and were appalled to think of an invasion by northerners and Indians. Why would a Mexican governor employ such tactics?[31]

Americans like Granville Swift and the Kelseys were not the sort of men to miss out on a cross-country spree which, with any luck at all, could turn into a shooting match. But their leader's pursuit of the enemy lacked dash. It wasn't until the end of January that Sutter and Micheltorena finally entered Santa Barbara. Soon some of Sutter's sharpshooters — including future Bear Flaggers Granville Swift and William Knight — were captured by General Castro's men. This was a blow to Swift's pride, over which he would brood for months.[32] While being held captive, he and his fellow immigrants received stray bits of information that worried them. Americans just as wily as they, such as Jim Beckworth and Bill Le Gros O'Fallon, were joining Alvarado's forces in Los Angeles. If Alvarado actually ended up winning the war, Sutter would be shorn of his holdings and the foreigners who had helped him might be tossed out of the country. More than a few of the volunteers felt their determination wilt. In fact, thirty-five men changed their minds, left the army, and returned to northern California.[33]

Sutter sent letters to his manager at New Helvetia, reminding him to keep an eye on Vallejo. Toward the end of January, he even suggested that it would be "very good" to capture Sonoma and "take the cannons and military stores up the Sacramento." He also wanted General Vallejo and Don Salvador arrested. It's possible Sutter and a lanky frontiersman named Ezekiel Merritt had already roughed out a plan of action before Sutter had started south, because the letter named Merritt as the right man to carry out the job.[34]

Rumors soon reached Vallejo that Sutter had left a company of men at New Helvetia to perform the raid. On February 1 the General issued a proclamation urging the people to prepare for their defense. However, Sonoma wasn't the only place in danger. Large numbers of Walla Walla Indians had been seen congregating in the Sacramento Valley. Fearing the tribesmen, the Americans at Sutter's Fort never made their expected attack on Sonoma.[35]

When Sutter reached Los Angeles, he had only 50 men left of the 150 riflemen who had marched out of New Helvetia. Support for Governor Micheltorena, which had always been thin in Los Angeles, shredded to nothing. On February 15 the Los Angeles Assembly named Pío Pico governor *ad interim* and deposed Micheltorena.

Hours before the battle rain and snow fell in the San Fernando Valley and the surrounding mountains resembled cold white tiaras. Castro and Alvarado placed their men on the uphill side of the Cahuenga Pass, thus blocking the governor's path into Los Angeles.

During the engagement of February 20, the cannons fired steadily, putting birds in more danger than soldiers, because the guns were firing high.[36] On this memorable day, an incredulous Sutter was shocked to discover that some of his men were casting votes, trying to determine who wanted to defect to the rebels and who wanted to remain with Micheltorena.[37]

Governor Pico accidently surprised another conclave on the battlefield. He promptly told the foreigners they would qualify to receive legal title to land if they surrendered — and no punishments would be doled out for their participation in the war.[38] This was welcome, even decisive news, and most of the men left the field.

The next day General Micheltorena surrendered, and on February 22 the Treaty of Cahuenga was signed, ending the war. Now the virtues of preconquest California began to shine with a burnished luster. Enemies jettisoned their fears, and friendships temporarily disrupted by the dispute traveled again along old channels. For instance, when Sutter was seized, his captors said they were glad to see him, and a messenger was sent to find Alvarado.

> The former governor rode up, dismounted, and embraced Sutter like a close friend. He ordered a bottle of *aguardiente* and poured drinks for Sutter and himself. Then he sent the cowboy to bring Don José Castro. When the general appeared, Alvarado called to him, "Castro, dismount and salute Captain Sutter." He did so, and clasped Sutter in the customary California *abrazo*.[39]

There were even some real tears shed by Micheltorena. He finally accounted for his actions during the war, explaining that if he had sent the hated convicts back to Mexico as provided by the Treaty of Santa Teresa, the supreme government never would have approved his actions or accepted his abdication. "Weeping like an infant," he told the people in a public speech that he had acted wrongly in taking up arms against the Californians.[40] The new secretary of state, Juan Bandini, pardoned the wily Sutter after the adventurer produced orders that proved he had "merely been obeying" Micheltorena's written commands when he took the field.

Sutter's Indians were turned into porters, lugging baggage and supplies to the harbor at San Pedro while preparations were made to put Micheltorena and his *batallón fijo* aboard the *Don Quixote*. The ship would sail to Monterey to collect Micheltorena's fifty-man garrison, then would head for Mexico.

Undoubtedly, there were few places on earth where matters of power, authority, and war could be settled so affably. Californians and Anglos alike tended to idealize the era when they wrote about it in later years. Perhaps they were right: why shouldn't civilized decorum, accompanied by forgiveness, receive more credit than the spilling of blood?

In Sonoma, Vallejo was totally unsurprised by the outcome. At age twenty-two, he might have joined Alvarado's rebels. But beginning with the ouster of Governor Victoria in 1831, he had seen many campaigns lead to battlefields in the south, and he had never been impressed with the results. If he had sensed a theatrical element in the present conflict, he was also aware that events in California often seemed like a series of recapitulations. The rift between north and south was as big as ever. Once again, a civil war had set the stage for a future showdown. (As it turned out, in less than two years, there would be another flight to the south by the Californians, another pursuit by an army of foreigners, and California's existence as a semi-independent country would end.)

For now, Pío Pico was governor in Los Angeles. He and the Los Angeles Assembly were not likely to relish Commandant General José Castro's control of the provincial treasury at Monterey. And the Montereyans would probably not accept Los Angeles as the permanent seat of government. If all went well, there would be a brief honeymoon period, a respite from armed conflict. Certainly something to be grateful for, but not to be confused with a genuine peace.

6

"Ojalá Que Lo Tomen Los Americanos" ("I Hope the Americans Take It")

"I often hear them say ojala que toma esta Los Americanos — They appear to be inclined to any kind of change that will free them from Mexico." [1]

General Vallejo had retained fewer illusions than most Californians about the province's ability to hang on to its modified form of self-rule. His financial security and political influence were so deeply rooted in the country's past that he had no reason to fear the loss of either one. Open-handed and possessing what might be called a "romantic readiness," he wanted something genuinely new to happen in California. His bride was the future. His mind was often preoccupied with dreams of material progress, education, and philanthropy, and he drifted forward like a cloud of seeds seeking the proper soil in which to take root.

Sutter represented a sticky problem, of course. But most of the time, Sutter, in Don Mariano's eyes, was like a shipmate with whom he shared a vessel that had desperate steering problems. Before anything could be done about the situation, the ship had to be brought to safety. One alluring shelter was the idea of an American protectorate. The pattern was slowly emerging: a red-white-and-blue future was an inevitability; it would happen almost by itself if no one interfered.

After the war with Micheltorena ended in public frolic, Sutter's aggressive impulses went into remission — at least for the time being. He returned to his fort somewhat ashamed of his performance in Los Angeles. The last thing he wanted to do was resume his stock-rustling forays against General Vallejo's herds. In his heart of hearts, he was hoping Vallejo would take little notice of him. [2] Like Don Mariano, Sutter assumed that incoming Americans would help put an end to the Indian troubles in the Sacramento Valley. His overall plan was to give

71

newly arrived families small grants of land along the grid of rivers (the Mokelumne, Stanislaus, Tuolumne, Merced) that flowed westward from the Sierras. Before long, a society of prosperous farmers would take root. He would be willing to devote a sizable share of resources to make this dream a reality.[3]

Though Commandant General Castro was somewhat suspicious by nature, his attitude toward Americans was nevertheless quite positive at this time and should have made the immigrants at Sutter's Fort feel safe under the new government. When Castro appointed Charles Weber captain of militia, he declared that Sutter's ex-soldiers would be permitted to settle permanently in California with full assurance of the government's protection. The guarantee would also apply to Americans in San Jose and elsewhere in the department.[4]

But Thomas Oliver Larkin, who had been appointed U.S. consul in California on May 1, 1843, began to see plots everywhere. When he learned that a fully equipped Mexican army would soon be on its way to California, he wrote Secretary of State Buchanan that these soldiers were being sent "at the instigation of the English Government" to make certain the United States did not seize California.[5]

In Sonoma, Vallejo doubted that an army capable of stopping American immigration would ever arrive from Mexico. Should one miraculously appear, he believed it would be used defensively, in case of war with the United States.[6]

Nevertheless, Larkin continued to let his imagination run away with him. From his New England–style home in Monterey, which had wide verandas facing the harbor, Larkin could see a number of ships rocking at anchor. Their flags seemed to tell an ominous story. He sounded another alarm for Buchanan when he reported that a new French consul, Louis Gasquet, had been appointed and was collecting

> a salary of over four thousand dollars per year, with no apparent business to do; we have the French Sloop of War, Heroine, twenty-six guns, and the French Transport ... from the Marquezas Islands ... now at anchor in this Port.[7]

In truth, the governments of England and France had no desire to seize California, though Larkin was ignorant of this fact. England's main objective was to block American ownership of the province; she did not want the territory herself.[8] Admittedly, because of the huge Mexican debt, papers signed in Mexico City or London could give the province to Britain without any need for war.

But silken-haired James Buchanan reacted quickly to Larkin's dispatches. If a game of intrigue were going to be played, he wanted Americans to take part in it. He issued orders appointing Larkin "Confidential Agent in California" at a salary of six dollars per day.[9] Larkin was urged to discover and defeat "any attempts which may be made by Foreign Governments to acquire a control over that Country."[10] However, Larkin was "not to awaken the jealousy of the French and English Agents . . . by assuming any other than your Consular character." Nor was the Mexican government to be given any "just cause of complaint." His primary role would be to "conciliate" the people of the territory so that there might be a peaceful convergence of American and Californian interests.[11] Buchanan's orders, sent in response to Larkin's letters of midsummer, were dated October 17, 1845, but the instructions did not reach the consul until April of the following year. Merely by following his own inclinations, however, Larkin had already begun to initiate Buchanan's policies.

While the worried Larkin tried to think of ways to stymie aggressive moves by England and France, and while directives forbidding further emigration from the United States to California were being drawn up in Mexico City, a bizarre election was held in Sonoma for the benefit (it seemed) of General Vallejo — an affair that puzzled most of the Americans who took part in it. In mid-summer a request that was "more like an order than an invitation" was sent out to foreigners living in the North Bay. They would be expected to vote on matters that were never spelled out.[12] A clear-headed millwright from Tennessee named William Baldridge and some of his friends obeyed the summons, traveling across the yellow knolls of the Huichica grant before descending to the Sonoma plaza. Once the election was under way, votes were cast by voice rather than by ballot. The institution of the ballot being sacred to the Americans, subsequent maneuvering came as something of a shock. The initial votes were tallied; then "there was a short earnest conversation held by two or three of the principal men." A member of the Carrillo family had been elected, but the officials thought General Vallejo should have been the victor. After the two clerks called for a second voice vote, Don Mariano was chosen, and the polls were closed.[13]

Much ink has flowed trying to explain what this was all about. Baldridge's employer, the wooden-faced Joseph Chiles, thought the gathering had been designed to gain American good will: Vallejo and his associates wanted to be able to depend on the immigrants' help in case of trouble with Mexico or the United States.[14] Baldridge guessed that a representative was being picked for a convention of Californian leaders in Monterey.[15] He may have been right. Carrillo was in all likelihood a "Blue," or British, partisan, and if a political convention were going to discuss the department's future, Vallejo, who favored an American alliance, would be the right choice for a delegate. The fact that the initial victor could be traded without much protest probably indicated the workings of the *patrón* system, which conferred almost absolute power on a region's leading ranchero. An inheritance of the Spanish political tradition, its feudal character was in direct conflict with the republican institutions so valued by the Americans and by Vallejo himself. Don Mariano would, in time, be willing to share political power with Americans — but he never would give up the belief that he knew what was best for Sonoma.

During the election, a former trailmate of the Kelseys, William Hargrave, was alarmed to see an officer counting foreigners. Hargrave feared that the immigrants were being placed under some sort of obligation for having performed acts of citizenship.[16] Whatever the election's purpose, one thing was clear, the request for a second vote and the swapping of victors further increased the immigrants' scorn for California's political system.

Following the election, there were no repercussions, but as fall approached, the pressure of American immigration could be felt everywhere in the north; the Swasey–Todd group arrived in September, followed in October by Sublette's party and the Grigsby–Ide company. Counting other arrivals for the year, the newcomers totaled some 173 people, nowhere near the 900 travelers Sutter had expected; still, the figure suggested their potential might.[17] Single men predominated among the newcomers, and for companionship they were dependent on the Indian women who congregated at Sutter's Fort. The majority of these young men found California disappointing. Contrary to all they had been told, land was difficult to come by. Some of them felt that the best years in the country might have already passed. They learned that a bloodless war had been fought between rival factions of Californians and that the Mexican governor had been tossed out; but nothing conclusive had been decided by the change. The immigration laws were downright discouraging. Being men who were used to a confrontational way of life, they were offended by the subtle language of Mexican protocol. As a group, these men did not satisfy Sutter's and Vallejo's hopes that a nucleus of hard-working farmers would take root in the Great Valley.

All this created uneasiness in Monterey. A number of distinguished leaders including General Castro, ex-Governor Alvarado, Subprefect

Manuel Castro, Andrés Castillero, along with an escort of some sixteen soldiers rode toward the Valley of the Moon in early November to see what was happening and to talk with the Americans who had come to the Sonoma and Napa valleys to find work.[18]

Alvarado and Vallejo had given up the petty feuding that had characterized their relationship in the early 1840s. Oddly enough, during these final years of provincial self-rule, the uncle and nephew were playing relatively insignificant roles in the government. Tall like Don Mariano, with heart-shaped face and turtle-like eyes, Alvarado was no longer the daring "Juanito" whose agility had permitted him to escape Governor Gutiérrez's troopers in 1836. His once-lithe figure was well cushioned now, transformed by long dinners and good wine. Castro, still encumbered by duties, was the most nervous of the three. Ruling the province was no longer inspirational for the boyhood triumverate. Unity could not be talked into existence, and the country's inherent political defects were winning out.

In answer to General Castro's summons, a handful of immigrants, representing all the recent newcomers, arrived at Sonoma. When Castro began his interrogation, he wasn't too surprised to learn that none of the Americans had brought passports. He delivered some ritual warnings about the Mexican laws. The Americans' explanations rehearsed old formulas, too. They said that their original intention had been to go to Oregon, not California, so passports hadn't been necessary. Moreover, when they had left the American prairies, relations between Mexico and the United States had been much friendlier than now. The immigrants were glad to be living in California and noted that with winter coming on, it would be impossible to cross the mountains until spring. Representing their intentions as peaceful, they agreed to obey the department's laws and leave the country when the snows melted if their petitions to settle were not granted.[19] They soon had reason to celebrate. Castro penned a decree which declared that he was extending

> the sentiment of hospitality . . . and considering that most of the said expedition is composed of families and industrious people, I have deemed it best to permit them provisionally, to remain in the department. . . .[20]

Arrangements were made for the immigrants to remain under General Vallejo's jurisdiction. They were to present bonds for their good behavior and would have to apply for a regular license to settle within three months.

But as far as some of the Americans were concerned, the interview could have been a lot friendlier. The haggard-looking Ezekiel Merritt was probably on hand. As mentioned earlier, Sutter had referred to him as the right man to rely on if an attack on Sonoma were going to be made.[21] Another recent immigrant, Pat McChristian, described the gathering as a sort of insult to the Americans. The settlers had been told they would have to leave California as soon as the snows melted, "without horses, arms, or cattle." According to McChristian's statement, after the settlers talked with the Californians, they chose Zeke Merritt as their leader and made plans to capture Sonoma.[22]

If a plan for revolt was afoot, José Castro knew nothing about it. The commandant general led his escort northeast toward New Helvetia. Although Alvarado and Subprefect Manuel Castro did not go with him, the list of ranking officials was still impressive. Victor Prudon and Jacob Leese accompanied Castro, as did Mexican diplomat Andrés Castillero.[23]

Having been notified of Castro's tour of inspection, Sutter (still chronically distrustful) was prepared for a violent showdown. Ever since the war with Micheltorena, he had found it impossible to credit the Californians' willingness to tolerate him. As related earlier, Castro and Alvarado had spared his life in Los Angeles, and recently, Governor Pico had increased his powers. Sutter saw a hostile motive behind Castro's visit. . . . Stories had reached him that the commandant general was stirring up the Indian leaders against him. When he was absolutely sure that Castro was going to arrive, Sutter wrote Larkin, begging him to come to the Sacramento Valley to help protect the Americans and their families. "But if it is not in your power or in the power of a man-of-war to protect them, I will do it. All are protected here, and before I will suffer an injustice to be done them, I will die first!"[24] The European told his guards to patrol outside the walls of the fort at night, and he arranged to have a canoe waiting so that a messenger could round up his employees from the surrounding region in case of trouble.[25]

When Castro, Andrés Castillero, and the others cantered up the slight rise to New Helvetia, brandishing no muskets and completely exposed to the fort's guns, Sutter thought better of his fears. Remembering his etiquette, he ran up the Mexican colors and told his cannoneers to welcome the visitors with a seven-gun salute.[26] He had assembled the American immigrants well beforehand (which was another way of strengthening the fort's defenses). Best of all, however, General Castro, on November 11, surpassed his recent generosity. He wrote a decree that was less restrictive than the one issued at Sonoma. The Americans at the fort did not have to post bond; with passes issued by Sutter, they could go either to Sonoma or to San Juan Bautista to find work. (Future parties of immigrants would have to accept whatever conditions might be imposed at the time.[27])

Sutter's fears evaporated. "People talk a great deal but when we meet one another, things are quite different," he wrote.[28] With his self-confidence restored and the status of the Americans settled, he was flattered to learn that the Californians were ready to buy his fort. He was offered the astonishing price of $100,000 for the place. So far, he had not erased even a hundred pesos from the $30,000 debt incurred when he bought Fort Ross from the Russians. Always betting on his cash crops, he trusted that profits from wheat would solve his financial woes. It would be some time before the grain could be harvested, though, and $100,000 was a very tempting sum of money — almost irresistible. In later years he "regretted that I did not accept."[29]

The tempting price having been offered and rejected, Castro and his men enjoyed Sutter's hospitality the night of November 11. The following day, as a courtesy, Sutter escorted the brightly uniformed party as far as the Cosumnes River. Then he returned to his busy schedule at the fort. Amazingly enough, Vallejo's secretary, Victor Prudon, reappeared within twenty-four hours, having backtracked in order to improve the offer of the previous day. Prudon was French, which in itself was enough to make Sutter dote on him. Sutter's concept of friendship, however, did not exclude bribery. That same year, he had tried to get Prudon to involve General Vallejo in a smuggling scheme. Partial duties, or perhaps no duties at all, would be paid on the cargo of a New York ship. Prudon's fee was not spelled out, but Vallejo was to receive "four or six thousand dollars to let the Ship enter."[30] Sutter had promised that if the secretary became adept at his work as go-between, he would find himself "wealthy very soon."[31] No money was paid because the scheme did not appeal to Vallejo. Persistent as always, Sutter had then tried to lure Prudon away from the General's "court of Sonoma," as he called it, to New Helvetia, where he hoped the Frenchman would build a hotel.[32] Nothing ever came of that idea, either.

As Prudon and Sutter began to haggle again over the price of New Helvetia, Vallejo's secretary surprised Sutter by offering him "all the lands and cattle belonging to the Mission San José" in addition to the $100,000 promised earlier. It wasn't just talk. A sizable down payment would be made after acceptance. Sutter — though fascinated by the hope of quick gain — seemed to have an entrepreneur's love for his own projects. More important, he did not like the fact that he would be paid in drafts on the Mexican government and that he would be forced to become an exile: the supreme government — hoping to eliminate the fort as a trouble spot — would expect Sutter to leave the country. Once again, he refused to sell.[33] Vallejo was aware of the ongoing negotiations and wrote ex-President Bustamente, urging him to approve the deal.

> I grant that this is a high price to pay for a few pieces of cannon, a not very scientifically constructed bastion, some fosses or moats, ten or twelve adobe houses, and corrals of the same material. . . .[34]

But, Vallejo added, "the security of the country is what is to be paid for, and that is priceless." Gaining possession of New Helvetia would deny the department's potential enemies an important rallying point. It would also remove from power a man who, because of privileges granted him by Alvarado, Micheltorena, and Pico, was able to sell or award land to anyone he liked. As Don Mariano characterized the frontier flotsam at New Helvetia, the majority "were not qualified to occupy landed possessions," but they "hold immense quantities of the richest lands in this part of the department solely by the title issued by Sutter."[35]

Don Mariano's predictions of some eight years before had "gradually come true." Many times he had described conditions in California as they were, with a minimum of exaggeration. The stream of incoming Americans had formerly been "only *considerable.*" Now, from Mexico's point of view, the numbers might be called "frightful."[36] Vallejo again stressed the need for funds and troops, carefully defining the character of the latter: "I understand troops to mean defenders of the public rights and not aggressors against private property."[37] In the same way a physician might describe an infection to a patient, listing symptoms with great clarity in hopes that the patient himself might be able to help with the cure, Vallejo carefully portrayed California's problems without embellishment. The letter, however, was the continuation of an empty ritual.

Larkin had already observed the disparity between Vallejo's personal views and his pronouncements as a Mexican official. Privately, Don Mariano was not opposed to American immigration, nor was he pessimistic about a future that included American settlement. Cultural inundation was unlikely — at least at the current rate of migration. (No one in the province could have foreseen the effects of the Gold Rush.) He certainly had nothing against the Anglo-Americans as a group, nor did he believe that the Californians, if prudent, would find themselves at a disadvantage.

By 1845 there were roughly 7,000 *gente de razón* in California and approximately 1,300 foreign-born residents, a large number of whom had arrived during the previous four years.[38] The Californians still held a numerical edge of better than six to one. Yet, considering the small military units employed in the province (35 to 50 troopers was an average force, 450 soldiers — about half the size of a single Civil War regiment — being the largest army assembled), the arrival of 150 armed men was sure to have a stunning impact.

In December 1845 Texas officially became a part of the United States. To the vast majority of Mexicans, a desperate calamity (if not a nightmare) had come true. In response to developments in Texas, orders had already arrived in California from Mexico forbidding all Anglo-American immigration from Oregon and Missouri.[39] Mexico, of course, had good reason to be worried. Daniel Webster had crooned that the bay of San Francisco was "twenty times as valuable to us as all Texas,"[40] and one of ex-President Tyler's spokesmen had described California as "the richest and most beautiful and the healthiest country in the world," compared with which, Texas was "of very little value."[41] Now President Polk was willing to pay millions of dollars for California. So far, however, Mexico had balked at every offer, always refusing to surrender territory.

The year's most important newcomers were recorded tardily by John Sutter, who reported them to Vallejo in December. They were some fifty well-armed U.S. topographical engineers who had entered the country by two separate routes. The travelers were under the command of Captain John Charles Frémont. No one realized it at the time, but Frémont was the catalyst for whom American malcontents like Ezekiel Merritt and Granville Swift had been waiting.

Frémont's presence in California was explained in various ways. Subprefect Guerrero learned that the American had come to the coast to fix the boundary between Mexico and the United States.[42] Sutter informed Vallejo that Frémont's mounted engineers intended "to pass the winter in a temperate climate before going to Oregon."[43] Before long, other explanations were given.

Frémont was already famous as an explorer, though he had emerged from a past that was clouded by the scandalous romance that had preceded his birth. The shame of his illegitimacy still haunted him. Biographer Andrew Rolle claims that although Frémont had acquired illustrious protectors through his marriage to Jessie Benton (Senator Thomas Hart Benton's daughter), the vacuum of his painful childhood remained, drawing him into endless conflicts with older men. Turbulent emotions were concealed beneath his cool exterior. Many Californians would later regret his arrival, and few would have better reason to do so than General Mariano Vallejo.

On the day the wiry Frémont arrived at New Helvetia, Sutter was away from the fort. Sutter's manager, John Bidwell, discussed a few practical matters with the captain, who said he needed sixteen pack mules, a half-dozen packsaddles, flour, and other provisions. Frémont also wanted to use the blacksmith shop. Even before Bidwell could respond, Frémont seemed resentful — as though having to ask for the favors was in itself an imposition. Bidwell didn't like to deny the requests; he only did so because supplies happened to be limited just then. Frémont made some barely audible remarks to a small, stoop-shouldered man who rode beside him. This was the famous Kit Carson, who had been employed as a scout for Frémont's expedition. Nothing in Carson's freckled face or soft blue eyes indicated "extraordinary courage or daring,"[44] but one thing was certain: Carson was as agile as a cat and worth twenty cougars in a fight. Bidwell could hear enough to gather that the words were unflattering references to Sutter.

Within a matter of weeks, Bidwell did his best to satisfy Frémont's requests, but the favors yielded even more complaints. Captain Frémont assumed, for one thing, that there were differences between the two countries: he was an American officer while Sutter was a Mexican official. What all this meant, Bidwell could only guess.[45]

When Sutter finally reported Frémont's arrival to Vallejo, the General — usually slow to anger — was infuriated. For one thing, the European had misdated Frémont's arrival by weeks. Scrawling instructions to Victor Prudon across the back of Sutter's letter, Don Mariano told his secretary to respond immediately:

> Inform him [Sutter] it was received after twenty days' delay and charge him, in the quickest way possible, to send detailed information about the new immigrants, a thing which has always been done in similar circumstances, even in the case of small parties, and which he inopportunely failed to do when it was most necessary and, even, urgent.[46]

7

Prelude to Revolt

*B*y the end of 1845, the Americans at Sutter's Fort were already look-ing up to Captain Frémont — the man about whom so many people had golden opinions — which made Vallejo, Sutter, and Vice-Consul Leides-dorff all the more disappointed when the explorer failed to discipline the immigrants. Throughout his career, Frémont proved to be a somewhat lax moral policeman and an inefficient administrator.

As a group, the immigrants of '45 and '46 were not easy to catego-rize. The unruly ones caused Vallejo and Sutter to be drawn into a closer relationship as the winter wore on. Before Sutter actually felt threatened by them, and before he became aware of Captain Frémont's hostile in-tentions, Sutter wanted Vallejo, Larkin, and Vice-Consul Leidesdorff to be impressed with the rugged overlanders. "Useful and decent," he called the members of the Clyman party, and he praised the Sublettes even more highly. "Not one Company has arrived before in the Country, which looked so respectable as this," he assured Larkin, adding that a few of them had "several thousand Dollars in gold."[1] Before long, however, he had to request Larkin's help in settling "a case of an attempt to commit rape by one of the late company from Oregon" (a member of the Clyman group). As 1845 came to a close, Leidesdorff told Larkin a bizarre story about meeting the famous "Mr. Sublitz," who arrived at Leidesdorff's door on Christmas Eve with five or six companions. In a letter filled with his peculiar misspellings, Leidesdorff complained:

> They fired a gun off, an made a great hurahing in the corador.
> I got up and asked who they were, and got no answer, so I was
> afraid to open the door. At last someone of them answered friends.
> I answered them, that If they could not give there names that I
> would not open the door, and if they had come to get liquor that
> I had none in the house. They then walked away. After awhile,

81

this Mr. Sublitz returned alone, and abused me shamefully, telling me that he had struck terror through all the towns he had
been at, and would strike terror through me before he left this
town. He finished by throwing two large stones on the roof of
my house, one of which I exspected would come through the
roof being so large. This is one of the last party which is said to
be such fine people. . . .[2]

Leidesdorff's unpleasant introduction to the Sublettes made an enduring
impression on him. Greatly trusted by Larkin, the vice-consul sensed
that the newcomers might turn the province topsy-turvy if they were not
controlled.

Though a captain in the United States Army, the moody Frémont
had no intention of restraining American immigrants. He and his engineers loved adventure and, as time proved, they enjoyed starting a little
trouble now and then. The explorer was already famous for his contri-
butions to the exploration and mapping of the trans-Mississippi West. In
many ways, he resembled his aloof predecessor, Lieutenant Charles
Wilkes, whose early efforts to chart the West Coast it was part of Frémont's mission to complete. (Before long, in fact, Wilkes and Frémont
would be carrying on a bitter exchange about whose mapping coordi-
nates were more accurate.) Gifted with a clear writing style (which his
wife, Jessie Benton Frémont, carefully polished), and having a broad
knowledge of the physical sciences, Frémont had all the talents needed
to concoct vivid accounts of his expeditions. Two of his published reports had already brought him national fame. Americans hungered for
information about the West, and by studying Frémont's narratives, they
could trace the best routes to the Pacific, get an idea of the weather they
might encounter, and marvel at the flora and fauna which only trappers
and a few emigrants had seen.

Most people attached great importance to the fact that Frémont's
father-in-law, Senator Thomas Hart Benton, was one of the most powerful men in the United States and an outspoken western expansionist.
Despite his belief that America's western boundary should be the Pacific
Ocean, Benton had a deep respect for Spanish tradition. Long before
Mexico became an independent republic, he had stressed the need for
closer ties with New Spain, and after independence had been declared,
he tried to make Mexico America's ally.[3]

Captain Frémont, whose mysterious imprisonment of Vallejo just
six months hence was to create so much animosity, had entirely different
ideas about Mexico. He ignored the fact that California had enjoyed a

modified form of self-rule for almost ten years, and he made no distinction between the tolerant, easygoing rancheros he encountered in California and their southern neighbors in Mexico who, for a variety of reasons, looked down on the Californians. Though the Californians had never created their own flag, the ties between them and the mother country had become quite tenuous. The turmoil and violence of Mexico's political life thoroughly alienated the provincials; wholesale abuses of the people were practically unknown in California.

In a letter to his wife, Frémont readily admitted that he was disgusted "with everything belonging to the Mexicans."[4] This blanket judgment covered practically everyone in power in Governor Pico's California.

Frémont's attitudes began to cause friction in the spring of 1846 when he angered some of the department's leaders. Not surprisingly, his first scrape with officialdom began over livestock. In a country as vast as California, any successful ranching or military operation depended on accumulating a good supply of horses. In order to cover sixty or seventy miles a day, travel had to be performed with replacement mounts that were usually driven ahead of the riders. A San Jose ranchero named Sebastián Peralta felt sure that some of his animals could be found among Frémont's herd; but when Peralta went to talk to the explorer about it, Frémont's men threw Peralta out of camp. Soon the alcalde of San Jose demanded an explanation. Frémont's reply, dated February 21, 1846, was not designed to foster goodwill. The explorer assumed that Peralta (a part-owner of a land grant that encompasses present-day Los Gatos and Campbell) "should have been well satisfied to escape without a severe horsewhipping. . . . You will readily understand," Frémont added, "that my duties will not permit me to appear before the magistrates of your towns on the complaint of every straggling vagabond who may chance to visit my camp."[5]

Until then, things had run fairly smoothly for Frémont. He had met with Consul Larkin, General Castro, and Subprefect Manuel Castro in January and had been given permission to winter his topographical corps in the San Joaquin Valley. At that time, Larkin had advanced Frémont eighteen hundred dollars to purchase supplies. It was understood that the explorer would keep his band of horsemen far from the settlements and would leave California when the snows melted.[6]

Late February found him still camped at Fisher's Rancho just south of San Jose. To reach the San Joaquin Valley from there, he needed to take the route that led east through the Pacheco Pass. Instead, he rode north through the Santa Clara Valley, with the green flank of the Diablo

Range on his right, then swung out toward the ocean via Los Gatos and the Santa Cruz Mountains. Deeply impressed by the redwoods, he took careful notes before circling to the south. It wasn't long before Frémont and his experienced fifty-man column were again within sight of the distinctive pines and red roofs of California's capital city, Monterey.[7]

Realizing that his presence so close to the capital might offend the touchy General Castro, Frémont hoped he could count on at least one friend, William Hartnell. During one of Frémont's earlier visits to California, the two men had enjoyed interesting talks. So the explorer rode toward the Salinas River, beyond which, on the plain of the valley, Vallejo's former tutor lived at Rancho Alisal. Frémont was now only twenty-five miles from Monterey. He rode up to the Hartnell dwelling on March 3, 1846, accompanied by a large train of extra mounts.

The thoroughly civilized Hartnell was a little shocked by Frémont's appearance. Another man who saw the explorer at this time noticed that his eyes were "deeper set than usual, with that look the Delewares said was like a stone."[8] Hospitable as always, Hartnell invited Frémont to stay at his house. Outside by a creek was a ghostly grove of white and tan sycamores beneath which Frémont's men were allowed to camp.[9]

Frémont, who had a keen appreciation for books, browsed a few hours in Hartnell's library. But the visit was cut short. Three of Frémont's men went to buy some supplies at the house of José Castro's uncle, Don Angel Castro, and a drinking party began. Under the influence of liquor, one of Frémont's men insisted that the ranchero's daughter become his companion. Perhaps other suggestions were made. The offender was hustled out of the room, but in the scuffle, the American drew his pistol. A fine of ten dollars was paid for the offense.[10]

Frémont assured everyone that his followers were "citizens," not soldiers, but Subprefect Manuel Castro referred to them as U.S. troops.[11] Jacob Leese testily informed Vallejo they were "a company of Dragoons."[12]

On March 5, Frémont wrote a letter to Thomas Oliver Larkin from Hartnell's adobe, admitting that "the presence of my little force might be disagreeable to the authorities."[13] A dispatch from Commandant General Castro arrived at Alisal that same day, ordering the explorer to leave California.

> . . . the Commandant General was given to understand that you and the party under your command have entered the towns of this Department, and such being prohibited by our laws . . . you will immediately retire beyond the limits of this same department.[14]

Frémont did not reply in writing. He merely told the messenger, Lieutenant José Chávez, that he had no intention of obeying an order which was insulting to him and to the United States.[15]

Frémont could no longer expect to receive friendly consolation from his host. Hartnell had held a number of important posts in California, and his sympathies were pro-British. He did not want to see a group of Yankee sharpshooters revolutionize the province. With firmness and tact, he advised Frémont that a peaceful withdrawal would be in everyone's best interests.[16]

Consul Larkin was, for the time being, quite impressed with Frémont. Larkin's letters to Secretary of State Buchanan minimized the explorer's challenges to the California authorities, calling the dispute over Peralta's livestock a minor affair and dismissing the fracas at the home of José Castro's uncle as "some insult to some Person or persons on a farm." He assumed that the Castros would "soon forget" the whole matter.[17] But no one would be allowed to forget the incident.

Captain Frémont abandoned Hartnell's rancho, riding along the northern boundary of the Salinas Valley past the site of Isaac Graham's old distillery. Before long, he reached the main road to San Juan Bautista, which ascends the green, undulating slopes of the Gabilan Range. Some of the summits of the range rise to several thousand feet above the valley floor. After stopping for a day at the rancho of Joaquín Gómez, he headed deeper into the mountains, riding toward a series of sharp crests that form the summit of Gavilán (Hawk's) Peak, today known as Frémont Peak. On a wooded flat beneath one of the crests, his men fashioned a makeshift flagpole, and while the American flag was sent to the top, the explorer's veterans cheered.[18]

It would be difficult to imagine a more obvious slap in the face to Commandant General Castro, who was informed of the Americans' location. Still wary of giving offense to U.S. citizens, Castro was convinced that, in time, Frémont could be persuaded to move on. First, the commandant general would assemble such a large force that the explorer would realize the foolishness of his actions.

Receiving news of Frémont's stand on Gavilán Peak, Larkin tried to maneuver Castro and Frémont out of their predicament. He wrote the captain on March 8, warning him that an army of about sixty Californians was being assembled. The process was taking place quickly, considering the military habits of the rancheros. He estimated that two hundred soldiers might be brought into the field and that the people would choose to defend the existing government. Larkin was cautious about offering advice, but he mentioned that Frémont's efforts to protect his men might not succeed. Whatever the results, the confrontation would probably "cause trouble hereafter to Resident Americans."[19]

At first, the explorer paid no attention to Larkin's warnings. By riding from one crest of Gavilán mountain to another, he commanded a 360-degree view of his surroundings. Toward the ocean, General Vallejo's youngest brother, Juan Antonio, lived on the San Cayetano Rancho granted to Don Ignacio Vallejo in 1824. To the south, Frémont could trace the curve of the Pacific shoreline as it looped back on itself at Monterey to form the cusp of the harbor. Another quarter-turn put him above the ranchos that William Hartnell and ex-Governor Alvarado had established at Alisal as a refuge from the Monterey fog. Frémont could also watch José Castro's military preparations at San Juan Bautista where Castro himself was drilling troops on the plaza.

Castro issued a proclamation that referred to Captain Frémont as a robber and noted that the intruder was still "encamped at the Natividad, from which he sallies forth, committing depredations and making scandalous skirmishes."[20] Frémont understood Spanish. Being called a robber was one thing, but the phrase "scandalous skirmishes" nettled him. He seemed to cling to the words, and the odd vocabulary crept into his own correspondence.

Despite his bravado, Frémont began to have misgivings. He was outnumbered by the Californians, and no American settlers were coming to his aid. In a dispatch to Larkin, however, he swore that "if we are hemmed in and assaulted here, we will die every man of us under the Flag of our country."[21] He pledged to battle "to extremity and refuse quarter, trusting to our country to avenge our death."[22] The phrase "refuse quarter" was mistranslated to mean "will not give quarter," but the overall meaning of his words could not be mistaken.[23]

Frémont's readings in history had alerted him to the fact that aggression in the name of defense sometimes greased the machinery of frontier conquest, and that flagrant bravery could be rewarded with soaring advancement. He had no written orders from President Polk regarding California and was unsure of just how far the President would go. Even allowing for the bluster normal to a posturing military commander, Frémont's proposal to defend Gavilán Peak was reckless. He had not been urged to start a war with Mexico. In fact, instructions were on the way from Washington asking him to take a conciliatory approach and give Mexico no "just cause of complaint." Nor was there any clear military objective that would justify the sacrifice of his men.

Consul Larkin sent a message to Mazatlán, asking American authorities there to send a ship north from the U.S. squadron. Conditions were ripe for a quick response. Within just forty-two days (perhaps a record for the times) the sloop-of-war *Portsmouth* arrived under Captain John B. Montgomery. Everyone was impressed with the readiness of the American warship to answer a call for help, in contrast to Mexico's apparent indifference to appeals during the past two decades.[24]

While Larkin was occupied with ploys to prevent a shooting war, Frémont continued to take stock of Castro's men and artillery. At one point, a detachment of cavalry moved along the road toward Frémont's position at the head of a long canyon. Quickly, the explorer led forty men down the slope to a place of concealment from which he could observe the enemy advance. The brightly uniformed troopers came closer, then stopped. There was something almost flirtatious in the maneuver. The Californians conferred, studying the thick brush and trees that screened the Americans. But they did not attack. General Castro had referred to "scandalous skirmishes." What could this be called? Led by one of the De la Torre brothers, the Californians finally turned back and headed the other way.[25]

On March 12 General Vallejo finally learned of Frémont's defiance on Gavilán Peak. Experience had taught Don Mariano to doubt sensational reports, and he had no way of knowing what a demonstration by Frémont might mean. For years Vallejo's main objective had been to create a union of some kind between the United States and California. He had no desire to fight American troops. He waited until March 14 to issue a proclamation that heaped criticism on those citizens who would close their eyes to the dangers threatening the country. Obviously, the warning was composed strictly for the record.[26]

Two days before Vallejo received notice of the Gavilán affair, Frémont descended the northeast slope of the peak, moving toward the expanse of green dips and spires that make up the lower Diablo Range. Once in the Great Valley, he marched toward Sutter's fort. As Frémont described the standoff to his wife:

> My sense of duty did not permit me to fight them, but we retired slowly and growlingly before a force of three or four hundred men and three pieces of artillery. Without a shadow of a cause, the governor suddenly raised the whole country against us, issuing a false and scandalous proclamation.[27]

By then, Captain Frémont was not likely to receive a very cordial welcome from John Sutter, whose feelings about Americans had undergone a sudden change. While Frémont had been staying at Hartnell's rancho, Sutter had been threatened by two future members of the Bear Flag party — gaunt, hollow-eyed Granville P. Swift and Franklin Sears — who had stolen goods from one of the fort's Indian employees. Sutter had told them that such actions were not the sort of thing he would tolerate at New Helvetia. Considering how helpful Sutter had been to the immigrants, their response was nightmarish. After subjecting him to insults, they offered to burn down the fort. Most of Sutter's employees were away at the time and he felt shaken. As he wrote later, "I was waiting every moment for a ball or a knife. . . . We had not one man who spoke in our favor and the whole mob assembled before the house."[28] Sutter, John Bidwell, and a few employees endured a harrowing night on March 5 after the immigrants seized the fort. According to Sutter's biographer Richard Dillon, the Swiss-born entrepreneur "was virtually a prisoner. Swift stabbed an Indian, and one of his confederates threatened to cut Sutter's belly open."[29] With this memory fresh in his mind, Sutter's attitude toward the U.S. overlanders changed. Even before the confrontation with Swift and Sears, he had thought of writing to "señor Vallejo for aid."[30] Now he was hoping he would "get a good supply" of Mexican soldiers at the fort — if and when a Mexican army should arrive.

New Helvetia's high walls did not prevent stories from reaching the men inside about Frémont's defiance of General Castro. Before long, everyone knew that a captain in the U.S. Army had challenged California's military authorities. Rumors increased as the men tried to puzzle out the many unknowns. Was there some political motive behind the explorer's reappearance in the country? Had he received special instructions? No one could say.

Having received no invitation to stop at the fort, Frémont marched beyond Sutter's stronghold as he headed up the Sacramento Valley on his way to Oregon. He was still bitterly disappointed that "not a single immigrant" had offered to reinforce him on Gavilán Peak, though he had sent out appeals for more men.[31] But the ubiquitous James Clyman had expressed his willingness to raise men, arms, and supplies, and Captain William D. Phelps of the merchant ship *Moscow* had volunteered to transport Frémont's command on his ship.[32] Neither offer, however, had actually increased Frémont's manpower during the crisis.

Considering California's lack of newspapers, word of the Gavilán flare-up was passed along rather quickly. Within twelve weeks, a revolutionary force of Americans took shape. One historian has claimed that the Gavilán affair "was a direct cause of the Bear Flag Revolt."[33] Frémont's provocation of the Californians, if not a direct cause of the revolt, was certainly a warning of what was to come.

Lieutenant Francisco Arce of Monterey had recently written a strongly worded letter to Vallejo, urging him to rally the department's leaders for the sake of California's security. This move would "furnish our compatriots and all cultured nations [with] an example of true citizens loving a just liberty."[34] Arce feared that if something were not done soon, the Americans would destroy "the political system and deprive us of our native country."[35] Amiable as Arce was, his brand of patriotism seemed hopelessly outdated to Don Mariano. The sources of Vallejo's disillusionment with California had roots stretching back more than twenty years. In the long run, Vallejo believed that American annexation would improve California's political unity, not destroy it.

Frémont had marched off in the direction of Oregon, but tensions in California remained high. Vallejo was summoned to Monterey for a council of war in the spring of 1846. The strategic *consejo* lasted from the end of March until the third week in April; its main objective was to provide Governor Pico with information about the crisis that was developing in the north. A document explaining the situation was signed by Vallejo and five other officers, including Castro. There was much talk in Monterey about Frémont: what his intentions might be, what he planned to do, and so on. Castro used poetic language to express his fears, complaining that the Americans had become so bold they thought they could "change the color of the stars" and "build ladders to the sky."[36] He also threatened to carry out defensive measures, such as going to the Sacramento Valley in July to prevent the entry of more immigrants.[37] Rumors based on his remarks reached Sutter's Fort, no doubt increasing the immigrants' fears.

Many Californians were still counting on the arrival of a large Mexican force to help with the department's defense, but this was a vain hope. Mexico's President Herrerra had tolerated the American annexation of Texas, but in December of 1845 he was overthrown by General José Paredes. The troops destined for California (an army of six hundred men ready to sail from Acapulco) were swallowed up by the Paredes revolution and would never reach the northern province.[38] In the absence of government troops, the Monterey *consejo* asked Governor Pico to come north to fortify the capital. Meanwhile, General Castro planned to move his headquarters to Santa Clara, a measure that would place the first line of defense closer to San Francisco Bay. He would take care of all necessities until Pico arrived or help came from the supreme government.[39]

When Governor Pico received the document in Los Angeles, he was suspicious of the northern officers' motives and was offended to see the signature of his would-be kidnapper, José Antonio Carrillo, at the bottom.

At informal talks that took place in April, Vallejo opposed the efforts of British sympathizers who wanted to maneuver California into an alliance with England. Those who favored English rule included men like Juan B. Alvarado, William Hartnell, David Spence, and Pío Pico. Either at Larkin's house or at José Castro's adobe, Castro himself surprised everyone by admitting his preference for an alliance with France, chiefly because it was a Catholic nation.[40] At the same gathering, the eloquent Pablo de la Guerra and Rafael Gonzales unearthed the old dream of an independent country: *"California libre, soberana, y independiente!"*[41] Soon afterward, David Spence and William Hartnell advocated British rule. The erudite Hartnell assumed that England would deal more impartially with Protestants and Catholics than France and would not be as likely to sanction slavery as the United States. He also believed California would retain its essentially Latin character under the British crown.[42] Vallejo realized that the time had come to fire a volley in favor of American statehood. The speech he gave became quite famous. The most important parts of the text are given below:

> It is most true, that to rely any longer upon Mexico to govern and defend us, would be idle and absurd. To this extent I fully agree with my distinguished colleagues. It is also true that we possess a noble country, every way calculated, from position and resources, to become great and powerful. For that very reason I would not have her a mere dependency upon a foreign monarchy, naturally alien, or at least indifferent, to our interests and our welfare . . . [F]or although others speak lightly of a form of government, as a freeman, I cannot do so. We are republicans — badly governed and badly situated as we are — still we are all, in sentiment, republicans. . . . Why then should we hesitate still to assert our independence? We have indeed taken the first step, by electing our own governor, but another remains to be taken.. annexation to the United States. In contemplating this consummation of our destiny, I feel nothing but pleasure, and I ask you to share it. Discard old prejudices, disregard old customs, and prepare for the glorious change which awaits our country. . . . Why should we go abroad for protection when this great nation is our adjoining neighbor? When we join our fortunes to hers, we shall not become subjects, but fellow-citizens,

possessing all the rights of the people of the United States and choosing our own federal and local rulers. We shall have a stable government and just laws. California will grow strong and flourish, and her people will be prosperous, happy, and free. Look not therefore with jealousy upon the hardy pioneers who scale our mountains and cultivate our unoccupied plains; but rather welcome them as brothers, who come to share with us a common destiny.[43]

Obviously, Vallejo favored the very changes men like Lieutenant Arce feared. Few Californian leaders believed that the *realpolitik* of the era would permit the province to retain its quasi-independence. The General's speech testified to his optimism. Indeed, he wanted to see the province enriched, defended by, and safely in the hands of a nation that was at least as futuristic as himself — the United States. He was not the sort of futurist, however, who wanted to see the past erased with a downward stroke of the sponge. But no matter who took over, there would be unforeseen cultural changes. The "discarding of old customs" referred to in his talk would be no easy matter, as the next three decades would prove.

Ex-Governor Alvarado, William Hartnell and other witnesses later vouched for the speech's tremendous impact.[44] But historian Hubert Howe Bancroft had doubts about the text and the specific place where the speech was given.[45] Since the pros and cons of the dispute have already been thrashed out by Bancroft and historian Myrtle McKittrick,[46] I will present my own conclusions: Vallejo gave the speech at one or more informal gatherings during the period of the military *consejo*. Because he was still a Mexican official, the General was wary of committing his pro-American views to paper, and he would not have wanted copies of his talk to circulate. But at social gatherings he tended to be free enough with his opinions. The text may have been doctored or even revised before being printed in Revere's *Tour of Duty*.

The Monterey council of war was about to end when — with dramatic timing — a red-haired messenger arrived aboard the *Cyane*. He was Lieutenant Archibald H. Gillespie, a marine carrying important orders from Buchanan to Larkin and Frémont. Gillespie, whose subsequent actions would hasten Vallejo's imprisonment by Frémont, had committed the Secretary of State's instructions to memory, destroying the written copies before crossing Mexico in a *diligencia* (stagecoach). He later put the words back into written form before he disembarked at Monterey. As mentioned earlier, Buchanan's instructions advised American leaders to "conciliate the feelings of the Californians in favor of the

United States," prevent any foreign government from gaining control of the country, and avoid giving Mexico "just cause of complaint." The lieutenant also carried a packet of Benton family correspondence for Captain Frémont.[47]

In keeping with his role as confidential agent, Gillespie had passed himself off as "an invalid merchant" traveling for his health. He spoke Spanish perfectly, and in order to create errors, he scrambled his words. Though skilled as a linguist, he did not prove to be a successful actor.

Larkin had served as American consul since 1844, and he was happy with California just the way it was, admitting that "the times and the country are good enough for me." He now took up his role of "Confidential Agent" for Secretary of State Buchanan, organizing additional support for the American cause. Foremost in his mind was the need to guarantee that France and England would respect the Monroe Doctrine. Larkin wrote Vallejo's brother-in-law, Jacob Leese, to find out all he could about pro-American sympathies in the North Bay.[48] Larkin prepared another letter in Spanish for the benefit of the Californian leaders. One of its main points was that the United States, though intolerant of European interference, would welcome California either as a sister republic, or as a part of the American Union. Within a week, Larkin could report, "I have had many of the leaders at my house. . . . I have said . . . to Castro, Carrillo, and Vallejo, that our flag may fly here in thirty days."[49]

A grand ball was held at ex-Governor Alvarado's adobe on April 19, and Gillespie tried to maintain his disguise. He was thoroughly scrutinized by Vallejo and the local leaders. Thinking the marine's identity a fake, Castro urged him to drink more brandy. Vallejo's own doubts were probably inspired by what he learned from an old flame, Adelaida Spence. Her husband, David Spence, had received a secret warning about Gillespie from someone aboard the *Cyane,* and she passed the information along to Don Mariano. Vallejo thought that Gillespie should be kept in Monterey under surveillance.[50]

With Larkin's help, however, Gillespie escaped. He was guided to Yerba Buena, where Vice-Consul Leidesdorff took care of him. While still at Leidesdorff's house, Gillespie received a letter from Larkin which said that Mexico was in a state of chaos, and war between the United States and Mexico would probably break out before long.[51] The marine continued northward to Sutter's Fort, arriving there on April 28.

Almost simultaneously with Gillespie's arrival in the province, a proclamation was posted at Yerba Buena by Subprefect Francisco

Guerrero, instructing all local authorities to forbid the sale of land to unnaturalized foreigners, and declaring that Americans who did not leave the country when asked to do so might be "expelled whenever the government may find it convenient."[52]

No hostile actions followed the order, but Gillespie undoubtedly relayed this disturbing news as he traveled from Yerba Buena to Sutter's Fort and beyond.

"Men With Nothing to Lose"

*G*eneral Vallejo's generosity as a colonizer (and his graciousness as a host) were proverbial, not only before but also after California's Americanization. Nicolas Carriger remembered that after he and his family had crossed the plains and camped by Sonoma Creek on the General's land, Salvador Vallejo approached the newcomers. Just ahead of the captain came

> three stalwart Indians, one groaning under a heavy load of flour,
> one carrying a basket of sugar and the other holding a basket of
> chocolate; the captain by means of one interpreter asked us if
> we were in need of any one of the articles his servants carried,
> and expressed his willingness and readiness to serve us to the
> full extent of his ability. On taking a farewell from us [he said],
> "Nearby I have one thousand cows. If any of you wish fresh
> meat, go and kill as many animals as you need for your daily
> support."[1]

To men like Carriger and David Burris, the frank and winning Don Mariano would say, "Land is plenty. God made it for us and I have plenty." Immigrants were able to buy parcels from him at reasonable prices. Even Archibald H. Gillespie's brother would receive an invitation from the General to settle in Sonoma. But in May of 1846 it was Lieutenant Gillespie who served as a harbinger of Vallejo's future.[2]

Because so much of Gillespie's early military experience had been acquired aboard ship as a marine, he had met quite a few American and British officers, as well as merchants engaged in the California trade. The disguised traveler was recognized by one of John Sutter's clerks at New Helvetia, and by Sutter himself, who had seen Gillespie as an officer aboard the *U.S.S. Brandywine* at Honolulu. Sutter knew the lieutenant was not a merchant traveling for his health.[3] Sutter had not forgotten the events of early March, and he wasted no time sending word to General Castro that Gillespie was an agent of the U.S. government carrying dispatches for Captain Frémont. Fearing, too, that the lawless element at New Helvetia might become more uncontrollable, Sutter wanted Castro to "station a respectable garrison at this point" before more overlanders arrived.[4]

Oddly enough, Gillespie's clumsy deception helped convince the Americans that he must be the bearer of important news concerning relations between the United States and Mexico. If this were not the case, why would he have rushed all the way to Sutter's Fort — only to make tracks for Oregon? There can be little doubt that he left wild speculation in his wake. Accompanying the lieutenant toward Mt. Shasta were two guides, Frémont's former blacksmith Sam Neal and Levi Sigler.[5]

The design of California's evolving scrimshaw pointed north, and its pattern acquired unusual dramatic intensity when Gillespie rendezvoused with Frémont on May 9 near Klamath Lake. The air was cold, and though summer was not far off, snow was still accumulating in the Cascades. Frémont thought the drifts were too deep for eastward travel. At a campground set up on the edge of the lake, beneath some low cedar trees, he received the instructions issued by Secretary of State Buchanan and Secretary of the Navy Bancroft. He read through the packet of letters from the Benton family by the light of the campfire and spoke with Gillespie about what was taking place in California.

The official orders urged caution and diplomacy rather than violence. In fact, their contents, in the eyes of many scholars, seemed almost too bland to justify Gillespie's haste in pursuing Frémont to Oregon. But Gillespie had been instructed to deliver the dispatches to the explorer; he was simply obeying orders. There was also the matter of international politics, for the marine was convinced that a conflict with Mexico was about to explode. While traveling through Mexico, Gillespie had seen clear evidence of warlike preparations, which few other men on the West Coast were aware of. Troops and military supplies were being assembled near Mexico City by the victorious General Paredes. As far as Gillespie could tell, no state of war yet existed between Mexico and the United States. But with military goods being assembled on such a large scale, it would only be a matter of time.[6] This startling information, along with what had been learned from Larkin and the settlers at Sutter's Fort, must have had a telling impact on Frémont; certainly the news was more compelling than the outdated instructions from Washington, which had been written in October and November of the preceding year.[7]

Gillespie's Mexican news (and other factors like the weather and deepening snowdrifts) had their effect: Frémont decided to halt his northward trek; he would return to the United States — via California and "the line of the Colorado River."[8] He had always wanted to be on hand during a decisive moment in history, and returning to the Sacramento Valley would place him in the vicinity of any military hot spots that might develop, either in Alta California or in the Southwest.

As the white crests of Mt. Shasta and Mt. Lassen receded behind Frémont, he once again encountered worried Americans. The overlanders were feeling less secure in late May than they had prior to Frémont's confrontation with Castro in March. (Of course, the Gavilán affair had, in and of itself, helped to make their situation less hopeful.) Subprefect Guerrero's orders regarding land had spelled out in blunt terms the legal restrictions that would bar Americans from acquiring property. Immigrants without naturalization papers would not be able to hold land "either by sale or cession."[9] To a handful of the frontiersmen, the words sounded like a direct challenge that would justify their taking up arms.

Frémont had not yet traveled as far south as New Helvetia. He encountered Ezekiel Merritt on May 29 in the Bear Valley, and their meeting — for the peaceful residents of California, at least — was unfortunate; for still in the foreground of Merritt's thoughts was a plan to capture General Vallejo and Sonoma.[10]

Because of his drinking habits, Merritt probably looked older than his forty years. He also stuttered, especially when excited. But the former Rocky Mountain trapper knew the country well, and he viewed the provocation of Californians as a form of sport. He assured Frémont that Castro's troops had not yet been seen, and that there had been no attacks by the Indians.[11]

Continuing his journey south, Frémont set up a semi-permanent camp at a small range of extinct volcanoes called *Histum Yani,* said to be the place where the World Maker deity of the Maidu Indians had created the first man and woman.[12] Known today as the Sutter Buttes, the jagged cones of hardened lava tower above the flat expanse of the Sacramento Valley to elevations of more than 2,000 feet. Especially in the morning and evening, their bizarre silhouettes seem unrelated to the surrounding landscape. Frémont's company of engineers found water and game plentiful near the old Indian campsites there.

On June 1 Sutter informed Vallejo of Frémont's return from Oregon.[13] Sutter had learned that the explorer had bought stolen horses from the Indians, and he feared that this would encourage more theft.[14]

General Vallejo saw nothing positive in recent developments and wanted to arrest the momentum that seemed to be driving the country toward conflict. Both Castro and Sutter had learned that numerous wagon trains were about to descend into the Great Valley from the Sierra passes; just how many were coming no one could say for sure. American immigrants on the Sacramento River began to think that General Castro (or the Indians) would try to set fire to all the wheat in the valley, thus depriving the incoming pioneers of food.

In Monterey, an increasingly nervous Thomas Oliver Larkin predicted that California would soon be "well [w]rung by the torsion of the world."[15] He was relieved to know that his sons were already on their way to Boston; before long, passage to Honolulu would be arranged for his wife and daughters. Because he was pro-Californian, partisan politics might cost him his reputation. Not wanting to lose his good name, he tried to gain the sympathies of important newspaper editors on the East Coast, including A. E. Beach of the *New York Sun* and James G. Bennett of the *New York Herald*.[16] Larkin also confided in Frémont, hoping that if he "were assailed," the explorer might "render me services."[17]

Larkin knew that Vallejo's pro-American sympathies were already well anchored. The consul tried to sway José Castro to the American side by telling him that if war between the United States and Mexico broke out, the American flag would probably be raised over California within a matter of days. Castro gave the melancholy reply that war was preferable to peace, "as affairs will at once be brought to a crisis, and each one will know his doom."[18] Larkin thought that "if their offices and salaries could be secured to them," the Californian leaders might be willing to cooperate in the change of flags.[19] This became an article of faith for him. Larkin wanted men like Castro, Alvarado, and Vallejo to be given "permanent employ" under the new regime.

Larkin also prepared a written assessment of Vallejo's character. Since the General had relinquished his military control of the region, he had undergone some personal changes. Larkin judged Don Mariano to be

> very studious for a Californian, of much knowledge and general information. Anxious to improve himself and country . . . he has been formal, stiff, pompous and exacting, towards his countrymen and Foreigners of the lower or middle classes. Within a year has become pleasant and condescending, anxious for popularity and the good will of others. In Sonoma he has immense tracts of land, herds of cattle and Horses, and extensive Houses. Is hospitable to those highly respected or recommended to him,

ostentatious and for a Californian a close observer of every passing event. As a private person has but little regard for Mexico,
and an Officer more. Is confident that Mexico will not assist or
protect California, and that his own countrymen have not the
capacities to do so. Has given much work and employment to
the labouring American Emigrants, always speaking in their
favour. . . . Has his part of California the most free from Robbery or insubordination, with more safety of life and property
than any other Town in California.[20]

Don Mariano was also in the thoughts of Governor Pío Pico. Pico
was an unassuming ranchero whose low-key manner and homely, pock-
marked face seemed to inspire affection rather than jealousy. He consis-
tently opposed José Castro's increased military expenditures, believing
that the civil government should predominate. While trying to assemble
allies for what seemed like an unavoidable confrontation with Castro,
Pico appealed to Vallejo and did not hesitate to flatter him. He thought
that the officers at the Monterey junta should have made Vallejo commandant general in place of Castro, and he referred to Vallejo as a true
patriot. Pico regretted, however, that the Monterey officers had not conferred with the Los Angeles Assembly before calling for a council of war.
He implied that if Vallejo's allegiances were properly aligned, he might
benefit from a final distribution of mission property.[21]

Vallejo still hoped he could disentangle the bickering leaders.
He responded to Pico's letter by telling him that the dangers in the north
were by no means invented and that the officers had acted in good faith
when they had called for the *consejo*. It seemed to Don Mariano that the
governor's political prejudices had blinded him to the realities of the
situation.[22]

Pico planned to call an assembly of his own at Santa Barbara, to
discuss how "to avoid the fatal events impending at home and abroad."[23]
The meeting was scheduled for mid-June, and Larkin pressured Vallejo
to attend. In the foreground of Vallejo's thoughts was the fact that the
governor and his allies favored a British protectorate. If a vote were
taken on the matter of California's future alliance, delegates from the
south would greatly outnumber the pro-Americans from the north. Without stating whether or not he would show up, Vallejo asked Pico to
explain why San Diego should have two delegates when Sonoma, New
Helvetia, and San Rafael taken together would have only one.[24]

By June 3 the Los Angeles Assembly had become incensed with
Castro. In a secret session, they formally suspended the commandant

general for what was termed his "illegal assumption of powers."²⁵ Almost immediately, the southern capital became the scene of frantic activity as Governor Pico called for volunteers — his intention being to march an army north to challenge Castro's authority.

Simultaneously, due west of Mt. Hamilton in the Santa Clara Valley, Castro and José Antonio Carrillo were putting together an army of their own. The soldiers would be used against Governor Pico — or Captain Frémont — should the need arise. None of the Californians knew why the explorer had returned from Oregon in late May, or what he intended to do.

Farther north, Frémont himself was in the midst of preparations, though his plans were still unclear. American settlers and frontiersmen milled about at Sutter Buttes, exchanging ideas. From time to time, Ezekiel Merritt came to the camp. As usual, he tried to make the overthrow of California's government sound easy. Men who had been in the territory for a long time knew that there had been loose talk of that kind ever since the days of Isaac Graham.

Would-be rebels like William Hargrave and Benjamin Kelsey decided to go to the Buttes to hear what Frémont had to say. When they reached the picturesque encampment, Frémont refused to assume responsibility for "any sudden action on their part" and "endeavored to delay or frustrate" their efforts. This left the men feeling "somewhat disgusted."²⁶ If these settlers from the Napa Valley had arrived a few days later, they would have received a very different reply.

A man who was indebted to Vallejo, Joseph B. Chiles, was also chafing at the uncertainties of the political crisis. His rancho was located some fifteen miles northeast of Yount's Napa Valley grant. The sober Chiles doubted that a revolt in California would help the settlers. His partner, the square-shouldered millwright, William Baldridge, had serious misgivings, too.²⁷ Not that everything in pre-conquest California suited the two men. It bothered Baldridge that lawsuits were usually decided in favor of the "party who had the most money or influence."²⁸ He complained that the native rancheros suffered from "California fever" (laziness), and that their government was too unstable to be of much use.²⁹ Like many of the men at Sutter's Fort, Baldridge had an irrational distrust of José Castro. When Baldridge was told that Castro was organizing troops and supplies for a struggle against Pico, not Frémont, he scoffed at the idea. In fact, Baldridge assumed "the whole movement was dezined against us."³⁰ He saw no reason for the settlers to strike the first blow, however, since Americans had been well treated by the Californians. Besides, the "greatest dread" imaginable for the immigrants was that their land would be confiscated if they opposed the government.[31] The wary Baldridge knew that few men with property would support a revolution. His view was later confirmed by John Grigsby, who recalled that a few days after Hargrave and Kelsey had left Sutter Buttes, Frémont tried to "get some of the Americans who daily visited his camp, to undertake the matter [of starting a conflict] but no one who was suitable for the work were willing to undertake so grave a responsibility. . . ."[32]

William Todd, cousin of Mary Todd Lincoln, had written his relatives in the Midwest, warning them to stay out of California. "The Mexicans talk every spring and fall of driving the foreigners out of the country. They must do it this year or they can never do it."[33] If there was a revolt, he intended to join, but he realized that the Californians might oust the Yankees. The odds against the Americans' overthrowing Pico's government seemed long just then, especially since the cooperation of the landholding settlers wasn't guaranteed. One of Sutter's former soldiers, Nathan Coombs, thought that General Castro would "raise troops enough in two weeks to eat us all up."[34] Frémont was not willing to commit his topographical engineers to the project, and unless a war broke out, American warships would stay out of the fight. "Without any assistance from other sources, it was evident to any reasonable man that we should all be killed or driven out of the country in a short time," Baldridge concluded.[35] Another future Bear Flagger, a man named Fowler, offered an alternative that had already occurred to many of the settlers: they should pack up and go back to the United States or Oregon.

The die was finally cast on June 6, when Frémont sent horsemen up and down the Sacramento Valley with notices designed to create alarm. The unsigned warnings claimed that a band of Californians "amounting to 250 men, have been seen on their way to the Sacramento Valley, destroying the crops, burning the houses, and driving off the cattle." (Castro, at this time, had not raised a force of even 100 men, nor was he anywhere near the Sacramento Valley.) Frémont's message invited "every freeman" to come to his camp at the Buttes and decide on a course of action.[36]

On June 5 Vallejo received a visit from Castro himself, who came to Sonoma with Lieutenant Francisco Arce. Castro's prime concern was the potential war with Governor Pico. Before paying his respects to Don Mariano at the Casa Grande, Castro told one of his men to stand by with a boat just in case Vallejo could be convinced to join their cause and return with them to Santa Clara.[37] In recent years, Castro's opinions had not always been in

harmony with the General's and, of course, it had been a long time since
Don Mariano had been enthusiastic about civil war. During their meeting,
Castro asked for arms, military supplies, and horses. Vallejo promised him
170 mounts pastured at the Soscol Rancho, most of which already belonged
to the government. Six soldiers were assigned to drive the livestock, and
Vallejo issued one gun plus fourteen rounds of ammunition for each man.
Brass cannons, stacked muskets, and other military supplies, however, were
to remain at Sonoma.[38]

When Francisco Arce, who was described as having the good looks
of a smiling Irishman, and Lieutenant José María Alviso arrived at
Vallejo's Soscol Rancho to collect the horses, eight soldiers came along
instead of six. The waterways being high, the officers planned to drive
the livestock in a northward loop, traveling through the Sacramento
Valley before turning south again toward Santa Clara. James Harvey
Porterfield, who had recently done carpentry work for Vallejo, learned
of Arce's mission and left Sonoma for the Napa Valley to sound the
alarm. Porterfield assumed the horses would be used by Castro's army
against the Americans.[39]

Arce and Alviso crossed the Sacramento River at Knight's Landing,
where Arce may have dropped a remark or two about the ingratitude of
the foreigners. Ferryman William Knight, who had marched with Sutter's
army in defense of Micheltorena, immediately sped off in the direction
of Frémont's camp. According to Knight, Arce swore that the mounts
were to be used by Castro in an action against the settlers. This may
have been conjecture, or Arce may have actually said it. He was angry
enough about Frémont's presence in California to have wanted to throw
a scare into the immigrants.[40]

A week of rumors, assumptions, and anxious talk finally produced a
decisive plan of action the moment William Knight arrived at Frémont's
camp with the news. On hand at the time were Ezekiel Merritt, Granville
Swift, and a deserter from the U.S. Army named Henry L. Ford. Frémont
realized that an opportunity like this might never come again, and he
was determined to keep the government horses out of Castro's hands.
The explorer was satisfied that he had found the right leader for a raiding party in Merritt, a man he described as being "tractable and not
given to asking questions."[41] Merritt, Swift, and Ford, along with eight
or nine others (including Vallejo's future business partner, Robert Semple),
set off to intercept the Californians before the horses could be delivered
to Santa Clara.

Not realizing they were being followed, Arce and Alviso spent the night of June 8 at Sutter's Fort and headed south the next morning, covering only a few miles a day as they drove the livestock. They reached Murphy's Rancho on the Cosumnes River on June 9.[42]

It was no small task for the Americans to catch up with the Californians, who were some fifty or sixty miles to the south, but Merritt's party made excellent time, and by the morning of June 10, they had reached Murphy's property. Just before dawn, they moved up on the sleeping encampment. Most of the well-armed raiders "had nothing to lose but everything to gain" — the prerequisites specified by Frémont.[43] They knew that careless boasting about a revolution had led to the arrest and deportation of Isaac Graham and thirty-nine foreigners in 1840. What would the Californians do now, when instead of being faced with mere threats, they were provoked by the theft of 170 government mounts, taken at gunpoint from California soldiers — and with further acts of defiance already planned?

9

The Revolt Begins

"Who with wolves would run must learn to howl."
— *Spanish proverb*

I

The Americans' raid was a success. In the light of dawn on June 10, 1846, Lieutenant Arce was not very happy to be looking at the rawboned features of "Stuttering Zeke" Merritt. It may have been the second or third time he had seen him. Among the uninvited frontiersmen who had settled in the country, Merritt was one of the most audacious and least apologetic of them all. His tobacco habit had stained his beard, and his worn buckskins were full of holes. He embodied some of the qualities that had already been celebrated in frontier humor — a playful abrasiveness complete with flawless killer instinct.[1] His companions — about equal in number to Arce's soldiers — were a forbidding group to face so early in the morning.

Arce realized that the situation was hopeless, but he protested the ambush anyway. He denied any wrongdoing on the part of the Californians, saying the raid probably would not have succeeded without the element of surprise. The whole affair confirmed Arce's worst fears: he had been warning his countrymen that they might lose control of the province. It now looked as though he would have to hand over the 170 government horses his troops had rounded up at Vallejo's Soscol Rancho.[2]

His protest was answered by a sporting offer from Merritt: the Californians — if they did not like the element of surprise — could pick up their weapons and mount their horses. Upon a given signal, the Americans would try to repeat the raid. Merritt's men were some of the best guerrilla fighters in the territory, and Arce did not accept the challenge.[3]

Arce and Alviso were permitted to keep their swords; then they and their escorts were given horses for the ride back to the South Bay. Merritt warned the Californians that Sonoma and New Helvetia would be the next targets. As for the two Vallejo brothers, they would soon be prisoners.[4]

The despondent Californians watched the valuable herd being driven off, then they hurried in the direction of San Jose, where they reported the incident to General Castro. Arce forgot one important duty: he failed to send a soldier to warn the Vallejos. Even if he had done so, the Americans would probably have been a jump or two ahead of the news. Merritt and his men had tapped only a fraction of their energy, and once they got the herd to Frémont's camp, they planned to attack Sonoma before a messenger could alert the pueblo.

While Merritt's band was driving the livestock north, Captain Frémont was receiving a courteous tongue-lashing from an ex-schoolteacher named William B. Ide, who had arrived from Red Bluffs the previous morning.

Frémont's plans by that time had evolved somewhat further. He wanted to find a handful of men willing to commit "depradations against General Castro the usurper" and thus supply the Americans with horses "necessary for a trip to the states." Another of his intentions was to make prisoners of some of the principal Californian leaders and "provoke Castro to strike the first blow in a war" with U.S. troops. This done, he would unite the immigrants and march them to a place inside American boundaries.[5]

The explorer's curious plan to unite California and the United States would certainly mark the end of a peaceful courtship. Perhaps Frémont, like Sutter before him, hoped to align himself with the cause of legitimate rule by aiding the "rightful" leader, Pico, against the "usurper," Castro. Or so Vallejo was informed later on.[6]

To William B. Ide, Frémont's scheme sounded more like a marauding expedition than an act of political revolution. In particular, it reminded him of the Gavilán affair, during which Frémont had double-dared the Californians into action, then had marched off to Oregon, leaving the immigrants to deal with Castro on their own.

Ide was a seasoned pioneer, a native of Massachusetts who had arrived the previous October as co-leader of a large overland party. He had no intention of leaving California — even temporarily. He had a wife and five children, no money, and few possessions. His skills with rope and tackle had aided his company's progress over the Sierras, and no emergency seemed to faze him.[7] For Ide, as for many of the incipient rebels, the Pacific Ocean was destined to be the western boundary of his final home. He was willing to be buried in the attempt to make it so.

To convince Ide that attacks on the Californians were justified, Frémont reminded him of the outrages committed against Americans during the Graham Affair and said that Castro's treatment of the settlers provided grounds for "any measure they might adopt" for their safety.[8]

The fifty-year-old Ide disagreed. He was a better-read man than most of his companions, and his political convictions had been steeped in Brook Farm idealism. Ide thought it would be a good thing, as well as a feather in his cap, to liberalize California's social order. But his plans were general rather than specific. He hoped to free the poorer classes of Californians from the peonage of the rancho system, scrap import duties, and help the laborers by taking the government out of the hands of the leading families. He thought that the theft of the Soscol horses, followed by the kidnapping of the Vallejos and a hasty retreat, would be dishonorable.

Ide's intensity may have surprised Frémont. Unlike most Americans, the pioneer was not awed by the importance of Frémont's family connections. He expected the settlers' actions to be worthy of "the American name," and he startled the explorer by using words like "honor." When he promised to distance himself from any actions in Sonoma that were not motivated by high ideals, "Capt. F. became exasperated. Rising hastily he said: 'I will not suffer such language in my Camp; it is disorganizing!'" Then Frémont left the tent. This talk took place on the evening of June 10.[9]

Frémont's changing aims were interpreted in a number of ways by his American followers. John Grigsby, after hearing Frémont explain things, was sure the explorer would eventually join them "in an active campaign." As noted in the previous chapter, Kelsey and Hargrave had not been able to get Frémont's promise of military help. William B. Ide thought that Frémont would expect the settlers to act independently, and "would not afford us the least aid or assistance."[10]

The only man who was in agreement with Ide's general plan regarding the upcoming Sonoma raid was dentist "Long Bob" Semple, whose brother was then serving in the U.S. Congress. An extremely tall man whose talents and energies were as remarkable as his size, he would one day be president of California's constitutional convention. Since the morning of June 10, Semple, along with Merritt and the others, had been driving the Soscol herd toward Frémont's camp, and before noon of the 11th, the men reached the explorer's headquarters.

Frémont showed his approval for what the raiders had done at Murphy's rancho, but he dodged the implication that either he or the

U.S. government owned the captured horses, saying that the mounts were the property of Merritt and his men.[11]

He entrusted Merritt with the leadership of the next stage of the revolt, and within a matter of hours the new-fledged Bear Flaggers were ready for their journey to Sonoma. The formidable group numbered some twenty men, including Ide, Semple, Swift, Grigsby, three of the Kelseys, and Frémont's ex-employee, William Fallon. On the afternoon of June 11, they started across the corridor of blinding yellow grass toward the first tier of mountains they would have to cross. In all, three mountain ranges separated them from the Sonoma Valley. Stopping at Cache Creek, they enjoyed some refreshments and were joined by a few more rebels, including William Todd.[12] They paused in the Pope Valley to eat dinner at the home of Elias Barnett, but did not spend the night. They resumed their ride almost immediately, following the dark forest trails, not slowing their pace until they reached the upper Napa Valley. Since many of the men were exhausted from the ride, a long rest seemed to be in order, and messengers were sent up and down the valley to find more recruits. Belligerent feelings among the valley settlers had been whipped up during the past months by malcontents like the Kelseys and Merritt. For some reason, Dr. Bale, who had been hostile toward the Vallejos in the past, did not join the rebels, but his mill was the scene of some spirited harangues delivered by Robert Semple and Merritt on June 13. Fearing the consequences if they failed to surprise Sonoma, the Bear Flag leaders used threats and all the eloquence they could muster to get the raiders to head toward Vallejo's pueblo.[13]

The Americans apparently did not believe that ex-Commandant General Vallejo would have allowed his headquarters to remain unprotected after the dismissal of his troops. William Knight, who was on hand to lend his services as interpreter, seemed to be as poorly informed as the others about the state of Sonoma's defenses. Even Sutter, who had run off some of Vallejo's livestock in 1844, seemed to be under the impression that Don Mariano had replaced the garrison.[14] Lacking better information, the Bears continued to use secrecy and haste.

Now totaling thirty-three men, the muscular horsemen left the upper Napa Valley and traveled southward, the old cone of Mt. St. Helena at their backs. Along the route another important matter was straightened out. Ide and Semple wanted to make sure that no trouble would take place between Zeke Merritt and the Vallejos. Don Salvador Vallejo had already quarreled with Merritt: one version of the story being that Zeke had "tried to stir up a revolution" a few years before and had been punished by Captain Vallejo, who had given him a "sound drubbing" before releasing him with orders to behave himself in the future. Another account alleged that "under the pretense that Mr. Merritt had harbored a runaway man-of-war's man, [Don Salvador] beat him severely with his sword." As far as Merritt and his friends were concerned, the score had not yet been settled. For the moment, however, the Americans seemed willing to forego revenge, and they agreed not to harm either of the Vallejo brothers.[15]

The steep mountains between the Pope and Napa Valleys had proven to be tortuous and wearisome. Determined to avoid the usual routes to Sonoma, the men now attempted to force their way through the animal trails of the Mayacamas Range, a high ridge which separates the Sonoma and Napa Valleys. Even today, cars have difficulty negotiating the curves. The land pitches downward at strange angles, and bluffs appear without notice. Between the ancient oaks and pine trees were thickets of poison oak. It was country in which Merritt felt at ease because of his frequent hunting operations there.

By dawn of June 14, the Bear Flaggers had reached the floor of the sunny valley that the Vallejos had administered since 1834. The raiders did not forget their caution, but only one man was out and about, and he was taken prisoner. No one else had yet ventured into the brilliant morning.[16]

The horsemen approached the pueblo's center and found themselves facing a wide plaza — the largest in California — which communicated a feeling of indolence and tranquility. General Vallejo's two-story Casa Grande was located on the square's north side. Impressive in scale, its overall length was 110 feet. Rising from its west wall was a *torreón*, a four-story tower from which more than a hundred square miles of territory could be seen. A high adobe wall extended from the base of the tower, with gun slits for defense. To the east of the house was the barracks. Except for the flagpole in front of the deserted barracks and some dry cattle bones, the parade ground was empty. The tile roofs of the old mission had been carted off by townspeople for use in nearby dwellings, and the weather had torn at the adobe walls, reducing them to picturesque rubble. Not very much had been left as a tribute to the Franciscans' energy. All the structures — especially the house and barracks — were on an impressive scale, and reflected Vallejo's desire to create an imposing headquarters from which to administer the region.

The rebels on the plaza might have seen a man's face appear in one of the upstairs windows, the imposing visage of Vallejo himself. The silence was broken by the handles of the raiders' pistols, as they began to hammer on the Casa Grande's entrance.

To Doña Francisca Vallejo, who stood beside her husband, the exotic menagerie of Anglo-Americans was frightening to look at. Well armed, travel-weary, dressed in torn buckskins and coyote-skin caps, some of the men had red bandannas wrapped around their heads, and she was surprised to see how many of them were barefoot. Most of the Americans were crack shots; the handles of their guns and tomahawks were notched to indicate the number of men they had killed. "Banditti" is how she later described them.[17]

While Vallejo hurriedly put on his uniform, Doña Francisca suggested he use the back door to make his escape. But he did not want to desert his family (at least six of his children were living in the house at the time), and it was not like him to perform an act that was undignified; besides, any attempt to escape would probably fail.[18]

When he went downstairs, Vallejo ordered the servants to open the heavy door. The armed men pushed their way in. What they saw must have surprised them, for the interior was something of a rarity in California. As described not long afterward by Edwin Bryant, future alcalde of San Francisco, all the rooms were scrupulously clean and presented an air of comfort. "The parlor was furnished with handsome chairs, sofas, mirrors, and tables of mahogany framework, and a fine piano. . . . Several paintings and some superior engravings ornamented the walls."[19] The rebels, with their powder-keg ideas of freedom, represented some of the worst and best elements on the western frontier. But here, about as far from the eastern seaboard as they could get, they found something which wasn't supposed to exist in the Far West: a grandee's house, sophisticated gentry! They thought they had left all that behind when they crossed the Rockies.

Most of the raiders remained outside, but there was noisy confusion in the sala. Vallejo raised his voice to ask the name of the leader and to find out what they wanted. A number of people answered, "Here we are all heads." Then, after a time, Zeke Merritt was pointed out as their spokesman.[20]

Quite possibly, Vallejo had seen the rugged hunter before. Merritt may have been one of Dr. Bale's cohorts during the attempted murder of Don Salvador in 1844. But the tobacco-chewing frontiersman did not impress Vallejo. In fact, the General later contemptuously referred to the men who had stormed into his house as "White Indians."[21]

Hauteur was a quality Vallejo had abandoned in recent years, but it again seemed appropriate. He asked Merritt, "To what happy circumstances shall I attribute the visit of so many exalted personages?"[22]

Merritt replied that the General and his family were in no immediate danger, but that they were under arrest. He described his companions as settlers with a justified gripe — honorable men who would no longer tolerate living under the Californians' rule. They had been insulted and threatened by the recent Mexican proclamations, and the rights of Americans would have to be respected. From now on, the territory of California would be independent.[23]

Although Merritt stammered badly and Knight's shortcomings as an interpreter were obvious, Vallejo was beginning to get a better idea of what was taking place. The violent advocates of American rule from the Sacramento Valley were trying to overwhelm the peaceful pro-American faction in Sonoma, using methods that might cause bloodshed in the future.

The General was one of very few Californian officials who knew how to deal with impassioned Americans, and it seemed as though he had already formed a plan. He suggested that Jacob Leese might be useful now, to help draw up any formal papers that would require approval and signature. Merritt and his men agreed, and a messenger was sent to the west side of the plaza to find the Ohio merchant, who had recently returned from Yerba Buena.

II

Before Jacob Leese could be rousted from his adobe, Don Salvador Vallejo and Victor Prudon were led into the General's sala, where they too were placed under arrest. Prudon was reported to have said, "Boys, you have been a little too fast for us. We were going to serve you in the same way in just ten days from today." The remark may have been modified slightly in the process of being relayed to a friend, but the brag would have been in keeping with the Californians' habits of loose talk.[24]

All the raiders from the Sacramento Valley knew that Isaac Graham and a couple of dozen Americans had been imprisoned at San Blas for merely uttering threats against the California authorities. Merritt's nabbing the government horses had dissolved any lingering doubts the rebels might have felt. They had broken the law, and it would no longer protect them.[25]

After a few minutes, Jacob Leese was brought into the room under guard. His past differences with Vallejo had been smoothed over, and he and the General were again on good terms. They both favored an American protectorate, as did Victor Prudon. If it were up to the three Sonoma leaders, the Stars and Stripes would already have been waving outside on the plaza flagpole.

Leese could read the shock of events on the faces of Vallejo's children.[26] At Don Mariano's request, the Ohio merchant approached the most conspicuous individual in the sala, a man who stood six feet, eight inches tall, "Long Bob" Semple. The Kentucky dentist was dressed from head to toe in grey buckskin and was wearing a fox-skin cap. In the not too distant future, he would publish California's first newspaper (making free use of its pages to promote his real estate ventures). Leese asked Semple for the name of their leader and the reason for the arrest of Vallejo and the other officers. Admitting that they had no official spokesman, Semple described the rebels as poor men who wanted to make California independent. He knew that the General possessed vast military stores and owned large tracts of property and that Vallejo was one of the most powerful individuals in the country.[27]

In fact, 250 stands of arms and other supplies were stored in the barracks — all belonging to the Mexican government. Already some allusions had been made to the notion that the Bears were operating under Captain Frémont's orders, and when Don Mariano heard others make references to the explorer's involvement, he surrendered the keys to the arsenal. In this way, Vallejo was given a convenient, politically discreet way to discharge his duties as a Mexican official.[28]

The absence of resistance, both inside the Casa Grande and outside on the plaza, created an unexpected situation. There were no opposing soldiers, no cavalry or Indian auxiliaries. The raiders had not "taken" Sonoma; they had merely occupied a sleepy village.

Meantime, a cask of brandy was being distributed on the plaza by a Canadian named Oliver Beaulieu. After it had made the rounds, some of the rebels seemed ready to forget their promises. Having received no news from inside the quiet adobe, they decided the time had come to loot.[29]

Their cries were loud enough to draw Robert Semple and some of the other leaders to the entryway. The dentist was furious. Bawling at the crowd, he promised to kill any of the men who tried to turn the takeover into a "looting expedition." His threats were backed up by Grigsby and Andrew Kelsey, and the commotion on the plaza died down.[30]

The sun was higher now, and there was a strong odor from the sweating horses that had brought the men over the mountains. Some of the rebels hadn't bothered to dismount, and dust followed in their wake as they rode across the plaza to talk and pass liquor back and forth. As it grew warmer, the horsemen found shade under the porches and balconies that protected the whitewashed adobe walls of Vallejo's hacienda. A handful of men closed their eyes for the first time in two days.

Indoors, Merritt and Kelsey continued to be confused by the unexpected calm. Don Mariano suggested that wine and brandy be served and negotiations begin. Once, he had been thought of as one of the most military-minded men in California.[31] As a young officer, he had treasured the idea of an independent California, but now, American annexation seemed like the department's most logical political solution.

Jacob Leese thought that well-defined guarantees needed to be written out by both parties "for the protection of all security and honour."[32] However, the documents that would give the Bear movement legitimacy were beyond Merritt's powers of expression.

So the men best suited to the job, Robert Semple and Jacob Leese, began to draft the articles of capitulation. They also composed a paper which guaranteed the safety of the villagers and granted a parole to all political prisoners who did not oppose the rebels.

Vallejo seldom took more than a few sips of wine, but on this occasion, neither he, his brother Don Salvador, nor Victor Prudon even tasted it.[33] Merritt was hardly the sort to pass up alcohol, and most of his companions joined in.

The wine made emotions flow more freely, and soon bad feeling erupted between Stuttering Zeke and Don Salvador. The American announced he would not repay the blows he had received from Don Salvador in the past, but he intended to put the Californian in irons. The threat was not carried out, and Leese and the others helped discourage further quarreling.[34]

Approximately three hours had passed since the Bears' arrival and it was now about 8:30 A.M. Some of the early morning guests complained that "they was hongery," and a bullock was killed for their breakfast. They were also given tea with sugar.[35]

For the raiders outside, the long wait seemed pointless. In the absence of a fight, they wanted to collect all the weapons and horses they could find and ride back to Frémont's camp. Merritt had done nothing to let them know what was taking place, and they cast around for a new leader. After a quick vote, John Grigsby was chosen to replace Zeke Merritt. The men asked Grigsby to speed up negotiations and report back as soon as he knew what arrangements were being made.[36]

But Inside the Casa Grande the American negotiators had turned their morning's work into a celebration. They shouted a welcome to Grigsby when he entered the General's parlor, and a barely-awake Merritt invited the Tennessean to have a drink.

Grigsby announced that he was replacing Merritt as the rebels' captain, but the hilarious mood of the American negotiators soon prevailed. For Grigsby, too, things were placed in a new perspective by the General's wine.

The men outside were forgotten. They had anticipated a shoot-out. What kind of revolution was this? Two former sailors, who had joined the Bears a couple of days earlier, went to the door of the Casa Grande and said they knew there was money in the house and they wanted it. This wasn't the sort of thing Semple and Grigsby would tolerate, and the men were shown the muzzles of loaded rifles.[37]

Meanwhile, the malcontents on the plaza repeated the electoral process and this time chose William B. Ide. Since he didn't drink, the odds for his success were more favorable.

By the time the teetotaler entered the Casa Grande, Merritt was cushioning his head on his arms and William Knight's function as a translator had been forgotten. The others were glassy-eyed and silent.

The conscientious Leese and Semple (the giant was now sitting in his stocking feet) were still at work on the official documents. To Ide, the picture was seriocomic, and he later complained, "The bottles had wellnigh vanquished the captors!"[38]

The documents were finally ready for signature. "Be it known," the Articles of Capitulation read, ". . . having been surprised by a numerous armed force which took me prisoner, with the chief and officers belonging to the garrison of this place . . . myself as well as the undersigned officers pledge our word of honor that, being under guarantees of prisoners of war, we will not take up arms . . . which guarantees our lives, families, and property, and those of all the residents of this jurisdiction, so long as we make no opposition."[39] There was room for the signature of General Vallejo and the others.

The spokesmen for the Bears signed their names to a separate declaration which expressed their desire "to establish a government upon republican principles." They would refrain from taking or injuring "any person who is not found in opposition to the cause," and they promised that property would not be destroyed "further than is necessary for our immediate support."[40]

Best of all, the Vallejos and Victor Prudon were to remain in Sonoma. The idealistic Ide had always admired the documents of the American Revolution, and he found nothing wrong with the wording of the Sonoma papers. Jacob Leese, feeling that he had performed a good morning's work, excused himself and went home for breakfast.[41]

Ide also went outside, but when he showed the Articles of Capitulation to the agitated men on the plaza, there were shouts of disappointment. Some of the raiders wanted to hold the Vallejos and Prudon prisoner.

Still slumped in his chair in the sala, John Grigsby roused himself and, not too steadily, went into the sunlight to find out what was going on. "What were Frémont's orders on this?" he demanded. There was no definite reply. "But," he cried, "have you not got Capt. Frémont's name in black and white to authorize you in this you have done?" Ide asked the crowd for written instructions but no one could produce any.[42]

"I thought we had the United States behind us," Grigsby shouted. Then he swore he had been deceived and said he would not go through with the plan.[43] He assured the men, "I can take my family to the mountains as cheap as any of you."[44]

These words were unsettling to the others. The raiders began to break up into smaller groups. Some of them considered the alternative Grigsby had just suggested: a journey over the Sierras back to the United States.

The confusion increased, and there was a renewed call for looting. Ide tried to bring the men to order. He expressed his contempt for any of the rebels who would not stay and follow through on the revolt.

> "I will lay my bones here, before I will take upon myself the ignominy of commencing an honorable work, and then flee like cowards like thieves when no enemy is in sight. In vain will you say you had honorable motives! Who will believe it? *Flee this day, and the longest life cannot wear off your disgrace!* Choose ye! Choose ye this day, what you will be! We are robbers, or we *must be* conquerors!"[45]

Amazingly, his speech kept the movement from falling apart. A few minutes before, the raiders had been willing to abandon him in favor of Grigsby, but now they again acclaimed the highly principled Ide as their leader.[46]

From the first, Vallejo had sensed the Bears' confusion. His patience and self-confidence had survived the morning. Now, there were no interpreters on hand to tell him what was going on. On the other side of the adobe walls, some of the violent rebels were saying they wanted to "tear down and pillage" the Casa Grande.[47]

A compromise had to be reached because a noisy faction of the group did not want to release the Vallejos. This development worried Semple and Ide.

The plaza's perimeter was nearly a half-mile in extent. Diagonally across from Vallejo's spacious hacienda was the U-shaped adobe belonging to Jacob Leese. Having finished his breakfast, the successful businessman again started across the dusty parade ground, heading for the Casa Grande. It was not difficult to see how unruly the rebels had become. Once inside Vallejo's parlor, the fact that his own life might be in danger was brought home to him. Semple admitted to Leese that it was becoming impossible to control the men and gave him the job of telling his friends that Prudon, Don Salvador, and Vallejo himself would have to ride to the Sacramento River under guard.[48]

The General was instructed to give the Bears eighty horses, and Leese had to surrender sixty. When Leese begged one of the raiders not to take horses that belonged to his children, the request was refused, and the explanation given was, "We go in for good horses."[49]

Soon the house was searched and all arms and ammunition were removed. Ide later said that nine cannons, 250 stands of arms, and "tons of copper, shot and other public property" worth approximately $1,200 had been "seized and held in trust for the public benefit."[50]

Staying out of sight during most of the morning's events was the powerful Chief Solano, Vallejo's principal Indian ally, who had been living at the Casa Grande as a houseguest. He now urged the General to permit him to organize a rescue party to free the Sonomans. Don Mariano was opposed to the plan. (Later on, feeling it to be part of his duty, Solano remained at the house and watched over Doña Francisca and the children.[51])

Vallejo expected the morning's riddles to be cleared up after a meeting with Frémont. Now, his primary concern was for the safety of his family and the townspeople. Though five-year-old Platon Vallejo had been fascinated by the arrival of the strange visitors, the older children and Francisca sensed the increasing peril of their situation.[52]

The Bears (and Vallejo) wanted Leese to accompany them to the Sacramento as an interpreter. Would he do this? The merchant agreed. At this point, Leese was hoping Frémont could be persuaded to "come to Sonoma and make that place his headquarters."[53]

Inevitably, perhaps, Don Mariano had to make the long ride to the camp of the enigmatic Captain Frémont. Before leaving, he asked a former Sonoma alcalde, Don José de la Rosa, to take a message to Captain Montgomery at Sausalito, urging the officer to use his influence to secure the safety of life and property at the pueblo. Would Montgomery also send someone to help pacify the Bears?[54] De la Rosa didn't know it, but he was endangering the lives of the captives by performing his mission. The alcalde of Sonoma was later told that "if any person in the place . . . attempted to notify other places of this act" the prisoners were liable to be shot.[55]

It was now approximately eleven o'clock in the morning. Don Mariano, Don Salvador, and Victor Prudon were being given an escort of about ten men for their ride to the Sacramento River. Jacob Leese, though not considered a prisoner, was also mounted for the eighty-mile journey.

There was still some drunkenness on the plaza, and Semple and Grigsby bawled violent warnings about the punishments that would be doled out if any looting took place. Remaining behind as commander of the twenty-five-man garrison was William B. Ide. But as the armed escort (which included Semple, Merritt, and Grigsby) led the captives away from the plaza, Ide accused his comrades of deserting the cause. He probably feared a challenge to his authority by the unpredictable rebels, or a counterattack by Castro.[56] The company headed east, crossing the hills that separate the Sonoma and Napa Valleys — country which was part of Jacob Leese's Huichica grant.

Don Salvador thought Merritt was about to forget his pledge and would kill the prisoners on the way to the Sacramento, and some of the guards did make hostile remarks to Don Salvador. Not that he was the type to keep his feelings a secret. The gritty Indian fighter was probably reflecting aloud on the inequities of the situation.[57] Reminding Don Salvador that Merritt was no longer in command, John Grigsby promised that the captives would be safe enough.[58] General Vallejo had by now struck up a friendship with the ambitious Robert Semple, whom he called "Buen Oso," Good Bear.

People along the road wanted to know where the horsemen were going, and they were told that the Sonoma leaders would return in about four or five days.[59] Their route took them between high, rolling hills. Near the streams, conical flowers of the California buckeye were in full bloom, and where the ground was rocky, madrones and manzanita shrubs had shiny new skin.

Approximately half the distance to New Helvetia had been covered when the Bears called a halt at Manuel Vaca's rancho (in the Lagoon Valley southwest of present-day Vacaville). Vallejo had no desire to rest and was hoping the ride would continue through the night. The guards, however, had finally tapped the last of their energy.

Undoubtedly, Don Manuel Vaca was surprised to see trouble arriving at his doorstep in the company of General Vallejo. It was Don Mariano who had encouraged Vaca to come to California from New Mexico, and had approved his land grant. Always the courteous gentleman, Don Manuel offered the travelers the best he had in the way of food and refreshments. A rumor soon reached the rancho that an attempt was going to be made to free the prisoners. Vallejo and Leese assured everyone in the house they would not "consent to any such movement."[60]

The weary Americans were grateful to lie down and close their eyes for the first time in days. This left the prisoners carelessly guarded. The Sonomans settled themselves on a bed of straw about one hundred yards from where Grigsby and the others were sleeping.

It was about 3 A.M. when Vallejo noticed a man coming toward him in the dark. Don Mariano and Leese were still awake, discussing the day's events. The man may have been Juan Padilla himself, or one of his lieutenants disguised as a woman — it has never been determined for sure. Vallejo later identified the messenger as Vicente Juárez, brother of the cavalryman Cayetano Juárez. Don Cayetano, along with Juan Padilla, had gathered a force of about thirty men to intercept the Americans and free the Sonoma leaders. The early morning visitor told Vallejo it would be quite simple to release them but it was up to the General to give the order, and this he would not do.[61]

He thanked the messenger, saying that since all the prisoners were being well treated and there had been no bloodshed, it would be better to settle the matter with Frémont. If some of the guards were killed during a rescue, the families of the Vallejo brothers would be the first to suffer.[62] The General's refusal was probably bewildering to Padilla's men.

Morning found the prisoners behind a low rim of hills on the western edge of the Sacramento Valley. To the southeast, rising from the valley floor, were the twin ridges of the old cone of Mt. Diablo. Extending in the other direction, toward the ocean, was the dark line of the Vaca Mountains.

Feeling refreshed now, the guards were ready to continue the ride. They left Don Manuel Vaca behind to puzzle over the possible repercussions of the visit. In the morning hours of June 15, as the horsemen passed through Chief Solano's old country, Padilla's men still trailed the prisoners. Honoring Vallejo's instructions about an attempted rescue, however, they stayed out of sight.

Soon the shallow, gently rising hills disappeared, and the land flattened out. It was now about thirty-two miles across the hot plain to the site of New Helvetia. Vallejo's impatience increased again when, at the end of the second day's ride, his escort called a halt near the green waters of the Sacramento. The captives spent the night at Thomas Hardy's rancho.[63]

The following day it was learned that the wandering Frémont had shifted his headquarters to the American River. Before the captives met him, the explorer was briefed by Grigsby and some of the others. Soon Jacob Leese (who had come along merely as a favor to Don Mariano and the rebels) received some bad news. Even before he was able to confront Frémont face to face, the Ohio merchant was placed under arrest by John Grigsby. Leese was American-born, and completely red, white, and blue in his sympathies, but he, too, would be treated as a prisoner.[64]

1. Vallejo As a Young Man

1864 painting by Arriolo Fortunato Courtesy, Vallejo Naval and Historical Museum, Vallejo, California.

2. Francisca Vallejo

Courtesy, State of California, Department of Parks and Recreation

3. The north side of the Sonoma Plaza as it looked in the mid-1840s. The artist incorporated General Vallejo's suggestions when she painted this representation in 1879.

Painting by Oriana Day
Courtesy, State of California, Department of Parks and Recreation

5. Thomas Oliver Larkin
*Courtesy, California State
Library, Sacramento*

4. Captain Thomas ap
   Catesby Jones
*Courtesy, California State
Library, Sacramento*

6. Isaac Graham
*Courtesy, California State
Library, Sacramento*

7. Manuel Micheltorena
*Courtesy, California State
Library, Sacramento*

9. Juan B. Alvarado
*Courtesy, California State
Library, Sacramento*

8. Jacob P. Leese
*Courtesy, California State
Library, Sacramento*

11. Robert Semple

*Courtesy, California State
Library, Sacramento*

10. John Bidwell

*Courtesy, California State
Library, Sacramento*

12. John Charles Frémont

*Courtesy, California State
Library, Sacramento*

13. José Castro

*Courtesy, California State
Library, Sacramento*

14. John A. Sutter

*Courtesy, California State
Library, Sacramento*

15. 1857 Daguerrotype of Pablo de la Guerra, Salvador
Vallejo, and Andrés Pico.

Courtesy, State of California, Department of Parks and Recreation

16. M.G. Vallejo in the Early 1850s
Courtesy, California State Library, Sacramento

17. Vallejo in the Late 1850s.
His appearance reflects his setbacks
and disillusionments during this
harsh decade.

*Courtesy, Sonoma Valley Historical Society,
Sonoma, California*

18. Dr. Platon Vallejo

Courtesy, Society of California Pioneers,
San Francisco

19. Salvador Vallejo in His Later Yea
At the time this photograph was take
it was often impossible for the don to
walk without a cane. Multiple fractu
suffered during a lifetime on horseba
left him crippled in his old age.

Courtesy, Sonoma Valley Historical Society,
Sonoma, California

20. William Hood Ranch in Kenwood, 1869.
This photograph illustrates how open grazing land in the
Sonoma Valley was broken up into smaller holdings. Hood's
ranch was once part of the extensive Los Guilicos grant,
obtained in 1837 by Vallejo's brother-in-law, John Wilson,
from Governor Alvarado.

Courtesy, Sonoma League for Historic Preservation, Sonoma, California

128

21. Fannie (Epifania) Vallejo

Courtesy, Vallejo Naval and Historical Museum, Vallejo, California

22. John B. Frisbie

Courtesy, Bancroft Library, Berkeley, California

23. Lithograph of Lachryma Montis.
Vallejo used this particular representation on one of his letterheads.

Courtesy, Sonoma Valley Historical Society, Sonoma, California

24. Vallejo As an Elderly
Distinguished Gentleman

*Courtesy, California State Library,
Sacramento*

25. Francisca Vallejo in Her Later Years

Courtesy, California State Library, Sacramento

26. The Petaluma Adobe in the 1870s.
It had fallen into disrepair but has since been restored.
Courtesy, Sonoma Valley Historical Society, Sonoma, California

27. The Reservoir at Lachryma Montis. After 1876, much of Vallejo's income was derived from piping water to Sonoma from the spring at Lachryma Montis.

Courtesy, Sonoma Valley Historical Society, Sonoma, California

28. The Sonoma Plaza in the 1880s. Directly behind the pavilion is the new train station where Vallejo's Casa Grande once stood. To the right, almost unrecognizable, is the Sonoma Barracks hidden behind a Victorian façade, which was superimposed over the old adobe front. The barracks has since been restored.

Courtesy, State of California, Department of Parks and Recreation

29. Vallejo and His Niece Carmelita Kune, 1887
Courtesy, Society of California Pioneers, San Francisco

10

Ordeal on the Sacramento

"The bed and the prison are the proof of true friends."
— *Spanish Proverb*

*A*t the time of his first interview with John Charles Frémont, Vallejo was like a man who — on the basis of his close ties with the relatives of a beautiful woman he has not yet met (one reputed to be very noble and desirable) — has agreed to marry an unseen bride. What he liked best about the future connection were some valuable documents possessed by her relatives (in this case, the Constitution and Bill of Rights). Now, at last, he was face to face with a bona fide representative of his intended. Right from the start, however, he was dismayed by the way Frémont was denying any connection between his men and the Stars and Stripes. The American flag was nowhere in sight and Lieutenant Gillespie had already been criticized for displaying one.[1]

Though Frémont was worried by the fact that his hair was "turning grey before its time,"[2] he was a handsome man whom one observer described as being "compactly knit," with thin face, bold aquiline nose, and eyes "deep-set and keen as a hawk's."[3] It was well known that his men would follow him anywhere; but very few of them were able to guess his thoughts; nor was it often that any two individuals could agree on the exact details of what Frémont had previously said.

Vallejo — admired for his self-command — was probably the most urbane Californian Frémont had met. Once Don Mariano was inside the explorer's tent, he expected to be treated with courtesy, if not friendship; and as a colonel in the Mexican army, he outranked the captain.

No confirmation of the United States' involvement in the Sonoma takeover had been made. Hoping to have some sort of reassurance spelled out, Vallejo alluded to the fact that he was the captain's prisoner. "No. You are the prisoner of these people." Frémont pointed to Merritt, Grigsby, and the others.[4]

To make up for the lack of campstools, Frémont's orderlies removed sacks of newly minted coins from a trunk. (These contained pay for U.S.

government employees.) After the heavy bags were placed on the ground, Vallejo and the others sat down on the improvised chairs.[5] Then there followed a "mysterious silence." Frémont refused to explain by what authority (or for what reasons) he was holding the Sonomans, even though he did not accuse them of any specific crimes. "I have been told you are the one who directed the action of those who invaded my residence," Vallejo began, "and . . . I wish you would inform me of what you propose doing with us."[6]

Frémont dodged the implication that he had been behind the Sonoma raid and said that he would have to consult with the rebels before making any decisions. He then began to recite what Jacob Leese called a "long rigamarole": a list of complaints which the immigrants had made against José Castro, adding that Vallejo and the other prisoners would have to remain under guard until these matters were straightened out.[7] A commotion was heard in a nearby tent. Trappers from Oregon had joined some angry Bear Flaggers who thought the prisoners should be executed. Robert Semple broke up the meeting and was later credited with having saved the captives' lives.[8]

What were Frémont's motives for holding the prisoners? The answer is by no means easy to come by. Don Mariano later offered two explanations: the first (blatantly generous) assumed that Frémont wanted to treat the Sonomans more humanely but was prevented from doing so by his angry followers. There was also a devious quality to Frémont's actions, which made Vallejo think that the explorer possessed a "very elastic conscience" and was "sheltering himself under the cloak" of his American citizenship.[9] Another motive — Frémont's political jealousy — was hinted at by John Grigsby when he told William Baldridge that Frémont was somewhat awed by the General's reputation and had a "'greater dread of [Vallejo] than any other man in the country.'"[10] Possibly, Frémont was already thinking of the California governorship and wanted Vallejo safely out of the way. According to Baldridge, it was generally accepted that Vallejo "had more sagasity and wielded more influence than any other man at that time, and it was desirable that [Vallejo's] sagasity, and influence should not be exerted against us."[11]

Frémont was in no mood to admit that the Vallejo brothers, Leese, and Prudon had given more help to incoming Americans than any other leaders in the territory, (with the exception of John Sutter and Thomas Larkin). This made their arrest all the more puzzling.

Don Mariano and the others now took their turn listing the wrongs committed against them: the loss of more than one hundred horses, the disruption of civil order in Sonoma, and the seizure of the Mexican military stores. To Jacob Leese, Frémont's replies seemed "arbitrary and offensive in the extreme." Leese's testy side was in the ascendant now, and he complained that he was being wrongfully held. As a courtesy to the Bears, he had volunteered to serve as an interpreter; Frémont was treating him as an enemy. Frémont bluntly replied that Leese "was a bad man." Leese asked for an explanation, but none was given.[12] As far as the confiscated horses and other personal property were concerned, Frémont promised that all "would be made right."[13] The talk was over. The explorer organized a company of his men and personally escorted Don Mariano and the others to Sutter's semifeudal but cozy fortress, which was a short distance away.

Sutter did not know what to think when he saw his friends Victor Prudon and Jacob Leese, accompanied by Don Mariano and Don Salvador Vallejo, entering the gates as prisoners. Nor did he believe the time had come for celebration. As mentioned earlier, the immigrants of '45 had paid him little respect. Sutter had condemned Merritt's seizure of the Soscol horses and had been equally outraged by Frémont's purchase of stolen mounts near Lassen's ranch earlier that year. The most critical problem in the territory was horse-stealing; it had spread like an epidemic from the Indians to the whites and was now being treated as a casual affair by almost everyone.

Without wasting time on explanations, Frémont ordered Sutter to take charge of the Sonomans and treat them as he would any other prisoners. The European was a famous host, always gracious to visitors. He had nothing against General Vallejo or the others. Being told what to do inside his own walls made him indignant. Frémont pointed out that Sutter was a naturalized Mexican citizen, and added that if he didn't like the way things were being handled, he could be relocated "across the San Joaquin River and he could go and join the Mexicans." According to John Bidwell, the scolding brought tears to Sutter's eyes.[14]

Still vexed by the way he was being treated, Sutter escorted the four prisoners to the large upstairs portion of his office. The room he assigned his charges was by no means a dark cell, but it was too small for four people. It lacked mattresses and blankets, there was only the bare floor to sleep on. The unwilling guests were not given any water. At 11 o'clock the next morning, a pot of soup and some meat were brought in, but without utensils.[15]

The thick walls of the fort were 18 feet high, and inside the tidy enclosure, a form of military order was kept, with daily drill and armed guards. Shops and storage areas were located along the inner walls of the fort. This arrangement created a slanting line of roofs that faced inward, leaving the interior plaza open except for Sutter's headquarters, which was placed almost exactly in the center. A night watchman rang a bell every half hour, and even when Vallejo succeeded in dozing off, he was reawakened by the gong.

At times like these, Captain Salvador Vallejo found living in the shadow of his brother's politics a bit hard to swallow. By not permitting their rescue, Don Mariano had either indulged in wholesale quixotism, or something worse. In a recollection of their imprisonment, Captain Vallejo remembered having to

> "rough it" as Mark Twain calls the life of the mountaineer. But my heart grieved for my brother. I went back to the days in which the house of General Vallejo was the rendezvous of every foreigner that visited California. I thought of the many English, Americans, French, and Russian officers that had received kind treatment at his hands. And when the light of day allowed me to see him lying on the damp floor without coverings or even a pillow on which to rest his head, I cursed the days in which our house dispensed hospitality to a race of men deaf to the call of gratitude, so perfect strangers to good breeding.[16]

For almost two decades, General Vallejo had been related to Americans by ties of marriage. He took his arrest and imprisonment personally, as a sign of ingratitude on the part of the very people he had tried to help. He lay awake inside the walls of the fort, wondering if his repentance "had come too late." He even regretted "not having accepted the offer of . . . Don Cayetano Juárez." Had Vallejo given the go-ahead at Vaca's rancho, he and the other prisoners could have been sleeping in a friendly adobe by now.[17] He considered Sutter to be "a foresworn man, a foreigner who had received many favors from me," but "had consented to become my jailor, in order to curry favor with a lot of men . . . who were not fighting under any recognized flag, and who apparently had no other objective than robbery and looting."[18]

Vallejo's anger with the European was understandable and perhaps justified, but it did not make Sutter's predicament any easier. When Frémont moved back to his own camp, he left behind a garrison of well-armed men — effectively occupying the stronghold.[19] "I can assure you," Sutter wrote American Vice-Consul Leidesdorff, "it is not very pleasant to have another as commander in his own house."[20]

Once Sutter got over his exasperation with Frémont, he reverted to his friendly style of treating the political prisoners. Sometimes the captives were left unguarded, and Sutter shared his meals with them. The heat in the valley was stifling: temperatures in excess of 105 degrees were common during the summer. An hour or so before the long brilliant evenings faded into darkness, Sutter allowed the prisoners to leave their quarters and walk outside. Across the valley to the east, they could see the high peaks of the Sierras. Though actually well behind a line of foothills, the blue-edged mountains seemed much closer. From north to south, they were covered with massive glistening snowfields.

Frémont spent a good deal of time at the fort and groused that Sutter was being too kind to the prisoners. "I told him if it is not right how I treat them, to give them in charge of somebody else,"[21] Sutter recalled. Frémont even threatened to hang Sutter from the branch of the old oak tree in a corner of the fort if he continued to treat the Sonomans like chums.[22]

General Vallejo and the others were worried about what was happening to their families in Sonoma. No contact with the distant pueblo had been allowed. Fortunately, the situation there was far better than what he imagined. The women were being treated well, and there were surprisingly few complaints against the raiders. From the first, however, Vallejo's wife was made to understand that she and the children were hostages. This ominous aspect of things was increased by the presence of men who were enemies of the General and Don Salvador. Threats — both implied and direct — were to be a part of her life until August.

The same day that Francisca Vallejo watched her husband being escorted from the plaza under guard, the plucky William Todd, encouraged by Franklin Sears and Granville Swift, created a makeshift flag for the rebels. Working on the ground by the Sonoma plaza flagpole, Todd used a piece of unbleached cotton and some red flannel. (The cotton piece may have been a petticoat belonging to Sears's wife.) Mixing some Venetian red that had been discovered in the barracks (or perhaps, as others claim, using berry juice), he blocked out the words "California Republic." Above the lettering he drew a lone star and a strangely shaped bear. Vallejo's inquisitive five-year-old son, Platon, wandered outside and stood watching the American make the design. When the breeze blew the cloth, the boy held the flag down with his toe.[23]

Todd's artistic efforts drew laughter from the men, because, to them at least, the image of the bear resembled a pig. When native Californians saw the flag later on, they repeated the word *coche* (hog) or *cochinillo*, when they looked at it.[24] The banner was raised on the northeast side of the plaza while the Bear Flaggers cheered and drank a toast.

Foremost in the minds of Ide and his lieutenants was defending Sonoma from an expected attack by General Castro. The much-harried

commandant general was far to the south in Santa Clara issuing proclamations that guaranteed protection to all foreigners not in arms. The
Sonoma rebels, Castro warned, would have to take their chances with
the fortunes of war, but he would never "lightly proceed" against any
residents until their crimes had been proved.[25]

Worried Americans from outlying districts brought their families to
Sonoma to ensure their own safety and to make the common defense
easier. It has been said (with some exaggeration, perhaps) that as many
as four hundred adults and ninety children were added to the pueblo's
population between June 14 and 19.[26]

Native Californians capable of bearing arms were rounded up and
kept under guard on the plaza.[27] When it was discovered that many of
the Californians were pro-American, it was then decided to release them.
However, Ide wanted to make sure of their allegiance, and he drew up a
list of stipulations.

Former Alcalde Don José de la Rosa, who had served as Vallejo's
messenger to Captain Montgomery on June 14, had succeeded in reaching the American ship. Montgomery realized he had no authority to
interfere in California's internal affairs, but in answer to Vallejo's request, he sent his own son, John Elliott Montgomery, and Lieutenant
John S. Misroon to Sonoma to study the situation and, hopefully, try to
keep the rebels under control.[28] They arrived on the evening of June 16.
Misroon was able to calm Doña Francisca's anguish by assuring her that
the General was in no real danger. She had been asked not to communi-
cate with her husband, but Misroon encouraged her to prepare an open
letter. Her brother, Don Julio Carrillo, was allowed to take the message
to the Sacramento River and was given a passport for the journey. As
might be expected, the letter disguised her true feelings:

> I and the children are well. Don't worry about the family be-
> cause the men are taking good care of us. We are sad because we
> don't know when you will come. My Mama sends you many
> greetings. She says for you to take good care of yourself. Julio
> can't do much on the ranches because the Indians are running
> away. . . . Senor Venterio is doing the slaughtering at Soscol.
> Your papers are well cared for. I am sending you a little money,
> a bit of cereal and bread. When you write to me, make the let-
> ters well, otherwise I don't understand them.
>
> Francisca Carrillo de Vallejo[29]

Her request, that Vallejo be careful of his handwriting, was repeated in
a number of her letters. She usually relied on others to copy down her

messages — a job which Don Mariano sometimes performed when he was at home.

Besides making it possible for Don Julio Carrillo to act as messenger, Lieutenant Misroon managed to secure a pledge from Ide that the Bears would be kept "from perpetrating any violence, or in any manner molesting the peaceable inhabitants...."[30]

In a letter home, Captain Montgomery's son gave a brief description of Vallejo's wife and the eccentric commanding officer, William B. Ide:

> She offered us beds in her house which we accepted[.] she is a very pleasant woman indeed.... [Ide is] a plain man about fifty years old in his Shirt Sleeves, with a pair of pantaloons which certainly had seen better days ... his Shoes looked as if they had not seen.. blacking bottles for six months & his hat was somewhat more holy than righteous....[31]

After making a slow and somewhat circuitous journey, Don Julio Carrillo finally reached New Helvetia. When he entered the fort, he received minimal hospitality. His passport was ignored, and without offering any explanations, Frémont ordered him locked up with the others.[32]

Vallejo was relieved to hear that Francisca and the children were safe. Separated from his family and friends, he realized that his political aims were beginning to make him look a bit naive. Nevertheless, he was hopeful that Frémont and the Bears would be discredited and that the legitimate American leaders would soon take charge.

Still yielding to his native generosity, Sutter ordered a demijohn of brandy and some tumblers for the captives.[33] This, of course, irked Frémont, who began to hunt around for a jailer strict enough to suit him. He gave the job to William Loker, one of Sutter's own clerks. After a short time, Loker complained that the task did not suit him either, and Frémont appealed to John Bidwell. In both cases, Frémont was being careful not to put a U.S. government employee in a position that might be politically sensitive.

Bidwell, like Baldridge, was a moderate man who found himself carried along by events touched off by the more radical immigrants like Merritt and Swift. He had no grudge against Vallejo, and he remembered that upon his arrival in California in 1841, the General had given him a passport at Mission San José without charging him any money for it.[34] Bidwell took up his jailer's duty more like a trailmate than a goaler, tutoring Victor Prudon in English in return for which he received Spanish lessons.[35] News of the peaceable arrangement reached Frémont, who then handed the task to Edward Kern, one of his own men. Having accompanied Frémont across the Sierras as an artist and topographer, and being unusually devoted to his captain, Kern tried to compensate for the lax routine established by his predecessors. The Sonomans had liked their daily exercise, but Kern imposed a ban on their walks. Don Salvador was especially annoyed when the jailers called in from time to time to see if "the damned greasers were still safe."[36] Salvador later claimed that the guards "almost invariably appropriated" the pinole and money his wife sent him.[37] As far as anyone knew, war had not yet been declared between Mexico and the United States, but the very situation Frémont feared — having U.S. government employees standing guard over California officials — had become a reality.

This was not the first time General Vallejo had been imprisoned. Once before, during the Joaquín Solís revolt of 1829, he had been crammed into a small cell with a group of friends. Then, after three weeks in the dingy jail, he had been banished to San Diego.

The experience had had its rewards. In the small presidio settlement in the south, he had met Francisca Benicia Carrillo, his future wife — along with Juan Bandini and other southern Californians who would later become his political allies.[38]

Now, Vallejo was probably the most optimistic prisoner in the New Helvetia lockup. The fact that there were individuals in the country like Captain Montgomery, Thomas Larkin, John B. R. Cooper, George Yount, and Joseph Chiles made him hope that the revolt's leadership would find its way into better hands. The present ordeal, like the 1829 imprisonment, might turn out to have future benefits.

11

Murder and Misdirection

*W*hile Vallejo puzzled over his future, William B. Ide — a man in tattered clothes, wearing a hat that looked as though it had been shot through with arrows — was proclaiming radical American principles in Sonoma. Much of what he had to say was beyond the intellectual capacity of his confederates, whose eyes were fixed on the main chance. Surely, any workable American plan *had* to include the cornerstone of the Yankee way: property rights. But some of Ide's followers seemed unwilling to guarantee even this much. Indeed, at that very moment, a war was being fought between Mexican and U.S. troops on the Texas border, but no one in California knew it.

From San Francisco south, California was in the hands of Pío Pico and José Castro. Pico was vainly hoping for English intervention. Castro had no hope at all, because his protector nation of choice, France, had never made a move. Obviously, the wheels had already come off the provincial cart; the belly of the vehicle was hanging over the embankment. It would fall, but no one could predict exactly which way.

In this summertime of threatening symbols, Commander Ide's promise of protection for Sonoma's townspeople did carry weight, and on the whole, good order was kept. This didn't mean that Doña Francisca and the other women felt safe. Vallejo's wife asked extra servants to sleep in her room at night. She had her near-hysterical sister-in-law, Rosalía Leese, to deal with, and there were extra mouths to feed. In the face of an occupying army, however, she continued to maintain her composure.

General Vallejo's sister Rosalía may have done more harm than good. Her anger could be formidable and she was rated as "quite expert" with firearms by William Heath Davis.[1] The fact that the Bears were experienced fighters did not protect them from her blistering attacks. She hated the inherent lawlessness of what was taking place. Robert Semple she considered to be "to all appearances the least inhuman of that god-forsaken crowd."[2] On the morning of the takeover, she defied four members of the rebel group, who, at gunpoint, demanded the key to her husband's storehouse. Eventually, of course, they got what they wanted. This and other incidents that summer made Rosalía Leese call the uprising a "thieving operation,"plain and simple.[3] The women in the village were not actually molested, but later in the month, Frémont asked Doña Rosalía to deliver a seventeen-year-old Indian servant to an officer at the barracks, and she refused.[4] She recalled that during those trying days, "Ladies dared not go out for a walk unless escorted by their husbands or brothers."[5]

Doña Francisca's outlook toward Americans was less hostile than Doña Rosalía's, and she carried on, in most respects, as General Vallejo would have wanted her to. Following the custom of the country, she baptized infants and also helped to deliver the newborn.[6]

A chance to test Ide's promises concerning the safety of property came up one afternoon while a workman was saddling a horse that belonged to General Vallejo. When the animal kicked him, the man picked up his rifle and shot the horse. Commander Ide and Alcalde Berryessa arrested him and asked him to pay the Vallejos thirty dollars. He replied that Don Mariano owed him fifty dollars for work previously completed, and he agreed to give a credit voucher for the horse. Francisca listened to the dispute and approved the settlement. When Vice-Consul Leidesdorff got word of what had taken place, he exclaimed to Larkin, "This was prompt and equal justice! Have you ever heard of such dispatch in a law suit in California before?"[7]

In outlying districts there was no one to enforce Ide's policies, and stories began to filter in about sizable property losses for which no payment was likely to be made. Livestock from the General's personal *caballada* — which included some of the finest horses in the country — had been stolen from pasturage in Lake County.[8] As time went on, American military leaders would find themselves helpless against the freebooting. In September, Captain Montgomery reported to Commodore Stockton that rancheros were being "entirely strip'd of their stock, by these unprincipled marauders, not Indians but Foreigners."[9] The looting angered Doña Francisca to such an extent that in later days, "Whenever a favorable opportunity presented itself, she would fire a full broadside at the Bear Flag crowd to whom justly or unjustly she attributed the loss of a great part of her husband's estate."[10]

By the third week in June, the pueblo of Sonoma needed food more than it needed horses. According to one of the Bears, "Our provisions consisted of the General's beef-cattle and some two thousand pounds or more of flour belonging to Berryessa, which had been seized at Mr. Yount's. These with pure water formed our rations."[11] Relying on his fledgling government's credit, Ide ordered additional flour and provisions. He also posted a proclamation encouraging all "peaceable" citizens of California to establish a republic that would foster "industry, virtue, and literature." The document took a swipe at the Californians for despoiling the missions, oppressing "laboring people," and imposing high tariffs. Ide promised that his new government would "unshackle" the fetters of commerce, end military despotism, and bring prosperity to Californians and Americans alike.[12]

When Commander Ide read the document to Alcalde José Berryessa, he discovered that most peoples' instincts for liberty travel along common channels. There was even a quiet moment; then, together, the commander and the alcalde pronounced the name of George Washington.[13]

In Monterey, information about the Sonoma takeover was fragmentary. "The Northern affair is beyond my comprehension," Larkin confessed.[14] Vice-Consul William Leidesdorff predicted there would be "very small collections" (on commercial balances due) because of the uprising.[15] Neither man yet suspected Frémont was behind it.

José Antonio Carrillo, banished the previous year from Los Angeles by Governor Pico, was planning to kidnap Larkin "as a reprisal or offset to the Señor Vallejo, according to how the war goes at Sonoma."[16] No one knew whether the chronic schemer would carry out his threat, but should he and his cohorts decide to play the hostage game, there was no force in Monterey large enough to stop them.

Larkin was more concerned for the welfare of his wife and three children than he was for himself, and he began to arrange passage for his loved ones to Honolulu. He also started to liquidate his storehouse of goods, offering a 25 percent discount for cash.[17]

Commandant General Castro was not at all encouraged by Ide's proclamation, which was circulating south of the bay. To make things worse, the document was accompanied by Alcalde Berryessa's signed testimony regarding the Bears' good behavior. Despite Vallejo's recollection that Castro detested Americans,[18] Castro was by no means anti-American to begin with, and, whether he disliked Yankees or not, he had no desire to carry out a long siege of New Helvetia or Sonoma against sharpshooting frontiersmen. As mentioned earlier, the sentiment among many of the Californians regarding annexation had been *"Ojalá que lo tomen los Americanos"* ("I hope the Americans take it"). Many of Castro's soldiers shared the commandant's apathy.

The nervous Castro posted notices reminding residents of "that indulgence" which had characterized his actions in the past — advising them that rash steps would never be taken against foreigners, as long as they went about their daily business in peace.[19]

A cavalry force under Joaquín de la Torre was sent across the choppy waters to the Marin side of the bay, but even after the troops arrived at Mission San Rafael, no attack was made on Sonoma. For a while, bewilderment permeated whole sections of the arid coast.

In the past, California's internal conflicts had usually been resolved in a style that would have delighted Gilbert and Sullivan. Relatives would go to battlefields, where icy stares or bantering remarks would be exchanged. There might even be an artillery duel or a series of flanking movements. But the leaders would soon find a way to make peace. A fandango would be held, there would be shouting and laughter, and perhaps a horserace. For the moment, it looked as though the Bear Flag Revolt might be resolved in the same old way. At least this was a possibility as long as the lull in hostilities continued.

At Sutter's Fort, Don Mariano and the other prisoners thought about what might be happening in Sonoma and tried to entertain each other by recalling stories from the past. The sweltering sun was a constant presence for sixteen hours a day. At night, the adobe walls trapped the motionless air. How long, they wondered, would they be kept in the sweatbox?

Then, on June 21, Doña Francisca's brother Ramón Carrillo was accused of having taken part in a grisly crime that caused men on both sides to overreact with senseless violence. This infamous affair — even after 150 years — has never quite been forgotten.

The trouble started when Lieutenant Henry L. Ford (Ide's second-in-command) sent messengers north and west in search of military supplies. William Todd and a guide headed toward Bodega. Two others, Thomas Cowie and George Fowler, were instructed to ride to the Fitch Rancho on the Russian River. The majordomo there was Kit Carson's brother, Moses, who would probably give them the gunpowder they wanted.

Cowie and Fowler scorned the Californians' fighting abilities, accepting the mission "against the advice of their friends and in a spirit of bravado."[20] At first the northbound pair took Ford's advice and avoided well-traveled roads. Then, tiring of what seemed like useless precautions, they followed the main route to Santa Rosa and were captured by Juan Padilla. (Padilla's horsemen had been among those who had tried to rescue General Vallejo on the morning of June 15 at Vaca's Rancho.) Until then, the twenty-five-year-old Padilla had made no reprisals against

foreigners or their property in the Sonoma Valley. One of his lieutenants was General Vallejo's brother-in-law, Ramón Carrillo. An avid
sportsman, Don Ramón was thought to be a "brave and good fellow"
by William Heath Davis, though this opinion was not shared by all.
Bancroft, for one, suggested that Carrillo was "not noted for his good
qualities."[21]

Two days passed and nothing was heard from Cowie or Fowler. But
rumors said that Castro's army was approaching from the south to
attack Sonoma. Frémont had promised help if trouble started, and a
courier was sent to New Helvetia to fetch him.[22] About this time, on
June 20 or 21, Francisca Vallejo sent a letter to her brother Ramón
Carrillo. William B. Ide had asked her to write the letter, and she
informed Ramón that Ide wanted to speak with him; but she warned
her brother that if Padilla's men attacked the Americans at Sonoma,
the Vallejo family would suffer.

Don Ramón did not like the implications of the message and wrote
a reply on June 22 from the coast range near Petaluma. He denied any
intention of "doing damage" to the Americans, explaining "the only
design for which we have united ourselves has been to guard our interests and lay claim in a legal way to the peace which has been promised
us in the articles of the proclamation which was given to the public."
Ramón admitted he was holding three of Ide's followers in his camp,
though he did not identify them by name. He expressed his willingness
to deliver them up as soon as he was certain the Californians' rights
would be respected. He also agreed to meet with Ide, but he wanted the
American commander to request the conference in writing.[23]

There was a more dangerous aspect to Francisca's dealings with her
family. It seems she was asked to smuggle arms not only to her brother,
Ramón, but also to her mother and to Juan Padilla. At first, the idea did
not appeal to her, and she refused:

> ... since I did not dare to jeopardize the lot of my husband
> and my young family, I refrained from doing what they wanted,
> notwithstanding that I had the greatest desire to do all that
> they requested of me. ... [Yesterday,] however, while I was
> conversing with my sister-in-law, *doña* Rosalía de Leese,
> Captain Ide came into the room and told us that unless we sent
> letters to Padilla and to Carrillo, begging them not to approach
> Sonoma, they would shut us up in a room and kill us, as soon as
> the California guerrilla men came in sight over the Sonoma hills.
> Filled with terror, *doña* Rosalía and I agreed to write the letters

that Ide requested of us and, in order to ensure the life of the messenger, we asked him to give us a passport. . . . He gave us the passport, so that the Indian Gervasio might travel freely with his oxcart loaded with hides. At night we ordered Gervasio to place among the hides a dozen pistols, ten pounds of powder, four flintlocks and six sabers. He left in the direction of Petaluma. On the road, he met my brother, Ramón, turned the weapons over to him and then continued on his way to Petaluma.[24]

The arms-smuggling probably took place between June 20 and June 22.

Meanwhile, near the Russian River, the search party that had been sent north from Sonoma on June 20 to find Cowie and Fowler learned that the messengers had never reached Fitch's Rancho. Moses Carson was able to supply the disappointed scouts with a keg of gunpowder; then the riders turned south. Before they reached Sonoma they were suddenly set upon by a small band of Californians. The Americans fought bravely and captured a troublesome individual, who turned out to be a notorious criminal named "Four-Fingered Jack" García — referred to by Vallejo as "the wickedest man that California had produced up to that time."[25] With the aim of making his listeners squirm, García gave grisly descriptions of his exploits. He admitted he had helped to kill Cowie and Fowler and willingly provided details. The two Americans had been tied to trees, he said; then they were stoned. Pieces of flesh had been cut from their bodies with knives, and García boasted of passing a *reata* through the jaw of one of the men and jerking the bone from his head.[26] (Edwin Bryant retold the story several months later, adding details taken from García's lurid newspaper account.[27])

Francisca's brother Ramón was quick to deny that any such atrocity had taken place. Counteraccusations were made against the American messengers, who were denounced for turning their mission into a foraging raid. They wanted to run off some of Padilla's horses and were charged with outraging one of the Carrillo women.

In August of 1846 Ramón Carrillo gave a sworn statement before Judge Santiago Argüello, describing the manner in which the two Americans had been killed: against Carrillo's advice, Padilla had picked five men to go out and shoot the Americans.[28]

In their rage over the affair, the Bears demonized the Californians. John Grigsby spread the word that the bodies of the messengers had been "horribly mangled," but this was questioned by his friend and companion-in-arms, William Baldridge. The millwright did not think any definite proof of mutilation had been found.[29] The notion that Ramón Carrillo had taken part in the murders did not die. Whether true or false, the belief eventually cost him his life. In later years, Carrillo moved to southern California, where he was shot in the back by vigilantes.[30]

General Vallejo, in his "Historical and Personal Memoirs," ignored the sensational aspects of the crime and said the murders had been carried out quickly: while Padilla and his soldiers were meeting in an adobe to decide the captives' fate, García had gone outside to where the men were tied to trees and had killed them with his knife.[31]

The affair stirred up ugly feelings that had remained dormant because of the lack of bloodshed. Amazingly enough, revenge was never taken on "Four-Fingered Jack" García for the murders of Cowie and Fowler. The Bears locked him up, then made a heroic effort to avoid being called bloodthirsty themselves. Time worked to García's advantage. He survived the summer and, during November of the same year, fought against American volunteers at the Battle of La Natividad. After the war ended in 1847, he committed many more crimes — so many that he entered the realm of folklore. Tales were circulated about his fondness for collecting strings of Chinese laborers' ears during the Gold Rush, and he was thought to have been a member of Joaquín Murieta's gang.[32] But if Bancroft is right, García finally kept his belated date with the hangman.[33]

One thing was certain: Cowie and Fowler were dead, and a war between Californians and Americans was soon to begin in earnest. But what had happened to William Todd, who had gone toward Bodega? Fortunately he was still alive, within sight of the steep forested slopes of Mt. Tamalpais. Lieutenant Ford and nineteen volunteers went out to find him. They picked up a trail that led toward San Rafael. By then, Todd had been transferred to the rancho of a former Indian ally of Vallejo's, Camilo Ynita. The Indian raised wheat on his Olómpali grant. A few years earlier, he had sold his grain to the Russians with Vallejo acting as middleman.[34] Near Ynita's adobe, which occupied a gentle slope above the mouth of the Petaluma River, Ford and Swift had spotted a corral filled with horses. The Bears had been pleased by the thought of having fresh mounts. They were still some yards from the corral when Joaquín de la Torre's uniformed troops began to stream out of the ranchhouse. Instead of rushing the Americans, the Californians hurried to their own mounts, which were concealed behind the building. (The Californians had a phobia against warring on foot; in fact, without a horse, a Californian was said to be "a wretched cripple."[35])

Lieutenant Ford turned out to be the better commander. Stationing his men at the edge of a grove of trees, he waited while the cordon of De la Torre's troopers drew closer. When the Americans fired, their volley killed one Californian and seriously wounded at least one other.[36] De la Torre then tried to draw the Americans into the open where his cavalrymen could use their lances and muskets to advantage.

During the worst of the fight, William Todd escaped from the adobe at "the top of his speed." Though more shots were exchanged at long range, the Battle of Olómpali was over. The Americans eventually returned to Sonoma without a scratch.[37]

This, the first significant encounter following the Bear Flag Revolt, had been a clear victory for the Americans, but it did not relieve the Bears' exasperation over the deaths of Cowie and Fowler. Nor did the Bears celebrate their victory or abuse the Sonomans after they returned to the pueblo. "All appeared to be serious and thoughtful," William Baldridge remembered. The rebels realized that they were in a real war now, though many of them had not yet "ascertained fully to [their] satisfaction what it was about. . . ."[38] "My own sentiments," the handsome Baldridge admitted, "were that making war upon the Californians was an act of great injustice, but as the deed had been done, I preferred taking the risk of being killed in battle, to that of being sent to Mexico in irons. . . ."[39]

Two days later, a fierce-looking group of men sped across the treeless, red-orange grasslands, following the road toward San Rafael. They were led by Frémont himself. He had hurried over from Sutter's Fort, stopped briefly at Sonoma, and then had continued on toward the Petaluma side of the valley. He was hoping to catch up with De la Torre and bring him to battle; but by the time Frémont's command had passed Novato and reached Mission San Rafael, the Californians had vanished.

The explorer encamped his men at the mission, which at the time consisted of some unimpressive buildings occupying a hill that overlooked the blue expanse of San Pablo Bay. Here occurred another tragedy, perhaps the saddest of the war.

Captain Frémont and his men saw a small boat approaching from the east. It had been the practice for travelers to land at the little inlet below the hill and obtain horses from the mission before continuing on. Preparing to get out of the boat were three Californians, who seemed to be in no great hurry, and who seemed unaware that they were being watched. When Kit Carson and two others were ordered to intercept them, Carson turned to Frémont and asked, "Captain, shall I take those men prisoners?" Frémont waved his hand and said, "I have no room for prisoners."[40]

As the boat neared the beach, the Californians who were coming ashore stood up. One was José de los Reyes Berryessa, the father of

Sonoma's alcalde and a man who had held public office himself. Berryessa was on his way to Sonoma to make sure his son was all right. With him were the twenty-year-old DeHaro twins, partial heirs to the large Sanchez holdings in present-day San Mateo County. The three men had lifted their saddles to their shoulders and were still on the beach when Kit Carson, Granville Swift, and a French-Canadian trapper, aiming from a distance of about fifty yards, brought them down where they stood. When Frémont was informed of what had taken place, he nodded his approval, saying, "It is well."[41]

Later on, Frémont claimed that the executions were in retaliation for the murders of Cowie and Fowler. But the elderly Berryessa was certainly a harmless individual, and his death was as senseless as the killing of the American messengers. No effort had been made to discover the travelers' identities or find out where they were going. It wasn't until the bodies on the beach had been stripped that a note was found in the shoe of one of the DeHaro twins. Before leaving San Pablo, he had volunteered to carry the communication, which seemed to contain information for Joaquín de la Torre about the movements of Castro's troops.

The murdered man's son, Alcalde José Berryessa of Sonoma, was a popular man with the Americans. The members of the Bear Flag movement were sickened by the murders. After passions had cooled, the rebels thought of the affair as the war's "most unfortunate event." Even a generation later, one historian would write that "Californians cannot speak of it down to this day without intense feeling."[42]

The most unforgiving of all those who witnessed the affair was Jasper O'Farrell, who was standing next to Frémont when the killings took place. He later sent a letter to the *Los Angeles Star*, saying that the events had been just as cold-blooded as they sounded. He condemned Frémont for the incident, referring to him as a man "I must always look upon with contempt and consider as a murderer and a coward."[43]

Frémont's turbulent nature was getting all the excitement it craved. That same day, he received a second message, which was taken from a captured Indian. Though it seemed genuine, it was a decoy communication that pretended to reveal Joaquín de la Torre's secret plan to recapture Sonoma while Frémont was still at San Rafael.

The explorer prepared his men for an all-night ride back to the pueblo. He had no way of knowing that William B. Ide had received a similar message at Sonoma. So while Frémont was galloping through the darkness, thinking to save the pueblo from De la Torre's attack, Ide was readying nine pieces of artillery to fire at De la Torre's men as they charged through the plaza's main entrance.

During the Bears' all-night vigil at Sonoma, Doña Francisca Vallejo did not know what the morning would bring, and she sheltered the town's women and children in the rear of the Casa Grande. At about 4 A.M., the approaching mounts could be heard. The matches used to ignite the cannons were lighted by Ide's men, and dozens of muskets were pointed toward the outer darkness. Kit Carson, riding a little ahead of Frémont, shouted, "My god! They swing the matches." Luckily, his voice carried far enough to be recognized. A few shots were fired, but the warning came soon enough to avert disaster.[44] Frémont had wanted a tangible victory; instead, he had come up with another fistful of air. Taking only a brief time to rest his troops, the explorer turned around and back-tracked toward San Rafael — traveling well beyond the mission this time. At Sausalito, he could see the churned-up ground where the Californians had boarded Captain William Richardson's launch, which had been used to ferry them back to San Pablo on the east side of the bay.[45]

This disappointment, added to the explorer's growing rage, caused him to change his tactics. By July 4, he had returned to Sonoma. While tensions between Californians and Bears were temporarily forgotten during an Independence Day fandango, Frémont continued to mull over his options. He "changed his shining uniform for a blouse, put away his hat and wrapped his head with a common handkerchief."[46]

On July 5 Frémont risked everything and put himself in command of the Bears, creating the "California Battalion." Now he would control the revolt, and his new headquarters would be at Sutter's Fort. Former Commander William B. Ide was practical enough to realize the change might be a good thing. Frémont's leadership could mean that government provisions would be added to the Bears' supplies. Even the U.S. Navy might be persuaded to help. Besides, Frémont had agreed to accept the principles of revolution which Ide had proclaimed in June. Not yet embittered by his fall from power, the displaced Ide became a private in the California Battalion.[47]

By committing his U.S. government employees to the movement, Frémont was daring the gods. As historian Ferol Egan bluntly states it: *If the United States and Mexico had managed to avoid a formal declaration of war*, Frémont (by leading the California Battalion) "would have been . . . destroying any chance for future government service . . . risking a court-martial, and a possible term in military prison. But his luck held out."[48]

Frémont managed to avoid only two of these unpleasant consequences. Before a year had passed, his disregard for the chain of command would force him to leave California. He would be placed under arrest and court-martialed, not because he had organized the California Battalion or approved the executions of the DeHaro twins and Berryessa, but because he had aroused the anger of a man who would soon make his appearance in California, General Steven Watts Kearny.

12

What Friend Larkin Will Do

$\mathcal{G}$eneral Mariano Vallejo had been locked up for three weeks now. Though not actually subjecting him to physical mistreatment, Edward Kern was using the vindictive approach Frémont had recommended. The sight of the outdoors — always a tonic for the Sonoma captives — was off-limits, and the food being served was no longer the savory fare Sutter had offered. At night, thousands of mosquitoes came to fraternize. Their breeding ground was directly behind the fort, a long slough filled with reeds and birds. In the years before Sutter's arrival, Indians had shunned the place because of the prevalence of malaria.

Frémont returned to New Helvetia from Sonoma on July 8 or 9, planning to make the fort his military headquarters. His men were driving four hundred of Vallejo's horses and also a herd of the General's cattle for beef.[1]

Not long before Frémont's arrival, Vallejo's weight had begun to drop and he had experienced chills and fever — the well-known symptoms of what in those days was called "the shakes." When Captain Montgomery learned that Vallejo had malaria, he sent Dr. Andrew J. Henderson to see what could be done. The doctor's escort was Lieutenant Charles Warren Revere, Paul Revere's grandson. "I found during this visit," Revere wrote, "that General Vallejo and his companions were rigorously guarded by the 'patriots,' but I saw him and had some conversation with him, which . . . excited a very ridiculous amount of suspicion on the part of the vigilant jailers, whose position . . . as revolutionists, was a little ticklish. . . ."[2]

Vallejo's fever retreated after the doctor's visit, but he continued to lose weight. Meantime, the prisoners could no longer stretch out or move around as before because three more captives were sharing their cell. Two were well-known South Bay rancheros, Vicente Peralta and José Noriega. They had been expecting to carry on some business at the fort but were suddenly imprisoned by Frémont's orders. The third man was a Britisher, the hard-drinking Robert Ridley, whom William Leidesdorff considered to be more enthusiastically Californian than most of the natives.[3]

Jacob Leese's confinement had rubbed him where he was already raw, because he did not like being treated as an enemy of the United States. He sent a message to Frémont, promising that, if offered a chance to serve his country, he would be happy to do so. However, no response came back.[4]

Vallejo's spirits had begun to mend within a few days of his being locked up at the fort. His resurgent futurism was probably responsible for his increased confidence. The theatrical maneuvering of John Charles Frémont did not destroy Vallejo's faith in an improved California, and he was the sort of man who was willing to suffer today if it would bring a better tomorrow. Encouraging, too, was the fact that he had been allowed to write an open letter to his older brother, José de Jesús Vallejo.

> I am sending this letter to you with the object of relieving your mind about the fact that we have not been killed, at least up to this time. Salvador is here and although we are all prisoners it is under the force of circumstances. We believe that our detention is no more than political, indispensable for the progress of the new order of things. We believe fundamentally that this is the beginning of a complete turnover in the country; but not without a change founded on justice and on the law that will be a relief from the present miserable state of things.... [A]ll together we owe much to Señor Sutter in whose house we are staying, we owe him for a thousand favors to us and we shall be eternally grateful to him.
>
> Our own persons, our families and our property have been solemnly guaranteed to be returned to us in due respect to us so we ought to rest assured of it under the safeguard of law as well as under the good faith of men so I hope it will turn out and your loving brother begs you to publish this letter.
>
> M. G. Vallejo
>
> Here also are Vicente Peralta, José Noriega and Robert Ridley. It would be well to notify their families.[5]

No one knew how long it would be before the captives would be freed. Certainly, Frémont's guards were a disagreeable bunch, and the explorer wouldn't release the Sonomans on parole. Without the exertions of Thomas Oliver Larkin, Vallejo and the others might have been stuck in their cell well into the fall.

On July 7, 1846, at Monterey, salutes boomed from the flagship *Savannah* in honor of the American banner as Commodore John Sloat took possession of the capital for the United States. He had arrived five days earlier, bringing news of battles between American and Mexican troops near the Rio Grande. Cautious at first about occupying Monterey, he had feared being "blamed for doing too little or too much"[6] — primarily because no formal declaration of war had yet been received. After his men marched ashore, the sound of his ships' batteries hung in the misty air above California's capital. Had Vallejo been there, he would have offered a toast.

For the second time in four years, the Stars and Stripes flew above the town. On this occasion, Sloat's lavish promises were reassuring: the residents could expect a "great increase in the value of Real Estate and the products" of the region, and he predicted that California would "rapidly advance & improve both in Agriculture & Commerce." If his proclamation sounded more like an investor's prospectus than a notice of military occupation, the cause might have been its co-authorship. California's canniest investor, Thomas Oliver Larkin, had helped Sloat write the announcement the previous day.[7]

Lieutenant Revere was given the job of taking the historic news of Sloat's occupation to the north. Carrying three U.S. flags, he made his way past San Rafael to the pueblo of Sonoma. On July 9, the Bear flag came down and was replaced with the Stars and Stripes. The three-week-old rebel banner was given to Captain Montgomery's son, John Elliott, who folded it and put it into his pocket. The youngster later made a drawing of it, and when he sent the sketch home to his mother, he remarked, "The cubby came down growling."[8] His comment referred to the Bear Flaggers' gloom over the change of pennants; they felt their accomplishments would now be minimized or forgotten. To a certain extent, they were right. Their lack of organization, Merritt's clumsy leadership, the theft of livestock, and the opera bouffe aspects of the takeover were placed in the foreground by most historians. The rebels' genuine efforts at self-restraint after June 14 were usually overlooked.

General Vallejo later theorized that financial disappointment was mixed in with the Bears' regrets. As he explained in his "Historical and Personal Memoirs":

I think I am not mistaken when I state that those who assaulted the Sonoma *plaza* intended to build up a great internal debt, issue bonds redeemable in five years and, when everything had at last been arranged in accordance with their desires, enter and become a part of the North American Union, provided the National Congress would assume the responsibility of paying the sums of money that Alta California owed to her residents.[9]

The rebels' brief reign did not give them the opportunity to issue the bonds. Before long, however, Frémont would amass a large debt.

Most of the Spanish-speaking residents of Sonoma were elated by the raising of the Stars and Stripes — especially Doña Francisca Vallejo — seeing this as the fulfillment of one of her husband's long-cherished dreams. She celebrated the flag-raising for both of them and described the event in a letter to the General. Obviously, she trusted that her message would not be censored and that the package she sent to Sutter's Fort would arrive safely.

I am sending you by Agapito and Tomás a basket containing loaves of bread. Inside all the loaves in the third and fourth layers you will find small gold coins which may help to buy you what you need most. For two nights the servants have not slept in my room; the danger is past, for a captain from Sauzalito, sent by Captain Montgomery . . . put the American flag on the staff where before was the Bear; and since then there have been no robberies that I know of although sister Rosa [Rosalía Leese] says it is all just the same. There have been great celebrations in these days, each and every one of us cheering heartily and waving our handkerchiefs. The Bears, however, have been very disconsolate. I heard the wife of Captain Sears say that her husband said that the American flag had come too soon, and all their work was lost. Sister Rosa and I no longer fear for your life and that of brother Salvador and *don* Luís [Jacob Leese].[10]

An American sailor staying in Sonoma at the time remembered that Francisca "threw open her house to all, friends and foes, and through the live long night she visited the door every half hour to be sure no daring hand would attempt to remove that flag on which she said hung all her hopes."[11] American servicemen were treated hospitably at the Casa Grande. The surgeon of the *Portsmouth* penned the following description of Doña Francisca:

Madam Vallejo is "muy gorda," very fat, but still has the evidence of much beauty. She seems to be femininely passive and voluptuous, contented and happy.[12]

To Edwin Bryant, who saw her not long afterward, the extra weight did not diminish her appeal. She was an individual of "charming personal appearances and possesses in the highest degree the natural grace, ease and warmth of manners which render the Spanish ladies so attractive and fascinating to the stranger."[13]

Doña Francisca felt certain that, had the Stars and Stripes been raised in mid-June (instead of July), the murders of Cowie and Fowler, the DeHaro twins, and the elderly Berryessa would never have taken place, and the transition to American rule would have been accomplished without bloodshed.

Eighty miles away at Sutter's Fort, on the same day the Bear flag came down at Sonoma, Frémont surprised his unhappy prisoners by agreeing to their request for an interview. The meeting was to take place the following morning.

The early hours of July 10 passed, but Frémont did not come to their cell. As the sun spread deep shadows southeast of the adobe walls, afternoon drifted into evening. Still there was no word from him. Vallejo's patience gave out, and he wrote the explorer:

> I have been awaiting anxiously all day long; but since this is already very advanced, I fear that you will no longer have time. As much to calm the uneasiness of the gentlemen who share my prison, as well as for my own satisfaction, I wish that you would let me know whether our imprisonment is now ended, which as you know has been made more severe by an absolute solitary confinement since the 16th of last June.

> I do not have to tell you anything regarding the way in which we have been deprived of our liberty, since you are not ignorant of it; but the national flag of North America which today flies over this fortress leads me to suppose that the change has already taken place, and to expect an advantageous future for this country whose fate cannot be a matter of indifference to me.

> Because of all this I flattered myself that today you would have told us of the proclamation which probably has been published on raising the flag, which today changes the future of California, and which can do no less than be of direct influence over us, whose intimate conviction is that the condition of the country cannot be any worse than that in which it was before the change.[14]

Obviously, by the time Vallejo wrote the letter, news of Sloat's possession of Monterey had reached him.

The next morning, Sutter's Fort witnessed an official ceremony for the very banner Frémont had been so reluctant to display in mid-June. One of the old cannons brought from Vallejo's arsenal was used to fire the salutes. More useful for decoration than for service, the gun became overheated and threw itself on end, firing a volley straight up in the air next to Sutter's windows. "Mein Gott, boys," the excited Swiss shouted after his glass panes were shattered. His worry about replacement costs didn't spoil the day, however.[15] As the American pennant went up, Sutter's relief was unmistakable. Too much lawlessness had taken place at the fort; he was counting on the U.S. presence to end it.[16]

From the captives' point of view, the flag's arrival turned out to be a disaster. The explorer forgot all about the promised meeting. Commodore Sloat had asked Frémont to bring a hundred men to Monterey. As much as Frémont would have liked to destroy Castro's army, a march to the capital now seemed more important to him. He might be able to talk Commodore Sloat into mustering the California Battalion into the U.S. service; in this way, the Bears' previous actions would receive the official stamp of approval. Any concerns Frémont may have had about Vallejo and his compatriots were forgotten.[17]

After Frémont's picturesque army set off for the capital, the diligent Edward Kern remained in charge of the fort.[18]

Captain Montgomery had been urging Vallejo's release for some time, and Commodore Sloat had been ready to issue the orders, but, according to Larkin, was "persuaded by Mr. Gillespie not to do so. . . ."[19]

Another person very distressed about Vallejo's condition was his mother, Doña Antonia, who was living at the San Cayetano rancho twenty-three miles north of Monterey. She wrote Larkin asking for more information about her son. At this point, the consul hired a messenger, John Murphy, to go to Sutter's Fort. Because the trip was risky, Larkin agreed to pay him three times the usual rate. The consul assumed that General Vallejo and Jacob Leese would "with pleasure" thank Murphy for his services, and Larkin debited Vallejo's Monterey account 100 pesos (approximately $1300 in 1990 currency).[20]

On July 22 Murphy arrived at Sutter's busy outpost. The resourceful Vallejo had been taking steps to make himself more comfortable. He had just written Doña Francisca, asking her to relay some messages to the majordomos at the Petaluma and Soscol ranchos concerning the annual slaughtering of cattle. Avoiding references to his health, he had also requested ten packets of writing paper and his miniature ivory chess set. "We are waiting daily for mail from Monterey and then perhaps we will be free to return to our homes."[21] As if in answer to his prayers, John Murphy walked into the prisoners' cell, and the Sonomans received proof that they had not been forgotten.

Murphy slept while Victor Prudon and the somewhat emaciated Vallejo prepared a formal statement for Commodore Sloat. It went over the events of their capture and mentioned some of the unpleasant aspects of their imprisonment: having their mail opened especially annoyed Vallejo. Now that the United States was in control of the territory, the General promised that he and his fellow officers would be ready to pledge their neutrality and would accept any conditions Sloat might impose.[22]

Vallejo also took the opportunity to write Larkin. The anger not expressed in the declaration to Sloat found its way into the more personal letter. Larkin's efforts were appreciated by the General, who directed his criticisms not at the consul or even at the men who had taken his Sonoma property, but at the Bears at the Casa Grande who had signed a parole agreement with him and then had broken all the conditions "before the signatures were dry." Though the American flag was now flying over Monterey and New Helvetia, nothing had been done to make things right.[23]

John Murphy set off for the capital the next day. The journey, which usually required four or five days, took him almost a week.

The much-feared English threat, the *Collingwood*, skippered by Admiral Seymour, had finally reached Monterey Bay. But the British jack tars treated their visit like a holiday. They were on hand when Frémont's tough-looking volunteers entered the capital. The Americans were driving a large herd of cattle ahead of them and seemed to have emerged from the pages of James Fenimore Cooper. Armed with two or three weapons apiece, they filed to their hillside encampment on July 19, making it clear that the United States was ready to defend its new coastal possession.[24]

The meeting between Frémont and Commodore Sloat aboard the *Savannah* unnerved both men. Sloat was anxious to see the orders that had authorized Frémont to take up arms against the Californians. Learning there were none, the commodore unleashed a blistering tirade. Frémont was taken by surprise and fell silent. Under the circumstances, Sloat had no intention of mustering the California Battalion into the regular service.[25]

Frémont had phenomenal luck, however. It so happened that Commodore Sloat was in poor health. Before another week had passed, Sloat transferred his authority to Commodore Robert Field Stockton.

More aggressive than Sloat, Stockton was a proud duelist and something of a power politician who had favored a war with Mexico long before its declaration. He was also quite sincere in the belief that, by imposing American rule in California, he would be replacing a despotic government with "the benign influences" of a free one. On July 23 he made Captain Frémont a major and placed him in command of the "California Battalion of United States troops."[26]

Steps toward completing the American occupation of California were now under way, but things had not yet improved for Vallejo and his companions. Larkin went to work again.

On the morning of July 29, the *Levant*, with the departing Commodore Sloat aboard, edged its way out of the bay, bound for Washington, D.C. Stockton was also preparing to leave the harbor in order to pursue Castro, who had marched overland to southern California.

Luckily, John Murphy arrived at the capital with Vallejo's letters that very morning, and the consul shuttled between naval officers, trying to end the prisoners' deadlock. Larkin took a small boat far beyond Point Pinos, and, with a favorable wind, was able to reach Sloat's warship. After climbing aboard, he was shown to Sloat's quarters, where he read Vallejo's declaration aloud to the commodore (thinking to himself that the wording was very "firm . . . and fully to the purpose").[27] Influenced by Vallejo's clear statement and Larkin's persistence, Sloat issued instructions to the new commander-in-chief to free the prisoners at Sutter's Fort.

Larkin took the new orders to Stockton and waited while they were translated. John Murphy carried the signed dispatches north, making much better time than on his previous journey. In fact, he covered the distance to Yerba Buena so quickly that Captain Montgomery questioned the date on the orders, finding it hard to believe that Murphy had made the trip "between sunrise and sunset."[28]

Larkin, at this point, was puzzled by Frémont's part in the Sonoma takeover: "The when, why and wherefore of it all I suppose the Authors will in proper time give with their reasons & motives," he mused in a letter to Jacob Leese. He also hoped there would be some compensation for the prisoners in the "increase of property" they would enjoy once their freedom was secured.[29]

Larkin informed Secretary Buchanan in Washington that the imprisonment of Vallejo, Leese, and Prudon "is yet so harsh on the feelings of the Californians that for the present they will not enter into any arrangement with the Commander in Chief of the American forces on this coast."[30] On the other hand, Larkin was satisfied to realize that some of his own patriotic objectives, which were identical to those of many immigrants (to say nothing of more than four American presidents), had at last been accomplished. Happily enough, he announced to James Gordon Bennett, editor of the *New York Herald*, "I am in the U.S.A. — as well as yourself."[31]

A Changed Man

Throughout the early 1840s, shrewd observers had predicted that one day, a game of international musical chairs was going to be played in California. In addition to the host (Mexico), the guests on hand would be the United States, England, and perhaps France. Three or four of them would dance in a circle until only one chair was left. But by mid-1845, England and France had, in effect, withdrawn. And at the time of the Bear Flag Revolt, Mexico was no longer a presence, for none of her troops had reached the province. Only America was on hand to vie for the chair. All the United States had to do was sit down. Most of the northern Californians — M.G. Vallejo in particular — were ready to hand the country over to the United States as a gift. But Frémont had wanted to make it look difficult. Could there be any real liberty without bravado and aggression? Considering his warlike stance, it was small wonder that José Castro, Pío Pico, and ex-Governor Alvarado had already said no to a meeting with Commodore Sloat and would probably not meet with Stockton either. Their aversion was more than a matter of ruffled feathers. The imprisonment of the pro-American Vallejo made everyone wonder if, in fact, American promises were going to be kept. When Consul Larkin theorized that the leading dons would accept government posts under the Stars and Stripes, he assumed the existence of a friendly climate for talks. A U.S. directive had already advised that "it would be wise and prudent to continue in their employment all such of the existing [Californian] officers who are known to be friendly to the United States, and will take the oath of allegiance to them."[1] But Frémont and Stockton were using violence. Gestures of conciliation were nowhere to be seen. The imprisonment of the Sonoma leaders had never been explained, and hatred had been fanned by the murders of Cowie, Fowler, Berryessa, and the DeHaro twins. In a letter to Larkin, Alvarado explained his reluctance to parley with U.S. officials and reminded the

consul that "the history of your country holds in remembrance the efforts of the immortal Washington, to make it independent of all foreign
rule." He then asked Larkin to judge "what you would do in my case, in
circumstances like the present."[2]

Encountering José Castro in San Jose, Joseph Warren Revere took
note of his impressive appearance: the stalwart figure and intelligent
black eyes. General Castro asked Revere whether the government of the
United States would give him a brigadier-general's commission in case
he decided to "pronounce" for the establishment of American authority.
Castro spoke "apparently in jest," Revere remembered, "but I could
perceive that the promise of such an appointment would have had its
effect."[3] Castro's beautiful wife was quite certain her husband had no
intention of fighting the invaders. To the men surrounding the general
(many of whom soon deserted the army), Castro appeared to be "careless and inexact" in his duties.[4]

As summer wore on, the heat was occasionally broken by a fog which
appeared behind the Sonoma Mountains. Pro-American sympathies in
the north remained strong. Castro finally realized that the only way to
make a stand against the United States would be to march his men to
Los Angeles. Arriving there during the fourth week in July, he joined
forces with his former enemy, Governor Pío Pico. Los Angeles had served
as a center for Californian resistance in the past and would again.

Finally, the ordeal of the much-weakened Vallejo came to an end. John
Murphy arrived at Sutter's Fort with Stockton's new orders on August 1.
The next day, a formal statement was drawn up for Don Mariano.[5] The
signature was witnessed by John Sutter. Dated August 2, 1846, the release stated that M. G. Vallejo would never take up arms "against
the United States of North America or furnish supplies or communica-
tions to enemies of same or leave his own district without permission
upon penalty of death."[6] Only three days later, Captain Montgomery
sent Vallejo a message that eased the conditions of the parole, enabling
the General to attend to his normal affairs "without hindrance or
restraint." In return, Montgomery wanted a simple "promise of friendship to the United States or of strict neutrality in all differences pending
between the existing and former governments of the Department of California...."[7]

Jacob Leese, however, remained behind bars. Stockton's orders had
stated that Vallejo's brother-in-law was also to be released, and it was
assumed that the person referred to was Don Julio Carrillo (Doña
Francisca's brother). Angrier than ever now, Jacob Leese fumed in his
cell beside Don Salvador and the others.

Once General Vallejo's release had been arranged, there was no need for further conversation. After crossing the Sacramento, Don Mariano, John Murphy, and Don Julio Carrillo headed toward the dark line of the Vaca Mountains. It was good to have the cloudy green river at their backs. The summer grass was crisp and almost white, and the clothes and saddles of the men broiled in the heat. The six-foot Vallejo guessed that his weight had dropped to some ninety-six pounds.[8]

The General continued to worry about Don Salvador and the others. On August 4 he sent a letter back to New Helvetia, telling his brother that a boat was on its way with orders to set the other prisoners free.[9]

Within a day or two, Vallejo reached Sonoma. Though Doña Francisca had been told that her husband would soon be coming home, she was not prepared for the physical changes caused by his illness. As he took stock of things, he too had cause for wonder: the pueblo was still occupied by the Americans and their relatives. The Bears — whose plan was to redivide the land — assumed that Vallejo would now organize the Californians and Indians against them; like Frémont, they greatly feared the General's power. On August 4 the Bears' special status was nullified when Lieutenant Revere enlisted fifty-two of the Sonoma rebels into "the Militia service of the United States." The Bears interpreted this as another blow to their prestige, but there was nothing they could do about it.[10]

During Vallejo's absence, a number of men had arrived to help protect his family. Among them were Joseph Chiles and Timothy Murphy.[11] When Murphy first reached Sonoma, he had been asked to state his nationality; he had replied that he was a Mexican citizen. The rebels wanted him to join their ranks, but he refused and "was ordered under guard, and remained a prisoner several days." Realizing he was doing no one any good in the Sonoma lockup, he added his name to the roll of the Bears and was freed.[12]

Soon after General Vallejo returned to the Casa Grande, he gathered up all his Mexican army uniforms, "made a pile of them and then burned them." According to messenger John Murphy, the General also shaved off his military beard. He kept the sideburns but never grew back the regulation whiskers.[13]

Jettisoning the appendages of his life as military commander was probably a relief. Vallejo had dismissed his Sonoma soldiers in 1844, and with them had gone all pretensions to military power. The mountain of correspondence he had carried on as the supreme government's advisor had been a meaningless duty. Any vestige of the Spanish military tradition represented a constraining burden he would just as soon do without. As a private citizen, he would now await the cultural advances, economic opportunities, and splendid future he had always expected under U.S. rule.

Despite his recent ordeal at Sutter's Fort, Don Mariano's sense of irony had not vanished with his beard. He intended to keep some epaulets President Bustamente had sent him in 1841 because, as Vallejo put it, they represented "the first instance of a present from a Chief of the Republic of Mexico to a native Californian."[14]

On August 7 Salvador Vallejo wrote his brother from Sutter's Fort, complaining that no boat had arrived, and, as far as freedom was concerned, present hopes were slim: "We go on always in our little room, telling a thousand stories and scrutinizing one by one, the words of our letters. . . ."[15] Captain Montgomery sent Dr. Henderson to Sonoma to check on Vallejo's condition. Montgomery also worked hard to make Edward Kern release the remaining captives. A third set of instructions, carried this time by Lieutenant Misroon, succeeded in unlocking the doors for Vallejo's brother. August 8 found most of the prisoners free to go home.[16]

Far to the south, off the arid coast of San Diego, some of the Bears were aboard the *Cyane* with Major Frémont, but their families were still living in Sonoma. Don Salvador's house was being used by John Grigsby's family, and by September, American soldiers were also garrisoned there. A part of Leese's adobe had served as Ide's headquarters earlier that summer, and it, too, was now housing Americans.[17]

Days passed before Don Salvador finally joined his brother at the Casa Grande. After having left Sutter's Fort, he discovered that his wife and four young children were "in a state bordering on distraction; my property scattered to the four winds, for whatever they [the rebels] could not carry away they had taken good care to destroy. . . ." But, he thanked God "for having spared my life and restored me to wife, children, brothers, sisters, friends, and freedom."[18] (In the 1850s, Don Salvador was partially compensated for his losses, the U.S. government allowing him $11,700 of the $53,100 he asked for.[19]) His rancho was still exposed to attack, however, and before long, he came to Sonoma to take up residence at his brother's adobe.

While Don Salvador continued to be nettled by almost everything that summer, Don Mariano's outlook became increasingly optimistic. Despite illness, the disintegration of the department's government, and his property losses, the General's basic premises remained the same. He told Captain Montgomery that the United States would speed California's development as no other government could. To Larkin, he suggested that a better future lay ahead for everyone. His letter to the consul revealed how destructive the political storm had been for him, and also disclosed the inner reserves that had enabled him to survive the ordeal:

> I left the Sacramento half dead and arrived here almost without life; but I am now much better. . . . The political change has cost a great deal to my person and mind, and likewise to my property. I have lost more than a thousand live horned cattle, six hundred tame horses, and many other things of value which were taken from my house here and at Petaluma. My wheat crops are entirely lost . . . and I assure you that 200 fanegas of sowing [approximately 350 acres] in good condition as mine was is a considerable loss. All is lost, and the only hope for making it up is to work again. . . .[20]

The transition would not be easy for Vallejo.

The lines of allegiance among the Californians were blurred and underwent many changes as the conflict in the south progressed. Don Juan Bandini received much better treatment than his godson, Vallejo. Like his political ally in Sonoma, Bandini was intellectually keen and famous for his hospitality. He also favored American rule, and the arguments he used — Mexico's neglect, the region's vulnerability, and the booming prosperity that would evolve under the American system — had no doubt been reconfirmed in conversations with Don Mariano. For some reason, however, after Frémont arrived in San Diego, Bandini was not subjected to mistreatment, nor did Frémont disgrace him. Instead, the explorer sought the don's aid. During the second week of August, when Frémont rendezvoused with Stockton in Los Angeles, he rode a beautiful gift from Bandini: a sorrel horse, its mane and tail decorated with green ribbons.[21] Obviously, Frémont did not consider Bandini to be a dangerous political rival.

In fall of 1846, the northern dons who had favored a U.S. takeover experienced a change of heart. Commodore Stockton staged an official welcome for himself at Yerba Buena, and "all the rancheros in the immediate vicinity . . . sent in a number of horses for the procession — the choicest from their camponeras."[22] The contributors included members of the Vasquez, Guerrero, and Sánchez families. But less than six weeks later, after being relieved of their livestock by John Grigsby and some of Frémont's other lieutenants, the outraged dons organized for a campaign against the Americans that led to the Battle of Santa Clara. In their zeal to provision Frémont's men, Grigsby and Charles Weber hadn't left the Californians enough mounts to work their land. The rancheros' hardships were well known to American authorities. Lieutenant T. M. Craven reported that the promises made by the American proclamations had been violated, and

> the people ... could not tamely see their rights thus invaded, & themselves stripped of their possessions. ... While all was thought to be quiet throughout the province a deep rooted & bitter feeling of hostility was fastening upon the minds of those who thought themselves outrageously wronged. ... .[23]

A few Californians continued to hope the United States would finally give up California and withdraw again — which is what had happened after Commodore Jones' capture of Monterey in 1842. But on August 12, a ship from Mazatlán brought news that war had definitely been declared between Mexico and the United States.[24] This meant that if the American soldiers defeated the Californians, the change in government was likely to be permanent.

A story was told after Admiral Seymour's ship, the *Collingwood*, anchored at Monterey. A few Californians mulled over the idea of declaring the territory a British protectorate. One man laughed at the idea, and said he was reminded of the strange remedy of a market woman:

> "A dog had robbed her hamper of a leg of mutton, and she sent another dog more powerful after him to get it away; when asked what good that would do her, she replied, 'It would be some satisfaction to see the *first* dog deprived of the stolen leg'. ... California is lost to us. ... The mutton is gone, and a choice of the dog only remains: others may prefer the bull-dog, but I prefer the regular hound; he has outstripped the other in the chase, so let him have the game."[25]

Present-day residents of the state who look back with envy and a poignant sense of loss at the simplicity of early Californian life might not be able to grasp all the circumstances that prevented the province from remaining independent. Larkin estimated that by 1846 four-fifths of the people in the territory were in favor of American rule.[26] His guess was too high, but once the conflict was under way, the extent of the Californians' apathy toward Mexico was obvious, especially in the way the people organized for defense.

General Castro, with barely one hundred men, had posted his soldiers near present-day Compton. Approximately fifteen miles away at San Pedro, Stockton was giving 360 American sailors and marines a quick course in land maneuvers. Castro told Stockton he would be willing to negotiate for peace if the commodore would suspend "all hostile movements" toward Los Angeles.[27]

One of the officers who carried Castro's dispatches was José María Flores, a Mexican captain who, by late October, would be at the head of the Californians' government. He had arrived in 1842 as General Micheltorena's secretary and, like most officers from the southern republic, had been exposed to prejudice from the Californians.[28]

Stockton treated Flores to some rude language and imperious gestures. As far as the commodore was concerned, Castro and the other California leaders were "usurpers" — at least that was the way he expressed it, perhaps for the record. His proclamation (which was condemned by Larkin, Sloat, and practically everyone else who read it), accused Castro of violating all principles of international hospitality by forcing Frémont to leave California. Now Stockton was picturing himself as the savior who had come to liberate the people.[29] He scornfully told Captain Flores that there was only one requirement for the ending of hostilities: Castro must raise the American flag over California.[30] General Castro's men melted away during the negotiations. Lacking a strong personal desire to fight the war, and badly outnumbered by the Americans, Castro withdrew his remaining troops from Compton. On August 9, 1846, he sent a dispatch to Governor Pico that was both an apology and a letter of resignation:

> After having done all in my power to prepare for the defense of the department and to oppose the invasion of the United States forces, . . . I am obliged today to make known to you with regret that it is not possible to accomplish either object, because, notwithstanding your efforts to afford me all the aid in your power, I can count on only 100 men, badly armed, worse supplied and discontented . . . so that I have reason to fear that not even these few men will fight when the necessity arises.[31]

Castro's intention was to leave for Mexico, and he invited Pico to go with him.

The melancholy General Castro had been given an unpopular role to play in California. Inclined at times to make aggressive threats, he had nevertheless been hospitable to foreigners, and by no means was he the native Belial that Frémont, Sutter, and disgruntled settlers had made him out to be. He wrote a maudlin farewell to the people, which was issued not long after he and his small band of followers headed toward the Colorado River:

> With my heart full of the most cruel grief, I take leave of you.
> I leave the country of my birth, but with the hope of returning to
> destroy the slavery in which I leave you; for the day will come
> when our unfortunate fatherland can punish this usurpation,
> as rapacious as unjust, and in the face of the world exact satis-
> faction for its grievances. Friends, I confide in your loyalty and
> patriotism. . . .[32]

One of the seventeen men who rode with him to Sonora was Francisco
Arce, who, only three months before, had surrendered Vallejo's herd to
Ezekiel Merritt. The majority of Castro's officers remained in California
and were paroled.[33] Years later, Castro's repeated promises to reconquer
the province would be satirized in the famous expression *cuando vuelva
Castro* (when Castro returns).[34]

Despite blowing dust and dollops of molten tar that fell from roofs
in the heat, Los Angeles was a prize worth capturing. Stockton's victorious sailors enjoyed the pueblo's abundance of grapes and peaches, and
there was good wine to drink.[35] Little remained to be done except establish a garrison. The job was given to a company of men under Captain
Archibald Gillespie.[36]

By late summer the situation in Sonoma had grown somewhat
complicated for General Vallejo, mainly because of Don Salvador. The
Indian fighter did not like having to live under the General's roof while
his own adobe on the plaza was occupied by Americans.

Whenever he had to choose between diplomacy and confrontation,
Don Salvador preferred the latter. He controlled his temper for a while,
then made an attempt to reoccupy his house. Of course, if he had used
armed force, it would have meant a bloody battle with Lieutenant Revere's
men. So he tried to make the eviction a private affair.

> One fine morning by means of a ladder, I entered my bed cham-
> ber through a window which had incautiously been left open,
> and once inside, I threw out of the window every article belong-
> ing to the intruders, who apprised of my proceedings placed
> around sentinels in front of each door of my dwelling, and in
> this manner they kept me a close prisoner. . . .[37]

Don Salvador thus found himself locked up for the second time that
summer.

The General got his brother out of the fix by offering both their
services to Captain Montgomery. A report had reached Sonoma that one
thousand Walla Walla Indians, under Chief Yellow Serpent, were about
to raid the Sacramento Valley. The chief's son had been murdered a year

before by an American. Since most of Frémont's men were stationed in other parts of the territory, the Indian leader had evidently picked an excellent time to take revenge. Vallejo let Montgomery know that he and his brother would hold the Sonoma frontier while Lieutenant Revere took the garrison to New Helvetia. As a result, the soldiers left Don Salvador's adobe. Captain Vallejo kept his end of the bargain. The Bears in Sonoma were alarmed when the Indians received navy handguns for their patrol work with Don Salvador, but no trouble developed, nor were any hostile tribes discovered.[38]

As it turned out, all the frantic commotion had been caused by a mistranslation of Yellow Serpent's words. The chief, instead of warning someone that nine hundred warriors were following a day or two's march behind him, had merely said that nine sick men had been left on the trail to recover from illness.[39]

Following the Yellow Serpent scare, Captain Montgomery thanked Vallejo for his assistance during the "emergency." Hostilities between American and Californian troops seemed to be at an end. Montgomery could see, however, that national prejudices had to be reduced as well as the "unfriendly suspicion among the various classes composing the Society of California."[40]

Vallejo knew that genuine attempts at mutual understanding, forbearance, and on occasion, a sense of humor, would be needed to nurture good relations between different national groups. For the time being, Don Mariano wanted to stay aloof from public affairs. In a letter to Thomas Oliver Larkin, he candidly asserted, "I am now only a farmer or merchant as you may please to call me. . . . I neither desire, nor wish, nor am I capable, to obtain any situation for the organization of the Government which is about to be established. . . . [A]s a private individual I will do what I can for the prosperity of the country."[41]

Prior to the uprising, Larkin had spoken to Vallejo about the possibility of their developing a commercial port on the Carquinez Straits. Plans for completing this project would occupy Vallejo's thoughts for years to come. Before the partners matured their idea, however, Larkin sought to buy a frontage lot which Vallejo owned in Yerba Buena. It would be ideal for one of Larkin's waterfront projects.

Vallejo answered by suggesting that they share the San Francisco property and perhaps build "a house on joint account."[42] The contents of Don Mariano's letter were nearly as convoluted as the message he had received from Alvarado in 1841 about the purchase of Fort Ross. And like the evasive message from Alvarado, Vallejo's answer to Larkin was really a polite refusal. A shrewd observer of men, Larkin probably knew that Vallejo could be manipulated in business affairs. When it was in Vallejo's power to give something, he usually gave it. And because of his feelings of gratitude toward Larkin, Vallejo eventually surrendered to the consul's urgings. By November Larkin had bought the property in Yerba Buena for $1,000.[43] This was to be expected, because when it came to real estate, Larkin usually won out.

The consul realized that the General, Jacob Leese, and Don Salvador "all chafe at your late treatment," but Larkin was determined to bring Vallejo back into public life. Talks took place between Larkin and Frémont about the formation of a legislative council, and Larkin wanted Vallejo appointed.[44] Larkin also thought it would be a good idea if Vallejo and his brother met Commodore Stockton. But Don Salvador was probably not overly eager to shake Stockton's hand. A letter had recently arrived for Captain Vallejo from his old aide-de-camp, Bonifacio Olivares, who was then in Los Angeles. Olivares revealed a plan to attack Gillespie's American volunteers and drive them out of Los Angeles. Two officers, Captains Flores and Noriega, were already on their way to help, but Don Salvador would be given a position of leadership if he came south.[45] In short, the General's brother was being asked to join in the war against the Americans.

Adopting the neutral stance maintained by Don Mariano, Don Salvador made no move to join the rebels. Months later, after a copy of Olivares' letter found its way to Larkin, General Vallejo wrote the consul to clear up any doubts the note may have raised about their neutrality. He told Larkin that neither Salvador nor himself had broken their pledge not to bear arms against the United States.[46]

In early October, when a warm haze hung between the Sonoma and Mayacamas mountains, Vallejo traveled south to shake hands with Commodore Stockton. Introductions took place aboard the *Portsmouth*. Vallejo was able to thank the commodore personally for securing his release from prison. Immediately following the meeting, Don Mariano helped stage an official welcome for Stockton at Yerba Buena. Much of the fanfare and extravagance of the day were in line with the commodore's own tastes, the opulent style being consistent with ostentatious military tributes popular in the nineteenth century. A barge of state was decked out, with Stockton aboard in full-dress uniform. He disembarked at the end of what is now Clay Street.[47] There he was greeted by a large reception committee, which included the elegantly dressed General Vallejo. Most of the local rancheros contributed horses to the parade. The chief marshal of the day wore a blue sash the ends of which corkscrewed in the breeze. As the procession moved away from the waterfront, there was an eruption of color as the brilliant uniforms of French, Russian, and Hawaiian sailors clashed with the bright *sarapes* and *saltillos* of the Californians. Some of the American newcomers went barefoot; others were dressed in buckskins. The day's official speaker was William "Owl" Russell, a former U.S. marshal who was fond of the "spread eagle" style of oratory.[48] His description of Stockton's career celebrated a life of heroism and privation, all the more remarkable, Russell thought, because the commodore's personal fortune made the sacrifices unnecessary.

Though things had not been going well for Gillespie's men in Los Angeles, Commodore Stockton tried to bolster Yankee ego. He admitted that a group of Californians under Captain José María Flores had successfully retaken the southern capital, but this made Stockton no less sure of a U.S. triumph. Flores' men had better not harm Gillespie's soldiers, he warned, or he would "wade knee-deep in his own blood to avenge it."[49] The absence of classical allusions may have disappointed public taste, but people liked his *pronunciamiento* style. Robert Semple's newspaper, the *Californian*, claimed that Stockton's words were "replete with beautiful and energetic thought."[50]

Vallejo enjoyed a grand ball that night. It would have been a dull affair if the guests had gone home early; but as the sun rose above the Diablo Range, the instruments and shuffling feet could still be heard.

After a week of party-going, the much-relaxed Vallejo returned to Sonoma. A meeting had just taken place, in honor of the Bears' midsummer revolt. Some of the Bears had set up a committee to "gather all the information in their reach" relating to the actions of the revolutionary group and report "at a subsequent meeting."[51] Though Vallejo knew that *some* of the members of the Bear Flag party had been freebooters, he was not angered by the presence of rebel leaders like William Ide or Robert Semple. But for Rosalía Leese and Doña Francisca Vallejo, even the word "Bear" caused distress.

In later years, the General would classify Frémont's mistreatment of him at Sutter's Fort as a sort of political prank and would speak of the Bear Flaggers with humor. If Vallejo ever wrote down his candid feelings about the takeover as the events were unfolding, his notes probably vanished in a blaze that destroyed the Casa Grande in 1867, and we have only his later writings to rely on. He realized that his former captors were now his neighbors. It wasn't going to be a matter of a curt goodbye. Former antagonists now had to live together. In the subsequent months, he would enter into business dealings with Robert Semple, Samuel Kelsey, and Jasper O'Farrell. A little more than ten years later, Granville P. Swift would elicit groans and protests from Natalia Vallejo when the Bear Flagger (his pockets then filled with Gold Rush profits) came to the General's house to pump her hand with vigor and woo her as best he could. (A later chapter will describe her response.)

Former Commander Ide made another trip to Sonoma in the fall, accompanied by journalist Edwin Bryant. They left San Francisco in one of the *Portsmouth*'s cutters and followed the winding course of Sonoma Creek to the embarcadero a few miles from the pueblo. It was a meaningful portent when the cutter's sailors offered Bryant a breakfast "of bread, butter, coffee, tea, fresh beefsteaks, cheese, pickles, and a variety of other delicacies. . . ."[52] The journalist appreciated the fact that Uncle Sam could give his sailors a superabundance of food. This would become a significant advantage in the coming weeks.

While Bryant was still at Sonoma, Thomas Larkin arrived to push along Vallejo's plan for a city on the Carquinez Straits. In recent months, the market for hides — a longtime staple of the rancho economy — had become "very dull indeed," and Vallejo and Larkin thought this might be a good time to begin their new enterprise.

Don Mariano and the consul were just about to leave for the Soscol Rancho when they received more bad news about American setbacks in southern California. Gillespie's men had been worsted more than once, and additional volunteers would be needed for increasingly bloody battles in Los Angeles and San Diego. Larkin and Bryant decided it would be wise to return to Yerba Buena with a military escort. As Vallejo and his partner said goodbye, neither man guessed that Larkin, who thus far had been spared most of the hardships connected with the conflict, would soon be made a prisoner of war by the Californians. He would experience ordeals very much like the ones Vallejo had known in June and July of this eventful year.

14

The Californians Retake the South

I

The warning Thomas Oliver Larkin had given Commodore Stockton was turning out to be prophetic. Though it was quite easy to occupy California, it would "prove much care" to remain in control of it.[1] Only now, in mid-fall, did the slow-to-react Californians seem to develop any interest in fighting the Americans. Devoting the majority of his time to personal affairs, Vallejo preserved his neutrality. He expected American arms to triumph, but he also wanted the thefts and other outrages against the Californians to stop. His ambivalence was understandable. His hopeful dream of an American protectorate had been replaced by realities that were sticky to live with. It is not surprising, then, that during the war he neither witnessed nor took part in a single battle. Somewhat more puzzling is the fact that Major John Charles Frémont was also a virtual noncombatant; as the winter campaign wore on, a chance to fight decisive conflicts eluded him.

In southern California, Captain José María Flores' successful operations had surprised the Americans. Flores' psychological advantage over men like Castro and Pico came from his believing, heart and soul, in the Mexican cause. Most provincial leaders continued to think of Mexico as "the bane of our existence," but for Flores the eagle and serpent inspired dedication. Since the war's development formed an important prelude to the success of Vallejo's and Larkin's efforts to make California a part of the United States, some time needs to be devoted to describing the kind of conflict it turned out to be.

Captain Gillespie and his fifty-man garrison controlled Los Angeles, and this became the uncertain anchor of the whole conquered zone. Gillespie imposed small tyrannies that were highly insulting to the locals. He ruled that any Californian seen galloping a horse across the plaza must go to the guard house. Men caught gambling received the same punishment, as did four or more people who stood talking on the street. One of the Americans noted that Gillespie "broke up their fandangos too, for I do not remember of them having one all the time we were there."[2] The Los Angeles señoritas dreamed up a curious revenge for the commander. They sent him some ripe peaches, which Gillespie misinterpreted as a token of respect. Before making delivery, however, the women rolled the gifts "in the fine fur-like particles of the *tunar*, or fruit of the cactus; and it was a full week before he got them all out of his mouth."[3]

On September 30, Captain Flores, leading more than three hundred Californians, forced Gillespie's garrison to abandon Los Angeles. The American volunteers followed a road that seemed to be a curse to unwelcome invaders. It went past low mesas spotted with cholla until the wide harbor of San Pedro came into view. Here, according to the terms previously agreed upon, Gillespie and his men boarded the *Vandalia*.

Instead of sailing to Monterey as promised, however, Gillespie remained a few miles out to sea, within sight of the beach. The reinforcements he was expecting finally arrived, and after reoccupying the sandy shore, the Americans were formed into a square with the marines ahead and the sailors in the rear. The company then marched without artillery across rocky ground toward Los Angeles, their flanks protected by Gillespie's sharpshooters.[4]

Against these troops, the Californians under José Antonio Carrillo employed hit-and-run tactics. They put their one cannon, "the Old Woman gun," into operation as a sort of flying artillery. The cavalrymen fired at close range, then dragged the gun away using reatas tied to their saddles. They were successful with the tactic almost every time. Four Americans were killed and six wounded. Once again, the sailors and marines marched back to San Pedro, boarded their ships, and abandoned the harbor to the defenders.[5]

Now referred to as the Battle of Domínguez Hills, this was the first in a series of victories for the Californians. How far would their triumphs take them? In mid-October, while the hills surrounding Monterey were still smoking from a recent forest fire, the Californians planned to "capture or drive out the small American force" there.[6] They probably would have succeeded if a company of marines had not sailed into view aboard the *Congress*. After the marines occupied the port, Monterey continued to have a wartime look. The streets were barricaded, patrols were maintained night and day, and no one was permitted to leave "without a written passport."[7] Even these precautions did not make Consul Thomas Oliver Larkin feel entirely safe. He knew the Californians had thought about kidnapping him "as an offsett to the Senor Vallejo." Sad to say, they eventually succeeded. While en route to San Francisco to visit his sick four-year-old daughter Adeline, he stopped for the night at Joaquín Gómez's adobe about seven miles south of San Juan Bautista. Learning of Larkin's whereabouts, Californian troopers under Lieutenant José Antonio Chávez woke him up, shouting, "Vamos, Señor Larkin."[8] By then, the Californians controlled all the territory between San Luis Obispo and San Diego. The departmental assembly in Los Angeles was holding regular sessions and had elected José María Flores to the civil and military governorship. Larkin may have been amused or flattered to learn that Governor Flores considered him to be Mexico's number one enemy. The newly elected governor even thought that if Larkin could be captured, the war might come to an end — so highly would his person be valued by American authorities.[9] Flores' awe of Larkin stemmed from the consul's great popularity. Larkin's wealth, astuteness, fiscal reliability, and his being a fluent Spanish speaker, made his concept of the future under American rule seem quite reasonable to a large number of Californians.

Larkin spent the rest of the night under guard, on horseback, heading back toward the Salinas River. The whole affair soon became hazardous. Several hours after sunrise he was shunted around a battlefield — a confused engagement known as the Battle of La Natividad. The Californians had approximately 130 men against a force of about 100 Americans led by "Hell Roaring" Thompson and Captain Charles Burass (sometimes referred to as Burroughs).[10] Burass was killed in the chaotic melee, as were three or four of his companions, and between five and seven Americans were wounded. The Californians admitted the loss of two men killed with seven injured.[11]

At the conclusion of the fight, Larkin — still a prisoner — saw a horseman racing toward him at top speed crying, "This man caused it all." Later identified as Lorenzo Soto, the angry partisan had just lost a nephew in the conflict. His pistol was drawn and he was aiming carefully. Larkin quickly backed his mount, ruining the would-be assassin's aim. Soto was prevented from taking revenge by Larkin's quickness and by the interference of others.[12]

This was not the only time Larkin's life was endangered, but on the whole, the Californians treated him well. When he was escorted to

Los Angeles, Governor Flores was kind to him, offering Larkin "a bed . . . furniture, clothes, food, at my own hours, and money whenever I might ask for it."[13] Such was the courtesy Larkin had always numbered among the Californians' fine traits.

As far as Frémont and Stockton were concerned, the kidnapping of Larkin was an unfortunate incident, but certainly not the diplomatic disaster the Californians had dreamed it would be. Since there was little reliable information arriving from the south, it was some time before news of Larkin's whereabouts reached Vallejo.

Many of Don Mariano's horses were being driven toward Los Angeles by companies of American volunteers who were hoping to rout Flores' army. The animals carried Vallejo's brand, and the General was known to be the rightful owner, but few, if any, of the mounts would be returned to him.

While the cities in the south were exploding like a string of firecrackers, the winter storms continued, and the weather created quagmires that made transportation by horse and wagon nearly impossible.

On December 6, 1846, at a place called San Pasqual, near San Diego, the war reached its unexpected climax. General Steven Watts Kearny and some 121 U.S. soldiers struggled over the crest of the Cuyamaca Mountains, where they were soon joined by Archibald H. Gillespie and about 50 reinforcements from San Diego.[14] General Kearny, who was already famous as an Indian fighter, learned from Gillespie that Pío Pico's brother, Don Andrés Pico, and his cavalry were not far off.

The Californian cavalry was thought to be hiding in a nearby Indian settlement. The officer in the vanguard of Kearny's forces, Captain A. R. Johnston, misunderstood the general's orders and led a charge. As his company swung around a low knoll, they could see Andrés Pico's troopers in the distance — a dense line of about one hundred horsemen blocking their path. Don Andrés, "a gentlemanly looking and rather handsome man," knew his weapons were poor, and he kept his men from shooting until the Americans almost collided with the human barrier. The Californians' volley, fired at point-blank range, killed Captain Johnston.[15] A brief skirmish followed, and after some maneuvering there was a sustained battle. The Californians' polished lances fastened to straight willow poles should not have triumphed over U.S. rifles, but they did.

The final results were appalling. Twenty-one Americans were either killed or died later of their wounds. Fifteen others were injured. Less than half that number of Californians sustained casualties.[16]

In Los Angeles, when Larkin learned of the encounter, his sentiments probably expressed Vallejo's as well: the fall of a man on either side was painfully "sad and disagreeable" to him.[17]

This did not end the war, but following the Californians' triumph, an odd reaction developed among them: it almost seemed as though their achievement had sapped their strength. This mystery can be explained by their original reasons for resisting. They had not struggled to restore Mexican authority, nor even to return Pico and Castro to power. Their stand was a way of satisfying their personal honor. By verbal abuse and unprovoked attacks, the Americans had driven the rancheros into the conflict. After the December 6 victory, the defenders felt they had exacted a high price. As the new year approached, they succumbed to apathy. Flores' men deserted. Worse still, he was having trouble with three of his most talented officers, José Antonio Carrillo, Manuel Castro, and Joaquín de la Torre. Their disobedience caused the governor to imprison them for fourteen days.[18]

The end of the war was a strange postscript to the battle of San Pasqual. Commodore Stockton and General Kearny planned to trap Flores between their combined force of 450 troops and the 450-man army marching south from Santa Barbara under Frémont. On January 8 and 9, the final confrontation, the Battle of the Mesa, took place. Fortunately, only a handful of men were lost. On the morning of January 10, 1847, a flag of truce was brought in and hostilities ended.[19]

Governor Flores was still holding Larkin hostage and intended to transfer him to Mexico. A courier was sent to escort the merchant to the outskirts of the battlefield.

As he crossed the sandy ground, Larkin could see American dragoons marching toward the pueblo in their accustomed square — too far away to do him any good. Larkin did not feel well enough to ride and for some distance walked his horse. When he reached his destination, a soldier who still held a grudge against him from Monterey days "came to me (drunk) with his musket lined to shoot me. Don Andrés Pico being nigh with some trouble took away his gun."[20]

With his typical generosity, General Flores released the consul on parole. Larkin returned to Los Angeles, only to learn of the death of his four-year-old daughter Adeline.

For most people, the suffering was over. There being little more that Governor Flores could do, he left for Mexico on January 10, the same day the fighting ended.[21] The always-composed Don Andrés Pico found himself in control of the Californian troops. The role of peacemaker, it seemed, would be left to him. General Flores and ex–Governor Pico would take no part in the talks. Oddly enough, neither would Commodore Stockton or General Kearny. A supreme irony developed: John Charles Frémont would sign the articles of peace with very little regard for the opinions of his superiors. And to the surprise of Vallejo and the others who had been imprisoned at Sutter's Fort, Frémont would show unprecedented respect for the Californians.

II

In January of 1847, the weather in General Vallejo's domain was bleak. Hard frost turned the trunks of the manzanita shrubs reddish-black, and the small oaks were entirely leafless and trailing moss; they stood like frost crystals on the tiers of hills behind the Casa Grande.

Vallejo's return to private life had given him definite satisfactions, but there were more than a few trials. The rustling of livestock hadn't stopped. Other Californians were faring just as badly, for Frémont's lieutenants paid them little respect. These rancheros constituted a population of pastoral agrarians who had been provoked — outraged even — by representatives of the very country they had trusted to put things in order.

The rainstorms that followed the New Year made it impossible for Vallejo to push ahead with his plans for a new city on the Carquinez Straits. But the most painful ordeal took place when one of his servants at the Casa Grande tried to harm Doña Francisca.

The house was filled with guests, and Vallejo's wife was dividing her time between making her visitors comfortable and taking care of her four-year-old daughter, "Guadalupita," who was ill.

Servants brought dinner to Francisca's upstairs bedroom, where she and her five-year-old son Platon were caring for the little girl. After taking a mouthful of soup, Francisca felt sharp chunks in her mouth and discovered she had taken a mouthful of glass.

A servant went downstairs to fetch Don Mariano, who was hosting the evening meal. When the Don reached the bedroom, he found more glass particles at the bottom of the soup bowl. Luckily, neither she nor Platon had swallowed any of the fragments. Apparently, a servant named Canulo had lost his reason. Some of the other domestics had seen him pounding a bottle to bits a few days earlier, and he admitted having wanted to kill Francisca because he had recently lost a shirt.[22] Canulo confessed to the crime, and Vallejo's deposition was given to Judge Nash on January 10, 1847. The servant was, by admission, guilty of attempted murder and was sent to Yerba Buena to await trial.

The day after Vallejo testified at the hearings, Guadalupita died. She was buried at the cemetery near the spring at Lachryma Montis. This was not the first child the Vallejos had lost. A total of six had perished in infancy or early childhood, leaving four boys and four girls at the Casa Grande. From time to time, the household welcomed surrogates, including Indian children after they had been orphaned or misfortune had left them no other place to go.[23] Vallejo was particularly troubled by the circumstances of one of his children, an adopted boy named José Altamira. Many people, including some of Vallejo's direct descendants, assumed that José Altamira was Vallejo's illegitimate son by an Indian mother whose name is not known. (Church authorities had documented some of the General's other illegitimate children: five *hijos naturales* were baptized — later to be listed in a genealogical register. [24])

Young José was, from the very first, an unusual child. When quite young, he had saved the pueblo of Sonoma from Indian attack. Overhearing some tribesmen planning a massacre of the pueblo's inhabitants, he had warned the General. Don Mariano and his ally, Chief Solano, learned that the raid was scheduled for that night and positioned their soldiers in the deserted mission buildings. When the attackers came down from the chapparal, they were routed. The General adopted the bright youngster, giving him the Vallejo family name and in at least one letter addressing him as "my beloved son." José was considered to be the equal of the other Vallejo children. As Platon put it, "He was my brother."[25]

José was sent to be educated in Valparaiso, Chile, where he received awards in second division mathematics and accounting. By the fall of 1846, he was ready to come home.

An optimistic and very tender letter from Don Mariano had not yet reached him, but José had learned of the General's imprisonment from other sources. He was so emotionally upset by it, he couldn't study. He hoped England or France would do something to stop the American takeover of California. More than anything, he wanted to return home and be of some use to his father. Nothing prepared him to understand that his own fierce hatred of Americans would create a crisis when he reached Monterey. First, however, he had to get there.

A year earlier, things would have gone smoothly; but now, politics got in the way. No American ship wanted to bring him back to Alta California. The captain of the *Independence,* Commodore William B.

Shubrick, was reluctant to welcome José Altamira aboard and "evidently wanted coaxing into it." His final decision was *not* to take the boy to California, despite everything one of Consul Larkin's friends could do.[26] Finally, a Chilean corvette under a Captain Jones gave him passage.

Young José thought things should have been handled very differently in the place of his birth. On the way home, he made insulting remarks to some of the Americans aboard ship (including Captain Jones), and suggested that the Yankees in California needed to have their throats cut.[27] He arrived at Monterey in June of 1847, when the allegiance of the Californians was still in doubt. In fact, Vallejo had just written Thomas Larkin, assuring him that neither he nor his brother Don Salvador had broken his pledge not to bear arms against the United States.

When Vallejo learned of his son's insults, his love for him was converted to shame. It was difficult, if not impossible, for young José to appreciate the General's dedication to a political passion, still largely unrealized, which no discomfort or frustration could change. And Vallejo did not seem to appreciate the fact that the strength of the boy's love for him was the same fuel that powered José's hatred of the General's former captors — the victorious Americans.

The American military presence was not very popular in mid-1847 — which created a rash of doubts in Vallejo's mind. His son's violent words only added another dimension to Vallejo's dilemma. In a later chapter, it will be seen that as the General's expectations for Americans dropped a few notches, his expectations for himself and other Californians rose higher. But his standards for his own family were very demanding, and he would never tolerate rudeness or discourtesy in his children.

He made José apologize to Captain Jones and warned the boy not to speak that way against Americans again. The General also told José that he and the rest of the Vallejo family had "received benefits" from the Americans. If the boy had pressed him for an explanation (which was not allowed in California), and if the General had permitted himself to defy tradition by being candid with his son, he would have explained that besides his affection for Americans, U.S. officers considered him to be a crony, and on legal, social, and political matters often deferred to his judgment. What's more, the Americans wanted land, and the General was willing to sell it to them. In short, they were all prospective customers for his real estate. Far more important, however, Americans were family. José Altamira had American in-laws. In addition to the uncles, there would soon be American nieces, nephews, and cousins. Finally, U.S. immigrants had set the stage for California's development, bringing with them an outlook that would enable California to progress. Young José's views, however, were *not* very different from Don Salvador's, and this further aggravated the General's own latent uncertainties.

Realizing José needed work, Vallejo gave him a job at the Petaluma Rancho and later employed him as a secretary.[28] But José continued to test the unwritten laws that guided relations between fathers and sons in California — sometimes acting with disrespect. Nevertheless, Vallejo made efforts to protect him. At one point, the General criticized Don Salvador for trying to involve José in the unwise sale of some horses. If Don Salvador intended the incident as an educational lesson, it was a harsh one. Before long the General complained to his brother, "I never would have said a word about it, if it were not for the deal you tried to make with José, in which I would have come out skinned."

After another unpleasant incident occurred at the Petaluma Rancho, the General was furious to learn that his son had treated the Vallejo family name "with insolence and contempt." Perhaps José thought that his feelings were being ignored. By then, things had gone too far. The boy had "just about exhausted" his father's good will toward him.

An anonymous mediator (probably Doña Francisca) sent José an unsigned letter explaining how matters stood, urging the adopted son to act affirmatively and with gratitude, and to avoid further acts of discourtesy. But José took no steps to change his ways. On the back of the anonymous message, he wrote, "If I am not to be forgiven, I hereby return this letter so that it will not be a painful reminder."

Though Vallejo later saved José from financial difficulties, the relationship never mended. The final break came when José left his Sonoma home. He married, raised a large family, and became an interpreter at the Contra Costa court house. Little remained between father and son except a pained silence.[29]

In January, while Vallejo was still upset by the attempted murder of his wife, moves toward a negotiated peace were being made in southern California — perhaps prematurely.

The flaws in California's military occupation were suddenly exposed. A tense camping arrangement placed the four-hundred-man army of Commodore Stockton a short distance from approximately fifty dragoons under General Kearny. The American personnel in Los Angeles should have been laboring to impress the Californians with U.S. knowhow and the advantages of American rule — especially while their army was bivouacked under the scrutiny of a newly conquered enemy. But at the very time that U.S. forces were bear-hugging the continent, the sleeves on their mighty arms started to unravel. Hostilities between Kearny and Stockton were so spiteful that the leaders were hardly speaking, and their respective armies taunted each other. The chain of authority being unclear, neither commanding officer felt inclined to begin negotiations with the Californian leaders. General Kearny's most recent orders authorized him to serve as California's military governor, and Commodore Stockton felt justified by his own earlier instructions to hold the same post.[30] This left the door open for Lieutenant-Colonel Frémont, who had been marching toward Los Angeles since late November and had finally reached the San Fernando Valley.

Frémont didn't bother responding to General Kearny's dispatches. But after reaching Mission San Fernando, he proclaimed a one-day armistice, asking Californian officials to join him for peace talks. One of the rancheros who arrived to talk things over was the six-foot, four-inch victor of the Battle of Domínguez Hills, José Antonio Carrillo. Argumentative as always, he was now ready to end the conflict to which the Californians had been driven by taunts of cowardice. But he was unwilling to accept the sort of harsh demands Stockton had made in the past.[31] Nor did he have to. The American commanding officers in Los Angeles were doing nothing to button up a treaty, and they were amazed when they received copies of the armistice. General Kearny assumed Frémont must be ignorant of his whereabouts. Kearny wanted to march some men to the San Fernando Valley to form a junction with the explorer's battalion. This plan was vetoed by Stockton. By that time the commodore had deduced that Frémont was deliberately ignoring him, too.[32]

On January 13, near a windy arroyo through which the Hollywood Freeway roars today, the conflict between the Californians and the occupying Americans officially ended. The leaders who put their names to the Treaty of Cahuenga were Andrés Pico, "Chief of National Forces," and John Charles Frémont, "Military Commandant."[33]

A former U.S. marshal brought a copy of the treaty to Stockton, who was furious to learn that Frémont had negotiated the terms without consulting him. There was even talk in the streets that Frémont didn't intend to recognize any authority higher than his own. When Stockton heard the rumor, he shouted out, "What does the damned fool mean?"[34]

These developments left unchanged the commodore's plan to appoint Frémont governor of California within a matter of days. General Kearny remained silent on the matter — undoubtedly because of his personal affection for Frémont's wife, Jessie, and his close political ties with Senator Benton.[35]

For once, however, Frémont's overreaching worked to the Californians' advantage. The treaty of Cahuenga — a far more generous agreement than Stockton or Kearny would have signed — allowed the defeated Californians to return to their homes with their arms, without the need for taking an oath of allegiance until the larger conflict with Mexico was settled. The ex-belligerents who chose to remain in California were guaranteed the same rights and privileges as other U.S. citizens. By an article added three days later, the remaining prisoners were released and the officers who had broken their paroles were pardoned. Andrés Pico's men surrendered two pieces of artillery, six muskets, and six charges of grape as a token gesture of capitulation.[36]

Had the conflict between the Californians and Americans taken place in Mexico, most of the defeated soldiers would have been executed as political criminals. And had the outbreak occurred in Sam Houston's Texas, a large proportion of the Spanish-speaking people (including pro-Americans like Vallejo and Bandini) would have been hounded from the country by the relentless Anglo victors of the campaign. But things were settled differently in California, where warfare seemed to end with refreshing nonchalance.

Though the final tally in dead and wounded might seem small by today's standards, the number was sad to contemplate. In the eight engagements from the Battle of Olómpali in July 1846 to the final Battle of the Mesa in January 1847, the Americans had lost (giving both high and low estimates) between thirty-two and thirty-six killed, and thirty-six to forty-four wounded; the Californians suffered between seven and nine dead, and thirty-two to thirty-five wounded.[37] The Californians sustained fewer casualties, but they lost far more in personal property and supplies than the Americans. Moreover, in less than eight months, the United States had built up a debt of more than half a million dollars. The cost of the conquest in human lives was made more painful because much of the bloodshed had been unnecessary. Frémont's generous peace terms seemed to signify an about-face for him, but in reality his concessions stemmed from his desire to gain the California governorship. He knew Captain Gillespie had ruined things for himself by mistreating the Californians in Los Angeles the previous fall. The defenders had since proven themselves to be a brave, resourceful enemy, and Frémont did not want to repeat Gillespie's mistakes.

A workable treaty now existed, but Stockton and Kearny were still feuding, and the troops became involved. Obviously, a military rivalry was not what Vallejo had pictured when he envisioned a stable government under American rule. Brawls started between men of the different U.S. commands and many officers thought a civil war might break out.

Kearny wanted to keep the mayhem from spiralling further out of control, so he asked Frémont to turn down Stockton's appointment as governor. But the explorer refused. Frémont was gambling that Stockton's authority would prevail. Hoping to prevent open violence between his small army and Stockton's men, Kearny withdrew to San Diego. As he explained to Commodore Stockton:

> I must, for the purpose of preventing collision between us, and possibly, a civil war in consequence of it, remain silent for the present, leaving you the great responsibility of doing that for which you have no authority, and preventing me from complying with the President's orders.[38]

The quarrel among the officers would go on for years, and not even Frémont's court-martial would put it to rest.

Despite the test of power among the military higher-ups, the *californios* were returning to their adobes. American volunteers also hoped to be discharged, but they would have to wait to be paid.

Vallejo was surprised to learn how far military rule had deteriorated in Los Angeles, but during the latter half of January, he received an invitation from Commodore Stockton to serve on a legislative committee made up of Thomas Oliver Larkin, ex-Governor Alvarado, Juan Bandini, David Spence, and two others.[39] Don Mariano had doubted the wisdom of returning to public life. He still had not made up his mind to accept the invitation when a second letter was handed him, this one bearing the signature of "J. C. Frémont, Governor, Commander-in-Chief of California."[40] We can only guess if Vallejo was bemused, or simply shook his head in wonderment.

At the time of Vallejo's last interaction with Frémont, the General had been locked up in close confinement at Sutter's Fort, without the privilege of exercise. Frémont had further soured the experience by canceling a planned meeting with the prisoners. Regarding the other events of June and July of 1846, there was no apology from Frémont. But a long letter from Larkin was enclosed with Frémont's invitation, perhaps to mollify Don Mariano's feelings.

Larkin confessed, "I would not act as one of the Legislature for $1000 per month as time is now very valuable to me." But monetary gain was not his chief concern. He stressed that "by degrees many Californians will receive office," and Vallejo's nonattendance would "sorely disappoint the Commodore, Governor Frémont, and myself."[41] Not entirely discouraged by the military conflict that had occurred, the consul was still trying to implement his original plan to give leading Californians political office under the new regime.

Robert Semple was convinced that Vallejo's "talents and suavity of manner" would help to "tranquilize the country and give confidence to the people. . . ."[42] Vice-Consul William Leidesdorff urged caution, as did many other long-term residents. In fact, a good deal of flattery and political cajolery went into putting the council together. With American leaders still at odds and contradictory sets of orders being waved by rival military commanders, Frémont's new governorship was obviously on very shaky ground.[43]

Vallejo's friend, Joseph Warren Revere, hoped the General would not compromise himself by joining a government that might be brushed aside by Washington.

> You now occupy a neutral position, full of dignity and I am sure General Kearny will have the support of the President of the United States and that Frémont and his transitory cabinet will not have much time to exist. . . .[44]

Vallejo's poetry-loving friend, Walter Colton, expressed worries many Americans were feeling at the time:

> There is no man in California who better understands her true interests than yourself. . . . We fear . . . should you decline a seat in the Council, it might be ascribed by the Californians to a want of confidence in the Government or a disaffection to it.[45]

On February 15, Vallejo gave up his brief retirement from public life and accepted the post. He hoped to promote legislation that would benefit the country, and this would vindicate his faith in the course he had taken. Vallejo's ambition and vanity were also factors — though the exercise of power itself did not mean as much to him as clear evidence of public confidence.

Technically speaking, the General was still a prisoner of war, or so he reminded Frémont in his letter of acceptance. Vallejo also noted that Commodore Stockton, not Frémont, had been responsible for selecting him. He modestly referred to his limitations and assured Governor Frémont that he was acting with California's future welfare in mind.[46]

It is fortunate that General Kearny and Lieutenant Colonel Frémont did not try to occupy the same town. After Kearny's post was confirmed, he took office as the territory's new governor at Monterey.[47] Frémont, sporting a large sombrero, paraded around as the governor in Los Angeles and amassed a stupendous debt. Soon General Kearny demanded that Frémont bring all his official documents from Los Angeles to Monterey and muster the California volunteers into the regular service, preparatory to Frémont's leaving California.

Not surprisingly, Frémont disobeyed Kearny's orders, and it would be another three months before the explorer — reluctant to take the necessary steps — would decamp. When Kearny sent his aide, Colonel Richard B. Mason, to Los Angeles to speed Frémont's departure, Mason and Frémont had to be prevented from dueling with "double-barrelled shotguns with buckshot at twenty paces."[48]

Though considered to be a good judge of political eventualities, Vallejo continued to be mystified by Frémont's motives and aims. Indeed, the showiest fireworks attending Frémont's governorship were still to come.

15

The Slip and Slide Transition

*T*he sooner the American presence could be translated into real gains for the Californians, the more secure Don Mariano would feel about the political developments that had unfolded since June of 1846. He had never known a Californian government that wasn't plagued by sectional squabbles intensified by threats of war. Certainly Mexico — the presidency of which had changed hands some twenty times in a single fifteen-year period — had never provided a stable model. Not that the General was looking for miracles; in fact, he took a somewhat ironic attitude toward human incompetence and rascality, which he knew to be as inevitable as the sunrise. He was disappointed, however, when the promise of a dramatically improved California was postponed for three years between July 1846 and December 1849. Seven American military governors replaced one another in that brief time — a performance which equaled the dizzying turnovers in Mexico. None of these governors seemed to know if California's residents were to be treated as an unclassifiable population in a territorial purgatory, or as fully vested citizens in a new American state. The governors' uncertainty along with their limited financial power froze the wheels of progress. The slavery issue in Washington made the question of California's statehood the toy of North–South politics. And in the middle of this three-year hiatus, an event took place which would have defied the balancing genius of any government: the Gold Rush.

At the very start of the transition, General Vallejo's optimism was nearing its apogee. He knew that the war between the Californians and Americans was indeed over, though he could do nothing to change the spiteful relations between General Kearny and Lieutenant Colonel Frémont. Larkin fumed when he learned that Frémont's imprisonment of Vallejo and the other Sonomans in June of '46 had not been justified by any known hostilities by Castro. But everyone set aside bitter feelings when news of the Donner Party tragedy reached the settlements in spring of 1847. In a famous dream, George Yount had pictured a caravan of men, women, and children on the edge of a body of water, the unfortunates "just as thin as they could be."[1] The image turned out to be all too accurate. Eighty-one travelers were trapped in the Sierras, thirty-five of whom lost their lives. General Vallejo and his brother Don Salvador immediately set to work organizing rescue parties. At one meeting, the General and Captain Joseph B. Hull of the U.S. navy raised $1,500 for the stranded victims.[2]

Shortly before sending Vallejo a handsome carbine "as a small mark of the high respect" he had for him, Governor Kearny appointed him sub-Indian agent of the Sonoma district at a salary of $750 per year. Vallejo's jurisdiction extended to Cache Creek and Clear Lake. This did not mean Vallejo would be called upon to improve the Indians' condition. From the first, American proclamations regarding the Native Americans confirmed the main features of old Hispanic abuses, and Indians still had to work without any monetary benefit — for food and clothing alone. Indians not employed could be arrested and forced to work, and their mobility was restricted by their need to carry a written pass from their previous employer.[3] John Sutter, whose control of Indian labor had been very similar to Vallejo's prior to the American conquest, was given the job of sub-Indian agent for the Sacramento Valley. A remarkable parallelism had developed in the two men's lives, and Don Salvador Vallejo growled in disbelief that two individuals with such different points of view should be yoked together by what he called "Masonic bonds."[4] Even after the war was over, Don Salvador could never bring himself to trust Sutter. The Bear Flaggers in Sonoma feared that Don Mariano would use his power as sub-Indian agent to organize the Indians against them. But this did not happen. In fact, Vallejo continued to provide cheap land to immigrants like Lorenzo Waugh and others who sought him out. He even gave work to the unfortunate Lewis Keseberg, the so-called ghoul of the Donner party, who had been falsely accused of reveling in the horrible feasts that accompanied the Sierra disaster. Vallejo trusted him, and Sutter knew that the lurid tales about Keseberg were untrue, but the Prussian immigrant was hounded and victimized for the rest of his life.[5]

Rather than devote all his energies to building his projected city at Benicia, General Vallejo gave Robert Semple and Thomas Larkin a five-square-mile parcel on the Carquinez Straits and allowed the two entrepreneurs to work on developing the port. Except for the one hundred town lots he reserved for himself and the nominal compensation of one hundred dollars,[6] Vallejo put his hopes for future gain in the thousands of acres he owned on the Soscol Rancho adjacent to Benicia. Their value would likely appreciate after the town's construction.

Some of the region's newly-arrived pioneers made it difficult to maintain order during this period, because they wanted to treat the country as though it were a vast lottery table loaded with prizes: the most attractive items only needed to be pointed out and claimed. Walter Colton, then alcalde of Monterey, was surprised one afternoon when a travel-worn woman entered his office and demanded a permit to cut timber on another man's land.

> I asked her if her husband had rented the land. "No." If he had any contract or agreement with the owner. "No." "Why then, my woman, do you claim the right of cutting the timber?" "Right, sir!" she exclaimed; "why, have we not taken the country?" I told her it was true, we had taken the country; but we had not taken the private land titles with it. . . .[7]

Other curious events occurred. For instance, an anachronistic pair of dispatches arrived for Vallejo from ex-President Bustamente. One contained a commission making him a brevet-colonel; the other increased his rank (for the third time, as he saw it) to full colonel.[8] Vallejo had already written shoals of letters to the supreme government, and he showed little gratitude for the new promotions, which were as unwanted as his incinerated uniforms. Tongue firmly in cheek, he complained that the Mexican government still owed him a sizable chunk of back pay, and he had yet to be reimbursed for the thousands of head of cattle he had slaughtered to feed the Sonoma garrison. Regarding California's present status, Mexico had abandoned the place to the invaders.[9]

There had always been a make-believe quality to Vallejo's correspondence with Bustamente, but even more far-fetched was a letter Don Mariano sent to former *comisionado* Andrés Castillero, then living in Mexico. It seemed like an outright tall tale: the General portrayed himself as being in dire straits and he begged Castillero to send cash at once since he was now minus "all my possessions and I am destitute along with my family."[10]

Vallejo dealt with American officials in a more businesslike way as he prepared a list of the losses he had sustained in 1846. He told Larkin that he did not intend to include personal effects stolen by the rebels from the Casa Grande; their sentimental value far outweighed their monetary cost, and he was hoping that Frémont would return them.[11] But Frémont had by then journeyed to the East Coast, where he endured an arduous court-martial that had been ordered by General Kearny.[12]

So it is doubtful that Vallejo ever recovered his items. But the General's claims against the U.S. government would give him cause to celebrate: in 1855 he was granted $48,700 of the $117,875 he had asked for. This was the largest payment made in the territory. It was rumored at the time that the generous settlement included partial damages for his long imprisonment at Sutter's Fort as well as for property never returned to him.[13]

Sonoma was growing rapidly now, and Robert Semple was making great progress at Benicia. Spirits in both places were high. Despite the advent of a few thousand Americans, old California had survived; but could it outlast a year like 1848? The grass was already lush on February 10 when Vallejo received a rather low key letter (considering the source) from Sutter. It described the location of a gold deposit at Coloma. Lucrative mines had been discovered in California before, but in regard to the new find, Sutter remarked guardedly, "According to experiments we have made, it is extraordinarily rich."[14] James W. Marshall had made the historic discovery on January 24, and Vallejo was one of the first men outside of New Helvetia to learn of it. From that day forward, finding gold, rather than cattle-ranching and dancing, would become the territory's ruling passion. As it turned out, gold did not hold the same fascination for General Vallejo it did for his brother Don Salvador, who during the relatively peaceful first year of mining operations amassed a small fortune. Unfortunately, most of this wealth was later lost in bank failures. For a brief time, the General considered setting up a mining partnership with Fort Ross's ex-manager, Alexander Rotchev, but nothing came of that. Rancheros such as Antonio Coronel and Dolores Sepúlveda had excellent luck at mining. But by 1849 it had become risky for Californians to go anywhere near the Sierra foothills, where they usually found themselves being treated as trespassers — unwanted "greasers." Racism led to such deep-seated resentments that within less than a decade, uncorroborated tales about a shadowy figure named Joaquín Murieta would gain currency until the Anglo-hating bandit would attain the status of a folk hero. Little wonder, then, that the majority of Californians left the gold deposits for others to find. Luís M. Peralta, whose holdings included a land grant that extended from Oakland along the East Bay to San Leandro, rationalized the situation with fatalistic altruism, telling his sons, "God gave that gold to the Americans. If he had wanted the Spaniards to have it, He would have let them discover it before now. So you had better not go after it. . . . You can go to your ranches and raise grain, and that will be your best gold field because we all must eat. . . ."[15] (Peralta's attitude is no doubt well understood by Californians today, who would just as soon leave offshore oil beneath the ocean.)

Vallejo traveled to Sutter's Fort to witness the gold excitement for himself. At Coloma prospectors stood knee-deep in the river, sifting the black sand for bits of metal. The General picked up some of the shining particles as mementos.[16]

By March 10 work on the sawmill at Coloma had been forgotten, and the Mormons who had built it began to prospect for gold full time. In April three of their party followed a creek upstream, discovering the famous Mormon Island, which seemed to enshrine an almost limitless supply of wealth. Four dollars a day was a good wage for laborers at this time, while on ten dollars a day, a man could become rich. Some of the Mormons were now pocketing $250 between sunrise and sunset.[17]

After financier Sam Brannan ran down the streets of San Francisco swinging his hat and shouting, "Gold! Gold! Gold from the American River!" the excitement became uncontrollable. One hardy miner, who in late April had traveled across the Carquinez Straits alone on Semple's ferry boat, returned two weeks later to find two hundred wagons waiting to cross the speeding waters.[18]

What a difference eighteen months had made: instead of mounted Californians galloping south to participate in the season's latest military ballet, long lines of men armed with picks and buckets followed roads that fanned out from Sutter's Fort toward the Stanislaus, Cosumnes, and American rivers. One of the best routes from San Francisco to the gold region went through Sonoma, across the Sacramento Valley, and into the foothills.

Don Mariano observed the whole spectacle from beginning to end. By mid-June of 1848, it was as though a plague had emptied all the towns from Monterey north. Laborers evaporated from Sonoma, and Bob Semple reported that soon there would be only two men left in Benicia, and he was one of them.[19]

The Gold Rush helped to make Sonoma a small social oasis. Anyone approaching the village along the Calle Principal (now called Broadway) could see the balconies of the large residences belonging to Don Mariano, Don Salvador, and Jacob Leese along the west and north sides of the plaza. Among the thousands of nameless miners passing through were a number of colorful individuals who paid their respects to the General at the Casa Grande. There was also an abundance of military men — leaders such as General Persifor Smith and Commodore Thomas Catesby Jones, who thought of Vallejo as a friend and enjoyed discussing the region's future with him. Other officers in the group would become legendary for their Civil War exploits: William Tecumseh Sherman and "Fighting Joe" Hooker. As the General expanded his reputation as host, the little village offered hotel accommodations, and before long, the Blue Wing Inn — just a few steps from the Casa Grande — had become a famous gathering place.

General Vallejo's daughters were undoubtedly part of the Casa Grande's appeal. Permission had to be granted by Don Mariano or Doña Francisca before meetings could take place with young Fannie or Adela. But for some of the callers, it was the mature beauty of Doña Francisca herself that helped offset the stark deprivations of barracks life.

The General's eldest daughter, Fannie (Epifania) Vallejo, was already a striking beauty. James C. Ward predicted she would create "a sensation in Washington, where her father intends to take his family before long."[20] She was later described by Gertrude Atherton as "that rarest of all Spanish beauties, a brown-eyed blonde" who might have been "an American girl, with her quick wit, her frank gayety."[21]

For General Vallejo, an important question had yet to be answered: what role would he play in Americanized California? Was he to be known in coming years as a cattle rancher and agriculturist; or would he try his hand at politics, railroad promotion — or perhaps capital investment? As it turned out, none of these occupations would ever completely monopolize his energies. But his line of direction was by no means defined in 1848 when he and his eldest daughter came under the influence of an energetic, handsome New Yorker — Captain John B. Frisbie — a man who within four years would dominate Vallejo's financial life. The twenty-four-year-old Frisbie was well-educated, ambitious, and had an excellent grasp of business affairs. His family came from Albany, New York, and on his mother's side he was related to Ezra Cornell, founder of Cornell University.[22] He had trained for the law in New York with Leland Stanford, a chance connection that would benefit him throughout his long career in California.

The influential Don Mariano and the American officer did not know it, but the glowing legend of General Vallejo would soon be put into partial eclipse by the financial exploits of the New Yorker. Neither individual would ever quite emerge from the shadow of the other.

Vallejo took an immediate liking to Frisbie. Perhaps the bond was so instantaneous and permanent because it involved the tender affections between the General and his favorite daughter Fannie. As Frisbie was drawn into the family circle, the new connections were steeped in a mixture of shared political dreams, paternal love, and commerce.

Frisbie's curly hair was abundant under his officer's cap, and his eyes shone with youthful intensity, but his gaze also revealed calm determination. There were clues to his inner strength. For instance, he had arrived at Sonoma in charge of a rough-and-tumble company of New York Volunteers. Described by some villagers as little more than Bowery toughs, the soldiers had moved into the barracks just as the war with Mexico was ending. The wiry Frisbie was able to control them. In his home state of New York, he had been elected captain of the Van Rensselaer Guard, reputed to be one of the best-drilled units in New York. Inexperienced in some ways (at least by comparison to General Vallejo), Frisbie was no mere child.

During the next four decades, the multitalented New Yorker would cobble together his own fortune, while taking command of Vallejo's business affairs. Prior to his being assigned to Sonoma, the captain had traveled to the mining regions for Governor Mason (Kearny's replacement) to discover what was going on in the Sierra. His extravagant reports had not sounded credible, so Mason had gone to the mines himself, where he had gained confidence in Frisbie's powers of observation.[23]

Fannie Vallejo was one of the most eligible girls in the territory, and Frisbie was strongly attracted to her. The General, though he would not eagerly sanction his other daughters' choices, permitted chaperoned meetings.

Before much time had passed, the parents of the thirteen-year-old Fannie were consulted and an engagement was arranged. The wedding would take place less than three years later on April 3, 1851. All this was done in keeping with family tradition. Fannie's mother had been engaged to Don Mariano at age thirteen, and Fannie's grandmother had married Ignacio Vallejo when she was fourteen — somewhat earlier than was usual in California during the Mexican period.

Within a few days of Frisbie's arrival at Sonoma, it was learned that on July 4, 1848, the Treaty of Guadalupe Hidalgo had gone into effect. According to its terms, all Californians had one year in which to decide whether they wanted to be Mexicans or U.S. citizens. Californians who did not take steps to reaffirm their Mexican status would automatically become Americans.[24] Article VIII of the treaty guaranteed that "property of every kind" would be "inviolably respected," which made land-holding Californians breathe a sigh of relief. It seemed from the wording of this and other articles that land grants from the Mexican period were to be fully protected. What Vallejo and his friends did not know was that prior to ratification, the U.S. Senate had stricken out Article X of the treaty, which had dealt specifically with Mexican land grants.

The treaty's provisions revealed a genuine desire to prevent wars from ever occurring again between Mexico and the United States. The Rio Grande became the southern boundary between Texas and Mexico, and the $15 million price tag paid by the United States secured not only Alta California but the Territory of New Mexico.[25] The majority of Americans were glad to put the Mexican conflict behind them. It had never been a popular war, and its opponents had included Henry Clay, Daniel Webster, Ralph Waldo Emerson, Abraham Lincoln, Robert E. Lee, U. S. Grant, and Henry David Thoreau.

Several states in Mexico, including Oaxaca, Jalisco, and Chihuahua, wrote formal protests against the treaty, but the majority of Mexican officials felt that an important vestige of their honor — if not their boundaries — had been salvaged. Some adopted a *mea culpa* attitude, blaming themselves for the conflict with the United States. The three Mexican negotiators who signed the treaty — Luís Cuevas, Bernardo Couto, and Miguel Atristain — theorized that California and the other northern territories had been "lost the day the first shot" was fired. "The singular circumstance of our being owners of remote and distant territories (like the Californias) which we were unable to preserve once the war was declared and without a powerful navy of any kind upon which to rely, should have prevented us from trying our luck by the use of arms." One of Santa Anna's former ministers, Ramón Pacheco, condemned the "political cannibalism" which had afflicted Mexico for nearly thirty years, draining the nation's energies and causing the presidency to change hands nine times in less than six years.[26]

Even before the war had ended, a number of Mexican intellectuals had conjectured that California and Texas had never really belonged to Mexico "except in name." Now the great decrease in Mexican territory was seen to be potentially beneficial: "A reduction in size might make for cohesion, concentration, strength."[27] To Mexican citizens who had experienced decades of bloody turbulence at home, these conclusions seemed appropriate enough — though opinions differed then, as they do today. California's new southern boundary was to be one marine league south of San Diego. The United States at last possessed a gateway to the Far East, a Pacific coastline 840 miles long.

In 1848 the American response to the terms of peace was probably best expressed by First Lieutenant William T. Sherman: "Great Jehovah!" he exclaimed. "What a treaty!"[28]

With the war over, Captain Frisbie and the New York Volunteers were mustered out of the service. Happy to resume civilian life, Fannie Vallejo's future husband continued to live north of the bay.

Don Juan Frisbie, as his friends now called him, became a popular local fixture, a thoroughgoing *californio*. He quickly learned Spanish and adopted the rancheros' style of dress. When the famous illustrator and diarist Frank Marryat arrived on the scene, Frisbie inspired some of his artwork and helped equip the globetrotter for a trip to the mines.[29]

A few weeks after their first meeting, Frisbie and General Vallejo decided to try their luck at merchandising. Following the example of successful retailers like Sam Brannan and Thomas Oliver Larkin, the partners opened a number of stores to serve the miners: the first was located on the ground floor of the Casa Grande; the second was in Napa (a chaotic young village filled with hard-drinking men), and the third was in Benicia.[30]

Vallejo was pleased that Frisbie was fluent in the language of law; he would make a gifted business ally, able to steer both their affairs through a difficult period of transition.

For the General and everyone else, there was the phenomenon of calamitous change to be dealt with. Following the war with Micheltorena, there had been five years of constant upheaval. California had needed time to regain its composure; but the only social stability it would know would be a long time in coming. The *californios'* preconquest anxieties about a few hundred more immigrants upsetting the balance of power now seemed absurd in light of the territory's astonishing growth. By 1850 the non-Indian population had reached 92,000 and by the end of 1852, the state had 250,000 people.[31]

The spectacle of foreign populations arriving by the shipload presented a daunting challenge, not only to the Californians but to the Americans as well. Compared to this human deluge, the ousting of Micheltorena, the secularization of the missions, even the Bear Flag Revolt now seemed like minor frenzies — easily comprehended events.

Vallejo later described the different nationalities who arrived without invitation at California's doorstep, all hoping to find wealth. Though his sense of outrage condemned some of them, others, he thought, deserved praise.

Australia sent us a swarm of bandits who on their arrival in California, dedicated themselves exclusively to robbery and assault. . . .

France, desiring to be rid of several thousand lying men and corrupt women, embarked them at the expense of the government on ships which brought them to San Francisco. Italy sent us musicians, and gardeners. The former, of course, lost no time in fraternizing with the keepers of gambling houses and brothels, while the latter, poor but industrious folk, settled in huts or dark caves near the mission, cultivated gardens, raised poultry, and in a short time, became rich since vegetables brought fabulous prices from '48 to '53, and eggs sold from $6.00 to $12.00 a dozen. . . .

Chile sent us many laborers who were very useful and contributed not a little to the development of the resources of the country. Their favorite occupations were wood-cutting and farm labor. There is no doubt that this group of citizens was highly desirable, and it is only to be regretted that so many of them were addicted to drinking and gambling.

China poured upon our shores clouds and more clouds of Asiatics and more Asiatics. These without exception came to California with the determination to use any means of enriching themselves by 'hook or crook', and returning immediately to their own country. . . .

But all these evils became negligible in comparison with the swollen torrent of shysters who came from Missouri and other states of the Union. No sooner had they arrived than they assumed the title of attorney and began to seek means of depriving the Californians of their farms and other properties. The escaped bandits from Australia stole our cattle and our horses; but these legal thieves, clothed in the robes of the law, took from us our lands and our houses, and without the least scruple, enthroned themselves in our homes like so many powerful kings. For them existed no law but their own will and their caprice.[32]

Vallejo's sense of foreboding about attorneys had a special validity for him. The following year, when California's constitutional convention met, he discovered that more than one out of every four delegates was a lawyer.

Despite this sudden abundance of attorneys, there was little regard for the law. Chaotic miners destroyed timber, squatted on ranchos, and ran off cattle. Americans and Californians alike — anyone who possessed land or livestock — suffered at the hands of the gold seekers. Even the former commander of the Bear Flag party, William B. Ide, complained that "All law and civil process is suspended — thefts, robbery, manslaughter and murder are perpetrated without inquest. Our cattle and hogs are killed to feed a foreign banditti, and ourselves are threatened with assassination if we resist."[33]

California's seventh military governor, Brevet General Bennett Riley, realized that something had to be done. No one seemed to know whether the alcalde's cane, the six-gun, or the U.S. Constitution should take precedence. Without waiting for instructions from Congress, the flinty officer called for a constitutional convention to be held at Monterey.[34]

As a seat of government, the old capital's days were numbered, but in September of 1849 Monterey was still a place where ravens set up a raucous din on the tiled roofs, fog created moderate temperatures, and beautiful, brilliant days had grey conclusions. Journalist Bayard Taylor much preferred the quiet port to the pandemonium of San Francisco, mainly because of the congenial circle of Monterey families who formed some of "the most pleasant society to be found in California."[35]

One of Vallejo's friends, Lillburn Boggs, had already given him a book containing the Constitution of the United States. In the back of the volume was Jefferson's *Manual of Parliamentary Practice*.[36] After Don Mariano, Boggs, and Robert Semple were elected to represent the Sonoma district, the General had the chance to put some of his new knowledge to work.

As mentioned earlier, more than a dozen of the forty-eight delegates were lawyers, and some fifteen of the representatives hadn't lived in California even a year. These newcomers wanted to speak of themselves as "the people" and bully the convention, but were they justified in doing so? A contentious Tennessean, William Gwin, who had already served in the U.S. Congress, was a very determined newcomer. Described by Josiah Royce as "the most admirable of all the unprincipled political intriguers in the history of California,"[37] Gwin would soon back the formation of the controversial United States Land Commission, a tribunal set up to challenge the Mexican land grants. His immediate ambition was to become president of the constitutional convention. He served notice early on that foremost in the delegates' minds should be "the great American population" (i.e., the itinerant miners), who then comprised four-fifths of the territory's people.[38] José Antonio Carrillo, impulsive as always, stood up to answer Gwin's challenge. With abrupt and polished belligerence, he announced that the vote of one permanent land-holding citizen from southern California should count for more than a transient miner's.[39] Carrillo's southern district faced its own problems, but it had not yet suffered the spectacle of thousands of foreigners rushing through the countryside searching for gold. Despite the fact that there were now approximately 76,000 Americans and only 13,000 Californians in the country, Carrillo realized that the Californians' influence was going to have a much greater impact than their small numbers would suggest. Congressional leaders in Washington, D.C. — especially the Southern members — hoped to prevent California's admission as a free state. If Carrillo and other Californians complained about the fairness of the Monterey proceedings, the Southern U.S. congressmen might be able to claim that the convention had not been truly representative.[40]

The Californians seldom addressed their opinions to the assembly directly; instead they allowed their viewpoints to be expressed by others. Their friendships with some of the long-term Anglo residents helped them achieve a political outcome that, on the whole, was satisfactory to them.[41]

Larkin, of course, was a delegate. So was his zealous business partner, Robert Semple, who was recovering from a bout of typhoid fever. After Semple was elected president of the convention, Vallejo, seeming like a man of only average height beside the six-foot eight-inch Bear Flagger, took one of his arms; the medium-sized Sutter took the other, and together they escorted the giant to his chair.

Semple's eloquent address reminded the delegates that California had not been settled by ignorant men exclusively. He hoped the "knowledge, enterprise, and genius of the old world will reappear in the new, to guide it to its destined position among the nations of the earth."[42] Gone forever were Semple's grey buckskin suit and the fox-skin cap he had worn into Vallejo's parlor in June of 1846.

Vallejo served on the committees dealing with finance, the preparation of the constitution in Spanish, and privileges and elections.[43]

William T. Sherman climbed the steps of Colton Hall to act as Governor Riley's observer, and John C. Frémont was also on hand. Though his court martial had convicted him of mutiny, disobedience to a superior officer, and "conduct to the prejudice of good order and military discipline," the explorer was not prone to soul-searching, and he had few regrets. President Polk had subsequently dismissed the charge of mutiny and had "remitted" the penalty of dismissal from the service approved by the court. But in a characteristic gesture, Frémont had refused the executive pardon and had resigned from the service. Soon he would run for one of California's U.S. Senate seats.[44]

Another rather mysterious individual, still greatly feared by the Americans, José Castro, was seen in a few public places. Bayard Taylor described him as gloomy, though still physically strong and "very handsome."[45] Word went around that he was planning to retake California. No doubt some of the long-term residents reported this with a wink and a smile.

Vallejo's future son-in-law, John B. Frisbie, made no secret of his political ambitions. He was hoping to run for lieutenant-governor on Sutter's gubernatorial ticket, and he began to generate support for their campaign.[46]

Bayard Taylor spoke with Vallejo between sessions and penned the following impression:

> One of the most intelligent and influential of the Californians is General Mariano Guadalupe Vallejo, whom I had the pleasure of meeting several times during my stay in Monterey. As military commandant during the governorship of Alvarado, he exercised almost supreme sway over the country. He is a man of forty-five years [sic] of age, tall and of a commanding presence; his head is large, forehead high and ample, and eyes dark with a grave, dignified expression. He is better acquainted with our institutions and laws than any other native Californian.[47]

Mexican statutes had long ago outlawed the owning of slaves in California, and the convention delegates quickly made slavery illegal.

Californian delegates also voted as a bloc to permit Indian suffrage. Vallejo's nephew, Pablo de la Guerra (whose colleague from southern California, Manuel Domínguez, was part-Indian), reminded the convention that land-holding Indians had voted under California law, and that besides exercising their political liberty, many had obtained educations. Unfortunately, the convention's majority ultimately decided that only "white male citizens" would have the vote.[48]

The right of a wife to hold separate property led to some grandiloquent debates. Property was an important matter to Doña Francisca and other Californian women who owned their own assets. A Virginian named C. T. Botts praised the advantages of the common law tradition over the California civil code. He claimed that a husband — who had been appointed by God and nature to be the woman's superior guardian — would "take better care of the wife, provide for her better and protect her better than any civil code devised." His phrasing sounds somewhat archaic today, but he insisted that there was "poetry and sentiment" to the theory. "I entreat you, not to lay the rude hand of legislation upon this beautiful and poetical position. . . ."[49]

His appeal did not convince the majority of delegates, however. It was probably no accident that Vallejo, De la Guerra, José Covarrubias, and Jacinto Rodriguez all served on the committee that wrote the provision guaranteeing a wife the right to her own property, "both real and personal."[50]

While appropriate motifs for the state seal were being talked about, Vallejo was reminded of the Bear Flag Revolt. Some of the delegates wanted a grizzly bear included as one of the emblem's features. There were other animals to choose from, and Vallejo's feelings were revealed in a formal declaration:

> *Resolved.* That the bear be taken out of the design for the Seal of California; or, if it do remain, that it be represented as made fast by a *lazo* in the hands of a Vaquero.[51]

The wording suggested that Vallejo's intent may have been humorous, but since the resolution missed passage by only a single vote, many delegates must have thought he had good grounds for his objection.

Vallejo's generosity was already well-established. But when he discussed the possibility of paying for three commissioners to draft a basic code of laws for California's new government, he took a stance of altruism that no one else in the country could match. The commissioners' work would later be submitted for approval to the first session of the state legislature. To some delegates, the matter seemed beyond the scope of their jurisdiction. Speaking in Spanish, Don Mariano clarified his aims: the commissioners would only be preparing a useful framework, not creating laws, and it would cost far less than the legislature meeting in full session later on.[52] Everyone knew he was referring to the fact that California was short of cash. Governor Riley had clamped a lid on the custom's house revenues, holding them in what he called a "Civil Fund," refusing to release even a part of them until authorization came from Washington. As a result, public works were at a standstill. Riley and General Persifor Smith had already traded some hot words on the subject. Roads, courthouses, and jails were needed. Who would pay for them? Since the territory had always lacked a reliable source of income, this was an old problem with no new answers.

Vallejo now offered to pay for the commissioners out of his own pocket. It was a grandiose gesture, prompted by a combination of motives: generosity, his wanting the new regime to prosper, and a desire to win the support of the delegates, since he was planning to run for public office. His prestige was already illustrious, and his pledge enhanced it, for there was no reason to doubt that Vallejo would make good on his promise.

Doubts about some underlying issues persisted, however, and the General's resolution was voted down by a margin of two to one — his nephew Pablo de la Guerra and his old rival, Sutter, voting in favor, while Carrillo and Larkin were among those opposed.[53]

The convention's last days spawned a frantic acceleration of the electoral process: there was to be a one-month campaign for office. On October 13 Governor Riley received and signed the new constitution. Candidates for the legislature now had a little more than four weeks in which to canvass for votes and get elected; following the election, they would attend the legislature's first session. The capital was going to be moved from Monterey to San Jose. Lansford Hastings and William Gwin were behind the removal measure, which carried in the convention by a vote of twenty-one to fourteen.[54]

Despite all the frenzied activity, Vallejo hoped to guide the new government during its first years of existence. Furthermore, about this time — after noticing the chronic animosity between Semple and Larkin — Vallejo envisioned what was to become the state of California's second capital rising beside the deep waters of the Carquinez Straits, not far from Benicia.[55]

Obviously, the gold miners' numbers could not be ignored. No one expected them to elect a Spanish-speaking Californian. But as the energetic Vallejo campaigned for office, he was encouraged by the homage paid him by the settlers — which helped restore his self-confidence.

By their own admission, the majority of voters had no definite idea of whom they were voting for. One flummoxed miner confessed:

> "I was determined to *go it blind*. I went it blind in coming to California, and I'm not going to stop now. I voted for the Constitution, and I've never seen the Constitution. I voted for all the candidates, and I don't know a damned one of them. I'm going it blind all through, I am."[56]

On November 13, 1849, Vallejo was elected state senator, winning his victory over popular miner-minister Jonas Spect.[57] Less than a year later, on September 9, 1850, Congress approved the admission of California — the republic's thirty-first state — into the Union. The enterprise that Don Mariano had worked so hard to bring about — the inclusion of California in the American political system — was a fact.

Consequences

*"I am human and weak. I regret to tell you I can't
pardon some things, although I know that sentence that
'God does not pardon the one who does not pardon.'"*
—Vallejo[1]

I

*F*ew of the prime movers who took part in California's American-ization — Frémont, Sutter, Bidwell, Ide, Larkin — enjoyed long-term contentment in the land they had done so much to change. Larkin died young, at age fifty-six. Before his death, his uneasiness about California's transformation caused him to write, "I begin to yearn after the times prior to July 1846 and all their honest pleasures. . . ."[2] Frémont and Sutter, despite the good fortune Lady Luck had showered on them, spent their final years away from California, financially embarrassed, one jump ahead of dire poverty. Sutter tried unsuccessfully to get Congress to grant him a pension. Frémont, who lost everything through unwise specula-tion, actually received a pension during the last months of his life — too late to enjoy it. He was buried on a bluff overlooking New York's Hudson River. The benefits of respectability and financial security did not pro-tect William B. Ide or John Bidwell from the painful solitude of their final years. Though their land grants were confirmed, both men com-plained of a sense of personal isolation, of having no one in whom they could confide.

But what of General Vallejo? How did the Golden State treat the prophetic Spanish-Californian as the cycle of his life swung from middle years to old age? People in the late nineteenth and early twentieth centu-ries often pictured him as a retired ranchero with courtly manners and rampant sideburns, buoyed up through financial reverses by the new society he had helped to create[3] — a man who could be found "sunning himself on his patio."[4] Gertrude Atherton told her large readership that Vallejo had been spared the fate of other rancheros through the support of John B. Frisbie and the generosity of "Count" Agoston Haraszthy's family. Thanks to the Haraszthys, Don Mariano "was not reduced to poverty."[5] Confirmation of this picture was found in the words of exiled Mexican poet Guillermo Prierte, who remembered Vallejo as being "as broad-shouldered and active as any youth. . . . Laughter comes easily to his lips and his speech is salty."[6]

The physical descriptions were true enough, but as the turbulent 1850s began, Vallejo's love affair with American democracy was about to undergo its harshest trial — far more grueling than what he had endured during the six-week imprisonment at Sutter's Fort. At first, few omens gave warning that a time of suffering lay ahead. In April of 1850, while still state senator, the General tried to settle the state capital problem by giving California 156 acres on the west end of the Carquinez Straits about seven miles from Benicia. He wanted to call the place Eureka, but his friends convinced him to name it for himself, Vallejo. The General also offered California $370,000 in cash, earmarked for the construction of public buildings (including a university, governor's mansion, capital building, orphanage, and insane asylum).[7]

State leaders happily endorsed the proposal, likening Don Mariano's offer to the legacy of a prince to his people. More than any other gesture, it caused the public to think of the General as California's most open-handed benefactor. The eruption of wealth during the Gold Rush had not yet created parallel extravagances in the fostering of culture. Vallejo — whose optimism was probably at its peak in early 1850 — hoped the gift would promote higher education and social change. His altruism was not without its personal motive: he expected the land surrounding the new capital to appreciate in value. However, the goodwill of his offer was never questioned.

But the Gold Rush was not a patrician affair. It was more like a hornpipe bacchanal. A Californian ranchero might gain status by this sort of potlatch giveaway, but Yankees in the early 1850s looked upon the phenomenon as a weakness. They expected things "to pay." If Vallejo hoped to establish himself as the state's leading *patrón*, he would have to do it alone.

Nineteen other cities vied for the honor of becoming the capital, and when the decision was submitted to a public vote, the Vallejo site received 7,477 votes, outdistancing its nearest rival, San Jose, by nearly six to one.[8]

Guaranteeing his splendid offer, Vallejo posted a bond for $500,000 and swore before Robert R. Pierpont that he was not only good for the amount, but was worth "in property, real and personal, one million dollars (some thirteen million dollars in 1990 currency) over and above all liabilities or demands against him."[9] John B. Frisbie, among others, helped Vallejo plan the new city. Then, on July 3, 1850, the son-in-law leapt into the foreground of the General's finances by obtaining his power of attorney.[10] This meant Frisbie would now be able to bargain, grant, or sell the General's holdings in Sonoma, Napa, and Solano counties. Such an arrangement was not uncommon in California, and it undoubtedly helped the partners fund their project. Regarding the new city's location, Vallejo won the first few skirmishes. With Frisbie's help, the General found prominent investors to underwrite the venture. But it soon became clear that some of these men were opportunists who could not be trusted. In fact, the battle was far from over.

On January 9, 1852, John McDougal became California's second governor, succeeding Peter Burnett. Described by his friends as a "gentlemanly drunkard," McDougal had only a hazy idea of how far construction had gone at the new capital, and he didn't bother to find out. Soon after his inauguration, he ordered the state offices to be moved to Vallejo. The premature shift was a portent of disaster for Don Mariano. In a year's time, he had only succeeded in putting up a frame State House. The building was considered to be superior to the "graceless unfinished crate" which had served the legislators at San Jose,[11] but for the most part, the hilly ground near the mouth of the Napa River, adjacent to the Carquinez Straits, was still a *tabula rasa,* justifiably called "an imaginary city." Men who favored Sacramento were gleeful, for the government's untimely move to Vallejo made it seem almost certain that Don Mariano's scheme would fail. The few accommodations available in Vallejo cost more than most men could pay. Luckily, a steamer was tied up at the wharf, and it housed approximately one hundred people — a fair share of the capital's population.

On January 12, the legislators voted to adjourn to Sacramento. The steamship *Empire,* which had been packed with men for about a week, became a sort of legislative ark which welcomed the rest of the local residents. Astute barkeepers tagged along behind the lawmakers. Even the town barber collected his razor and trotted aboard. Carpets from the State House were "torn up from the floors. . . . China chairs were tumbled in a heap . . . and carried . . . down to the wharf."[12] Then the *Empire* began its historic journey to John Sutter's old domain.

If it had not been for the disastrous floods of 1852, the capital probably would have stuck fast then and there on the banks of the Sacramento.

Understandably, General Vallejo assumed that the removal might be permanent. On January 27, 1852, he wrote a letter to the legislature, referring to the group of men who had helped him develop the capital:

. . . This organization after much fruitless effort, gradually ceased to have any practical life or vigor, and I proceeded myself to provide a temporary State House and offices of the State. . . . The credit and resources dedicated by me . . . have been shattered and destroyed.[13]

Realizing that his partners might leave him high and dry, the General lost enthusiasm for the project. By late 1852, another rival appeared —Thomas Oliver Larkin — who wanted to make Benicia California's capital city. To lure away Vallejo's backers, Larkin gave sizable payoffs to some of the General's former allies, notably General Estell and Major James D. Graham.[14]

But Sacramento didn't give up. One steamship had already served as the legislative ark; now another acted the part of flirtatious bawd: Sacramento promoters loaded the steamer "with provisions and liquor which cost them some $13,000." In the short run, their attempt failed, but the festivities were never quite forgotten.[15]

For a while, the capital staggered about like the crazed Io, returning to Vallejo in January of 1853, then a month later, migrating seven miles to Benicia. In the wake of the Benicia move, the General was released from his bond. In terms of capital, he had spent some $98,450, of which Frisbie had received $1,200 in fees.[16] Larkin, like General Vallejo and most of the other hopefuls who spent money to lure the fickle legislature, lost his investment. By 1855 Sacramento had won out.

As Vallejo's dream shredded to nothing, some people characterized him as a rainbow chaser, a man "addicted to idealistic fancies. [to the] concoction of magnificent schemes and projects difficult of being realized."[17] In reality, his ideas were sound enough, but he was a careless businessman and — when it came to relying on others — a stoic. This was not the last time he would be disappointed.

The failure of the capital project created the first noticeable crack in his serenity. He had staked a great deal on the scheme, lavishing not only money, but pride and energy. Understandably, he was wounded by its lack of success. His children noted his sudden shortness of temper, and he was bad company for everyone, including himself. Part of the problem stemmed from the fact that Vallejo wanted homage from California's newcomers — not just some of them, but all Americans. It grieved him that the respect he received was partial, marred by individuals who didn't want to help him at all, who wanted to see his power base dismantled and moved elsewhere. For the first time, Vallejo's futurism began to ebb. The man who had rolled out the welcome mat for the Americans began

to assume a defensive posture. He had been willing enough to suffer for
a better future, but he had not expected that future to turn bleak or
threatening. From his eminence of pride, it would be a long dismal reach
down to touch his humility, but he would do it.

He decided not to run again for the state senate. During his brief
first term, he had served on no less than seven committees, had promoted the so-called "Act for the Government and Protection of the Indians" (about which more will be said shortly), and when a bill had
circulated that would have kept "Free Negroes and Persons of Color"
from entering California, he had voted to postpone it. His famous report
on the derivation of California place names received wide circulation.[18]
Not only would remaining in the senate have meant daily confronta-
tions with hostile men who wanted to undermine his influence, but he
would have had to parry sharp criticisms from home as well: Doña
Francisca accused him of placing his legislative work above the needs of
his family. He explained to her that his objective was to organize
"a government by fair means," if that was possible. Thinking of his
political job as a temporary but important duty, he hoped she would
appreciate the work's redeeming features.[19]

But when we look at the "government by fair means" Vallejo worked
to establish, it's clear that, despite his capacity for hope, he could operate as
a servant of the status quo. The clearest evidence of this was the "Act for
the Government and Protection of the Indians." With John Bidwell and a
Southerner named David F. Douglas, the General helped patch together the
senate and assembly versions of the law. The resulting statute ought to have
rejected the old mold into which the relationship between master and worker
had been poured during Hispanic times, but it didn't. True, an Indian could
now obtain a trial by jury in a dispute with a white man, but the law's other
provisions revealed a robust duplicity: Indians could not give evidence against
white men in court! Native Americans who had been arrested as vagrants
or for other minor offenses could be hired out for up to four months to the
first white man willing to pay their bail. One single refrain seemed to accompany all the provisions of this legal song and dance: the Indians' time
and labor belonged to the white man. Agricultural entrepreneurs like Vallejo
and Bidwell wanted to make sure the Indians would serve the economy as
they had under Mexican rule. But the law had unforeseen consequences,
and in 1863 it finally had to be repealed.[20]

Fearing defeat at the hands of the increasingly militant squatters in
his district, Vallejo withdrew from state government. In a gesture that
was perhaps symbolic of the second half of his life, he moved his family

away from the commotion of the Sonoma plaza to a new residence known as Lachryma Montis (Mountain Tear), one-half mile west of the plaza. It was located near a spring which unfailingly produced pure artesian water.

The house itself had a placid exterior, but in actuality it was a maverick structure — a two-story "Boston House" — Victorian in style with arpeggios of decorative gingerbread along the eaves. Wide courses of adobe bricks insulated the building's walls. Its Anglo exterior thus concealed an Hispanic interior. The Indians had built the Casa Grande, but they had not fashioned this house. Much of the woodwork was cut with a scroll saw in the United States and shipped around the Horn. Prices for labor and materials being extravagantly high during the Gold Rush, Vallejo had to pay close to ten times as much to build Lachryma Montis as it would have cost him in 1847.[21] He turned the old Casa Grande into a schoolhouse, St. Mary's Hall, which educated many of the local children, including his own.

John B. Frisbie hoped to interest his East Coast business associates in the General's land. In 1853 Frisbie went to New York, taking along his wife Fannie and her brother Platon. The little boy who had held the Bear flag down with his toe was twelve years old by this time, and he was amazed to see the great eastern cities that had spawned the thousands of Americans who had migrated to California. While acquainting his friends with the advantages of speculating in West Coast property, Frisbie tried to find markets for the General's wheat. Before many years had passed, Frisbie's associates either bought General Vallejo's land or held mortgages on it. Frisbie also raised capital for the planned Benicia and Marysville Railroad.[22] A born lobbyist, he would see to it that the U.S. government purchased Mare Island (on the Soscol) instead of Sausalito for its naval station.

In referring to Frisbie, the General would say, "My esteem is unlimited." Frisbie, in turn, realized that he had obtained a well-connected friend in Vallejo, and he believed that the General deserved all the praise people showered on him. "If there is a person on earth from whom I entertain a sincere affection, it is yourself," he once wrote the General, "and it ever has been . . . a cherished object with me to merit yours in return."[23]

The mid-1850s saw profits from the Gold Rush fizzle while immigration fell off. The state went into a depression, and cattle prices spiraled downward. A cow that might have netted the General seventy or even ninety dollars in 1852 was worth about sixteen dollars four years later. Cattle-rustling, combined with a drought in the late 1850s, helped to destroy the rancho system. As the Gold Rush lost momentum, merchant ships arriving in California added their cargoes to the surplus goods already stacked on the wharves. Cash became king. Always accustomed to the luxury of ready money, the General did not like to lose face. His solution was to sell and mortgage his land. In most cases, it was his son-in-law who arranged the transactions.

There were other reasons why Vallejo's empire couldn't sustain him. Squatters tied up some of the region's biggest claims, making it impossible for owners to sell their acreage or raise stock on it; fences were torn down and timber carted off. As late as the mid-1870s, Vallejo could walk out the front door of his Lachryma Montis estate to find that "whole lengths" of fence had been dismantled. Uninvited guests had milked the cows during the night and carried off livestock. He complained that if the thieves were taken to court, he as landowner would "lose the suit and moreover will pay for it."[24]

It wasn't typical of Vallejo to look around for people on whom to blame his misfortunes. He made a catalog of high priority items he required for happiness, and first on his list was "a good home." Another important entry echoed Pindar's famous lines regarding the importance of worldly goods; gold placed only second; first, and "best of all things is water." The smooth operation of Lachryma Montis depended on "water in abundance for everything."[25]

The General valued pleasure, but his fun-loving side had to struggle to survive after his finances went into a slide. Perhaps this was the reason he took an overly tolerant attitude toward the antics of his mischievous son Napoleon. The boy seemed to be magnetized by the outdoors; he was also reckless, and his closest friends were Indian children. Though the town no longer had to fear Indian attacks, the tribes had by no means disappeared from the Sonoma region, and Vallejo was maintaining friendly relations with his Indian neighbors.

As Vallejo wrote, "childhood has the right" to joy,[26] and he liked to indulge all his offspring, especially "little Nap." When the father bought a $2,000 silver-mounted saddle for himself, he also bought one for Napoleon valued at $1,500.[27]

In the Sonoma Valley and within the confines of his estate, Vallejo sought a haven from the turmoil of California's agitated economy. Wealthy families had already found themselves impoverished, and poor immigrants were rising to opulence. As his finances became shaky, he wondered if the troubles plaguing him might not be avoided by his daughters, and he sought rich husbands for them. He encouraged his daughter Natalia to marry Bear Flagger Granville P. Swift, who had made a fortune in the mines. Swift had found so much gold that he was burying it at his ranch. His gaunt, spooky good looks were appealing to the opposite sex, but he was hopeless at the formalities of courtship. Sometimes he couldn't even mutter answers to a young woman's questions. A distressed Natalia told her father that Swift needed to learn how to shake hands. "He pumps instead of shakes," she complained, and added that he was not "the kind of man that I . . . could admire."[28] The marital plans of the General's other daughters tested the family's flexibility and exposed touchy social issues. This was especially true when Adela Vallejo, a year younger than her sister Fannie, wanted to marry Dr. Levi Frisbie, John B. Frisbie's older brother. The subject never failed to inspire violent mood swings in the General. Adela fell in love with the doctor when she was seventeen years old. Levi was almost sixteen years her senior, and both Don Mariano and Doña Francisca had hoped she would marry a younger man. The General even had a likely suitor picked out, William A. Cornwall, Secretary of California's senate and a political ally.[29] Compared with the seasoned Levi Frisbie, Cornwall may have seemed unappealing to Adela for any number of reasons. Her heart was solidly fixed on Levi. Vallejo asked her to wait four years, thus placing both her feelings and Dr. Frisbie's on hold. As a guiding principal, the General believed that parental authority should not be questioned in the early years. But after a child matured, this authority had "very sacred limits and when children are old enough to contract marriage, they should be advised and nothing more."[30] The theory was sound, but he ignored it in Adela's case. Her twenty-first birthday came and went, and her father remained adamantly opposed to the match. The source of the problem wasn't money. In fact, the reason for the General's resentment has never been made clear, but he definitely had an aversion to John Frisbie's older brother.

In early 1858, Vallejo's rejection of Levi Frisbie began to undermine his own sense of well-being at Lachryma Montis, because some of his older children as well as Doña Francisca sympathized with Adela.

One of the things standing in the way of Vallejo's capitulation was the strict obedience required in the California *familia*. Sir George Simpson had been surprised by the "profound respect" children showed parents in California — even after they were grown up. A son with his own home and a large family would never presume to "sit, or smoke, or remain covered in presence of his father," nor would a daughter, "whether married or unmarried, enter into too great familiarity with the mother."[31]

Vallejo's friend, William Heath Davis, remembered his own ordeal while courting Maria Estudillo, and could testify that young couples engaged to be married

> were permitted little association by themselves. They were scarcely allowed to see each other or to converse together except in the presence of their parents. . . . The courtship was usually arranged by the mother of the young lady, or sometimes a favorite aunt was sought and first consulted by the young gentleman who desired the daughter or niece in marriage. If the suitor was considered a worthy person by the father, the young lady was communicated with, after which a request in writing came from the young man to the father. If the application was deemed satisfactory, he sent a written reply.[32]

Vallejo had not yet heard Adela "plead her case in her defense," so she had to endure a drawn-out trial of her will. When the General was suddenly summoned to the San Cayetano estate on family business, it probably eased tensions at Lachyrma Montis. Adela might, in fact, have suspected her father would take a different view of her marital plans after he was away from the house. If so, she understood his psychology well. But the change wasn't sudden.

Vallejo's work at the Watsonville rancho involved his acting as court-appointed family administrator following the death of his youngest brother, the popular Juan Antonio Vallejo, who had been killed in a riding accident during a rodeo. Adela, however, was still very much on Vallejo's mind, and he wrote a letter to Francisca from San Cayetano, stubbornly defending what he termed "the domestic rules of the family."

Francisca knew that both in his personal life and in his political affairs, Don Mariano could proceed by indirection. This was an unconscious tendency, and he was probably not aware that his unspoken dissatisfaction with John Frisbie was influencing his attitude toward the older Levi. In view of the fact that John Frisbie now wielded more financial power than Don Mariano in the family's business affairs, the thought of having two Frisbie sons-in-law may have seemed irksome, if not stifling.

Before long, the General set aside his personal objections and sent Adela his parental consent. But this did not signify approval, for he had no desire to attend the wedding.

The bride-to-be chose July 26, 1858 as the date for the ceremony. She wrote her father to say "how much happier I would be if you come to be present. . . . It is my only wish and I pray you will not be angry with me.[33] Mail delivery between Sonoma and Monterey was by this time quite fast, and appeals for his presence at the event continued to reach him from Lachryma Montis.

Doña Francisca tried to get him to return home, complaining, "I myself cannot take care of everything." Her letter included many *abrazos* and "little kisses."[34]

Vallejo's answer sprang from motives that can only be guessed at. He praised Francisca for having penned her last message herself, instead of finding someone else to write it for her, but he completely sidestepped the matter of Adela's wedding. He probably wanted his letter to be as overwhelming as a sudden kiss.

> I still haven't forgotten what you said to me the night before I came away. You were seated at the foot of my bed, taking off a stocking . . . and I was looking at you. What different sensations in that moment. I don't want to remember it almost but no, I do, too want to remember it. How many things you said to me. And as I was looking at you . . . how beautiful you seemed to me. Do you believe me and if you don't — I would die of grief. I believe that you will be happy with this letter and moreover, more than happy as I am coming to see you soon. Keep in mind that as soon as I arrive I am going to plant a kiss on you, straight from the heart and will you return it?[35]

We know only one thing for sure: the absent husband did not return home for several months after writing this letter. Perhaps the words came from the pen of an erring spouse. Vallejo had more than one old flame in nearby Monterey. Or it's possible his passion for Doña Francisca had been revived by their long separation. Who can say? But there were other elements of this kind in his married life, and Vallejo sometimes wrote Francisca about the attraction he felt for other women. She once asked him to look up her cousin, Doña Amparo Ruiz de Burton in San Francisco, a highly talented woman with whom Vallejo had already corresponded; and when Vallejo finally located her, he sent his wife an explicit account of their meeting.

> Pleasant and very amiable as she is, I did not kiss her (but I had a great temptation to do so) as I found her very beautiful. After the usual greetings we had a conversation, holding hands for two and one-half hours. To be sure I was charmed with her. I do not know

whether she or I talked the most. I had a very pleasant time with the lady whom I liked very much, a lady with a good disposition, frank, gay and engagingly provocative, I believe like you. I also believe she understands and appreciates my character and intentions. I have invited her and her husband to pay us a visit.[36]

On another occasion, after the attorney Henry Gaston had walked into the Occidental Hotel, leaving Mrs. Gaston seated in a carriage outside, she was approached by a man with abundant "mutton-chop" sideburns, who took off his hat, bowed, and spoke engagingly. She protested that she knew no Spanish and almost immediately her husband, Mr. Henry Gaston, came out of the hotel. He smiled and made a formal presentation of General Vallejo to his wife. For a moment, Don Mariano was nonplussed. Then he paid his compliments:

"... a thousand pardons, but with such an exquisitely beautiful wife, you will understand the great temptation of any gentleman to become acquainted with her. So there may be no misunderstanding, Señor Gaston, I merely asked the gracious lady in Spanish if I had not had the honor and pleasure of meeting her previously."[37]

Don Mariano remained in the Watsonville area long after giving Adela his parental consent, and Francisca took the persevering daughter to San Francisco. The women spent several days shopping for a trousseau and stayed in one of the better hotels. The cost of the trousseau alone came to $1,700 (almost $20,000 in today's currency).

One of Vallejo's attorneys, Benjamin S. Brooks, received a visit from Doña Francisca and politely granted her request for a $1,300 loan on the General's account. Vallejo later received a letter from Brooks which complained, "You well know I have no money and it put me in a difficult spot and I beg of you to tell your wife not to ask me for such things."[38]

After the wedding ceremony took place in Sonoma, Adela and her sister Natalia wrote to their father again. Adela's letter showed she was still stung by his absence at the wedding; her tone was formal. She ended it, "I hope you will find yourself in good health and that you may come soon." Natalia was more frank when she admitted, "How often I . . . wished [for] your presence. How bad it looked without you being here."[39]

Marriage or no marriage, it almost seemed to require the death of Vallejo's youngest daughter, María Benica, and a near-fatal accident involving Napoleon Vallejo to affect a reconciliation between the General and Levi Frisbie.

In autumn the exuberant Napoleon was carried into a doctor's office, unconscious. The eight-year-old had accidentally stumbled and fallen on a knife he was carrying, opening a deep chest wound. The bleeding had resulted in a severe hemorrhage. Doña Francisca held one hand, Don Mariano the other, while they kept a long vigil, praying for him. At one point, the boy felt a prickling sensation in his veins, his hands suddenly felt warm and his pulse began to beat strongly. From that moment on, he began to improve.[40] It did not seem necessary to send for Dr. Frisbie at the time.

When the boy was almost well, the General decided to throw a two-week celebration in his honor. Some seventy-five Indian leaders came, as did numerous Indian tribesmen. Each day five bulls from the Vallejo herd, as well as hogs and chickens, were slaughtered to feed the guests. Indian sporting events took place in the afternoons, and at night Doña Francisca wrapped Napoleon in a blanket and brought him to the place where the Indians performed sacred dances. The boy watched his young friend, Comola, leap and spin in the firelight with fox tails tied to his heels. The Vallejos also enjoyed it when one of Chief Solano's sons, Joaquín, sang to them in the Suisun dialect.[41]

After Napoleon had recovered and the General was away from Lachryma Montis, other members of the family asked Dr. Frisbie to examine Napoleon's little sister, María Benicia, who was gravely ill. The doctor tried to get Vallejo's permission before entering the house, but no one could find him. The General did not take kindly to the idea when he learned of the visit, and Frisbie withdrew from the case. A week later, the little girl died. Regretting he had not accepted Frisbie's aid, Vallejo could not help blaming himself for her death. He grieved a long time for the child, and in his journal consoled himself by thinking of her as being "transplanted to the Land of the Sun."[42]

Later that year, Napoleon experienced a relapse. His lungs had been affected, and this time the distraught General welcomed Frisbie's help. The examination yielded a favorable report: the boy's lungs were functioning normally again. Napoleon completely recovered, thanks to the doctor's care. Thus began a warm friendship between Vallejo and Levi Frisbie which lasted until the General's death.

II

All during the late 1850s, the United States Land Commission, brainchild of Senator William Gwin, had been doing its work, using the basic assumption that every California land grant was invalid until "proven up" by the owner. This seemed to contradict Articles VIII and IX of the Treaty of Guadalupe Hidalgo, which guaranteed that the residents of the territories affected by the treaty "shall be maintained and protected in the free enjoyment of their liberty and property."[43] Vallejo had been forced to hire a battery of lawyers to represent him in the courts at prices comparable to today's high legal costs. Delays were common, and seventeen years was the average length of time a California landowner had to wait for his patent to be granted after filing a petition.[44] The losses the General had experienced during the previous decade had taken their toll, and as 1860 approached, Don Mariano realized that his affairs were approaching a crisis. As mentioned earlier, his income from hides and tallow alone had once been estimated at $96,000 annually,[45] which was approximately tenfold the amount his investments were yielding in the early 1860s. John B. Frisbie, who received a fee of approximately 10 percent for managing the General's assets, was trying to look on the bright side of things, and reported with more hope than accuracy that good fortune was "manifestly getting in our favor." But he could only guarantee Vallejo $10,000 a year from their investments.[46]

Unlike Larkin or Frisbie, Vallejo hadn't built wharves or commercial buildings. The majority of his wealth was in ranch and agricultural land, which made him particularly vulnerable to the heavy blow that fell on March 24, 1862. The U.S. Supreme Court overturned a lower court's confirmation of Vallejo's Soscol grant.[47] By then, Vallejo had spent tens of thousands of dollars defending his land claims in the lower courts, and he had already disposed of more than half of his Soscol property. To lose title to what remained was an enormous setback which carried the onus of disgrace, since the friends who had bought his property — Semple, Larkin, Revere, and scores of others—had believed in the security of the General's title.

A policy change in Washington stood behind the justices' decision. At first the Supreme Court had taken a generous attitude toward California land grants, deciding almost all disputed cases in the owners' favor. But during the court test of José Limantour's claims in 1857, some of the documents proved to be forged.[48] As time passed, the federal judges' skepticism increased. Newly-appointed U.S. Attorney General Jeremiah S. Black, aided by future Secretary of War Edwin M. Stanton, began to scrutinize all grants for fraud; during Black's tenure, twenty-five claims "were either rejected or remanded to the district court for further consideration. . . ."[49] Whenever possible, large holdings were broken up or invalidated. The new policy was in high gear by the time Vallejo's Soscol grant came to the Supreme Court's attention. Though the lower courts had established the legitimacy of Governor Micheltorena's grant to Vallejo, Judge Black objected to the transfer on three grounds: he claimed Micheltorena had the power to *give* the land to Vallejo, but not to *sell* it to him for five thousand dollars; secondly, the grant (though not considered to be a forgery) was in excess of eleven leagues; finally, the sale had not been duly recorded. In his dissenting opinion, Justice Wayne referred to cases of a similar kind that had been approved by the California Land Commission, including a twelve-league grant made by Governor Pío Pico in return for a payment of twelve thousand dollars. Furthermore, the language of previous Supreme Court decisions indicated that a money payment did create "a just and equitable claim against the government." Governor Micheltorena himself had deeded the land directly to General Vallejo for cash, stating in the document that he had by "virtue of the faculties with which I am invested by the Supreme Government of the Mexican Nation, sold him [Vallejo] the said land, Soscol for the sum of Five Thousand Dollars, which this government has received to its satisfaction."[50]

Another dissenting Justice, Robert Grier, rapped his colleagues for challenging Vallejo's right to a grant that Mexican authorities had never repudiated. He proposed this question:

> . . . [W]hy should we forfeit a property for which a large price has been paid to the Mexican government on the assumption that the Mexican government would not have confirmed it but would have repudiated if for want of formal authority? Vallejo was an officer of the army, high in the confidence of the government. His salary as an officer had been in arrears. In time of difficulty he furnished provisions and money to the government of the territory. How do we know that Mexico would have repudiated its sale of 80,000 acres as robbery of its territory when two decent colonists having a few horses and cows could have 100,000 [acres] for nothing. I believe the Mexican Government would have honestly and honorably dealt with their valued servant and the same obligation rests upon us by force of the treaty [of Guadalupe Hidalgo].[51]

Vallejo was badly shaken by the High Court's ruling. Most Americans who reviewed the matter felt that he had been robbed.

Frisbie found himself with more to lose on the Soscol than Don Mariano. In 1854 he had paid the General $25,000 for the town of Vallejo and had begun to work on projects that gave Frisbie control of local transportation, banking, and farming interests. After the Supreme Court handed down its unfavorable decision, Frisbie used all his skills as a power broker to lobby for a preemption bill, which passed the U.S. Congress in 1863. This enabled him and his friends to retain their Soscol holdings by purchasing land at the government price of $1.25 an acre.[52] It worked out well for men with ready cash, but poorly for land owners like Vallejo, who were already paying high rates of interest on mortgages.

Immediately following the Soscol reversal, the General wrote his son-in-law a letter, which showed the extent to which Frisbie controlled Don Mariano's finances. Considering the circumstances, Vallejo's restraint was remarkable. He said he did not want Frisbie to "be bothered in any way in helping me get out of the sad, critical, and agonizing state" in which he had found himself. Nevertheless, he was "reduced to asking you to tell me if . . . I have some right to the Sobrante, the Zabacca and the Potrero" properties. Frisbie's answer indicated that he thought of two of the properties as "our joint property," and that the third holding (the Zabacca) "is practically the property of Mr. Atherton who loaned me the entire amount of the purchase money and now holds the mortgage upon it about $42,000 quite as much as it would sell for."[53]

It does not seem possible that a friendship — much less a business partnership — could have survived such a debacle, but it did. Perhaps the answer can be found in the close ties Vallejo retained with his daughter Fannie and the fact that Frisbie had given her as much security and comfort as she could want.

Nevertheless, the General and Doña Francisca were at times acutely bitter about the way things were turning out. Vallejo noticed in the paper one day that Frisbie and some of his associates — still ascending the trajectory of their good fortune — had received patents on their land. "Frisbie has told me nothing which is very strange; but perhaps some day he will remember that I exist and that there is a *'General Vallejo'* *who remembers him at all times in all circumstances.*"[54] When the scale of Frisbie's mismanagement became evident, one of the first words Doña Francisca applied to him was "ingrate." In writing to her son, Platon, she said, "I am going to tell you why your Papa is so silent; why he is very poor. Captain Frisbie has given bad accounts to your father. . . . You wouldn't think the Captain capable of treating your papa so badly, would you? But he is the worst of all. The others hardly knew us but this one is married to one of my daughters, is an ingrate, and a shame, but he is an American and we can't hope for anything but tricks."[55]

For native Californians, gratitude was always considered to be a virtue, as important as the debt of hospitality had been to the ancient Greeks. Once it was betrayed, the offender could be written off; he was nothing, an "ingrate."

General Vallejo, however, did not agree with his wife's blanket judgment of Americans, and he forgave Frisbie. He had relied heavily on other men, including Martin E. Cook, Benjamin Brooks, and Henry Clement without feeling betrayed by them. But the General's changed status created friction with his wife. Doña Francisca was a proud, somewhat conventional woman, conscious of her social standing and fond of dressing in expensive Parisian silks and velvets. During the Bear Flag Revolt, she had exercised considerable independence, and one of her sons later described her as a level-headed woman "who believed in Woman's rights." As the Casa Grande's *patrona*, she had worked hard to organize the cooking, sewing, washing, sweeping, and gardening. She had been equally devoted to the needs of her children, and her example to her daughters was one of service and self-sacrifice within the family. She accepted Church dogma without question and gave religion a high place in her life. On the whole, her strengths were emotional rather than intellectual.

In her relations with the General, she could by no means be called a voiceless minion, performing her duties in silence, always complying with his wishes. As frugality became necessary, she took the initiative and tried to help him. Figs, apples, and grapes yielded well in the Sonoma soil, and she marketed the produce both locally and in San Francisco. When, in the mid-1860s, the General had to return to the San Cayetano Rancho in Watsonville to resolve the legal melee which was still going on years after the death of his youngest brother, she suggested that the time had come to open a public bath at Lachryma Montis. Vallejo's ego, at this point, was in bad repair. All his inner defenses were marshaled to protect his ever-increasing vulnerability. And here was another blow. In his response to her letter, he told her that this recent suggestion of hers had "shattered" his brain. For one thing, their bathing area was too small for the *public*, it was suited to "the privacy of the family." And something in her letter made him think she had already put her plans into effect without consulting him. He felt ashamed to think that they now had to "give everyone access" to their home in order to hunt up a few dollars. Old resentments rose to the surface in the exchanges that followed. "We think differently," he complained. As husband and wife they seemed to be "poorly matched in some ways."[56]

Using the sarcasm for which both the Vallejo and Carrillo families were famous, she replied, "As you know I have a husband; I asked for his opinion. . . . [in order] to help you in some way on my own." She then revealed the depth of her pain. "What small consideration you give to me. . . . I well know the indifference with which you look upon me after so many years that I have served you as wife, as friend, as companion. . . . Always the same problems, always the same difficulties. I think one way, you another. I think I do well and you say I do poorly — then which of the two is right?"

The public baths had only been a suggestion; she'd gladly forget about them. But what about the truck gardening projects? "I am delivering to the Hotel: vegetables; I'm delivering hens' eggs to the bakery . . . I am telling you now and if you don't like it, tell me so that I won't deliver any more."

Not long after sending his angry note, he had studied her first message with a clearer head and realized his mistake. Hastily, he wrote an apology, admitting that his diatribe had not been "very loving." In another letter, he assured her she was "doing right" by selling the produce.[57]

But things got worse. She was a proud woman and he, by his own admission, was a high-toned, unusual man, who hated to see her and the family suffer "on my account." From the fall of 1869 through late 1870, the husband and wife lived apart. People gossiped on, but divorce, of course, was unthinkable. She stayed with her daughter Fannie in the town of Vallejo, while Don Mariano remained at Lachryma Montis. He was used to a house full of children, but now his youngest daughters were away at boarding school. He did much of the cooking himself, dusted, took care of his voluminous correspondence, and kept things in order. Chief Solano's widow, La Isadora, ironed Vallejo's shirts, but he pressed his other clothes himself.

Don Salvador was living at Lachryma Montis too, which was another reason Doña Francisca had gone to live with her daughter. She objected to Don Salvador's crude ways with women, especially his treatment of her sister María de la Luz (Don Salvador's wife).

The Indian fighter's life on horseback had left him crippled from multiple fractures of his arms and legs, and he spent his last years dependent on his brother. The estate did have a cook, a Chinese who wasn't always on hand. Sometimes the companionable brothers made "a very good stew, with corn and really fine beans."

An Italian neighbor's little boy, Jacobino, made sympathetic gibes about the General's marital status. Vallejo drew sketches of a nearby train for the youngster, and the eight-year-old responded with poignant remarks: for instance, the boy didn't like the way the *patrona* left the *patrón* alone. It seemed odd to him that Doña Francisca should go off and "spend money" while the General remained at the house without even "a little meat and tobacco to smoke."[58] The General couldn't help but laugh at Jacobino's simplistic view of things.

But as far as Doña Francisca was concerned, she could be devoted to only one man. Faults or no faults, she would always love Don Mariano. By the mid-1870s she and the General had adjusted to their changed circumstances, and they were reunited.

Very different from Señora Vallejo was her intellectual cousin, Amparo Ruiz de Burton, a novelist married to Colonel Henry Burton, former commander of the *Susan Drew*. Acutely aware of the Vallejo family's plight (a condition that was shared by almost all native Californians), Doña Amparo expressed her thoughts on the subject to the General's son, Platon. She referred specifically to the U.S. Land Commission: "We are a child's handful in their mighty grasp; they can crush us with impunity." Unfortunately, the liberty and equality of rights so valued by Americans seemed to "stop when it meets a Californian." To heal their bruised hearts, the Californians should cultivate loyalty to their own group. This allegiance ought to be pursued "without bitterness and aversion, which some seem to think, is the best proof of patriotism; without the narrowness of view which will not see virtues in others...."[59]

Probably the most literate Hispanic woman in California at the time, Doña Amparo was, like Vallejo, a failed entrepreneur who had tried her hand at various schemes to make money. She owned the Rancho Jamul east of San Diego and another large holding in Ensenada, Mexico. Her property cost her harrowing litigation. In 1885 she published a novel, *The Squatter and the Don*, which was half historical romance, half diatribe against the U.S. Land Commission for its mistreatment of the native Californians. The depth of her affection for General Vallejo led her to base one of the book's main characters on Don Mariano himself, and she rendered General Vallejo's intellectual clarity and humane pragmatism with considerable skill. Like his real-life prototype, Don Mariano Alamar (as Vallejo is called in the book) is hated by some of the very settlers he has graciously tried to help. They occupy his land and shoot his cattle, but Alamar does not despise them. Capable of a high degree of objectivity, Alamar sees that the squatters are losers, too. The law has deceived them into thinking they can occupy another man's land, but when Alamar's grant is finally confirmed, the squatters lose their crops and their homes. As Alamar explains:

"No, I don't blame the squatters; they are at times like ourselves, victims of a wrong legislation, which unintentionally cuts
both ways. They were set loose upon us, but a law without eq-
uity recoils upon them more cruelly. Then we are all sufferers,
all victims. . . ."[60]

Doña Amparo and Vallejo credited the Californians with remarkable restraint in their ongoing battles with injustice and impoverish-
ment. But the General resisted drawing hostile lines between Americans
and Hispanics. A cosmopolitan at heart, he preferred to deal with individuals one at a time. Like the talented Doña Amparo, however, Vallejo
wanted the Spanish Californians to outshine the Anglos in public virtue
and respectability. Therefore, Californians should avoid squabbling
among themselves. In 1849 he had censured Alcalde Antonio Pico of San
Jose for banishing Teodoro Robles, a Californian against whom no crime
had been proved. Obviously, the punishment was "unjust to a son of the
country. . . . Where are we heading if our own countrymen turn against
us?" Robles' banishment also made the Californians appear to be less
sophisticated than they actually were. An unflattering, inaccurate impression would be created in the eyes of "the new people who are watching us."[61] In all things, the Californians should attempt to unfold an
exemplary image based on their superior qualities.

Because of these and other considerations, when the General's daughter Jovita and her husband Arpad talked of divorce (an event that could
have created open scandal), Vallejo battled relentlessly against the
breakup. He served as mediator, spending weeks in San Francisco, plead-
ing with the estranged couple. Only after a reconciliation was worked
out could he get any rest. As far as Don Mariano was concerned, "the
family is the only thing which keeps up society." Outsiders shouldn't
"have to see such things among our own people that are so disagreeable."[62]

But could any single group maintain these impossibly high standards?
For how long and to what purpose? The very attempt would tend to
create prolonged contests as native Californians fought with the spectres
of public shame and embarrassment. At least, this is what happened to
the General. His battles went on and on. The most scorching flare-up
was caused by his son Uladislao. Vallejo had been proud of his soldier-
son when "Ula" had gone to Mexico to fight against Louis Napoleon's
puppet, the Archduke Maximilian. But when the young officer came
home, Don Mariano realized that "Ula needs what a little tree needs —

a great big post for support." All of the young man's business ventures failed, and he climaxed his unlucky career when, as Town Marshal and Tax Collector for Sonoma, he pocketed the proceeds of the annual tax levy and sailed to Mexico. The shock almost killed the General, who was eighty years old at the time. But before many hours had passed, Don Mariano had obtained loans from two friends and had repaid the city treasurer, so that he could state publicly and truthfully that Uladislao Vallejo did "not owe a cent to the city of Sonoma."[63]

Another arrow found its mark after Don Mariano's daughter Jovita died of a heart attack at age thirty-four. Religious authorities would not bury her because they could not locate proof that she and her husband had been joined by a Catholic priest. She lay in a mausoleum for a week while the matter was straightened out.

For Don Mariano, the situation was intolerable. Not only had a priest performed Jovita's wedding ceremony, but the event had been one of the most glamorous weddings of the decade, and a certificate of marriage had indeed been issued. At last, the documents were found and she was duly buried. Vallejo demanded to know from Archbishop Alemany why the prelates had been "obliged to submit us to shame with an insult that only misconduct would merit . . . [when] Death had closed the lips of the innocent accused. . . ."[64]

These were traumatic events, but in Victorian California, a breach of family honor might originate — anywhere. Personal conduct had to be unimpeachable, outwardly discreet, laudable. Though many of Don Mariano's children had artistic talent, imagine the stigma if a son of General Vallejo should pursue a career as a musician or painter, work that had always been performed by the Indians. Could one of his daughters become an actress? Surely, there could be no thought of a daughter of Vallejo going on the stage. To be successful in the arts might involve censure, vulnerability, and displays of passion — which could shatter the mirror of social respectability.

Several of Vallejo's sons lacked direction. His eldest boy, Andronico, penned complaints during his early manhood that made unflattering comparisons between his status and that of the General's employees. One of Vallejo's secretaries, Señor Estrada, was obviously well paid, but Andronico was expected to work on the family farm: "My Papa's secretary is always aided from my Papa's purse. I, his son, go about with a worn-out suit and Señor Estrada with a new one; my shoes aren't shined but those of Señor Estrada are; Papa's son walks without a cane; but Señor secretary has one that cost five pesos."[65]

Like his younger brothers Uladislao and Napoleon, Andronico could not imagine himself being committed to a life of farm labor. But what *could* a son of Vallejo be? Even a successful career in business might imply a fall from caste. Obviously, Vallejo's offspring had to shrug off all inhibitions and carry through on strong inner volition, which is what Platon Vallejo achieved. During his stint on the East Coast, he cared for both Union and Confederate wounded after the Battle of Bull Run and graduated from Columbia University's medical school near the top of his class. Platon then returned to California and thrived in the new culture — as he would have in the old. While establishing his reputation as one of the region's most gifted doctors, he continued to study the myths of the local Indians, compiling a dictionary of the Suisun (Patwin) language. He raised fighting cocks, created interesting sculptures, and could joke as easily in English as in Spanish. Like his father, he was a sophisticate, at home in several cultures. Most of the other Vallejo children, however, found themselves dwelling in a painful hiatus between conflicting aims.

The exuberant generosity of pre-conquest California, its carefree economics and seigniorial display had given way to legal subtlety, mistrust, and parsimony. No people has ever been able to adjust to such radical changes in a single generation. Sometimes the adjustment can take five or six generations.

Gifted with considerable powers of introspection, Vallejo must have realized that his financial reversals were largely a result of his own failings. During the 1830s, he had acquired the habit of delegating authority to others — at first relying on people like Don Salvador Vallejo and Jacob Leese, whose trustworthiness was a proven fact. In those days, it had been alright. But after the American takeover, his habit of depending on others continued, even after the usefulness of his advisors' help had been discredited by red ink.

Vallejo did not have to listen to Amparo Ruiz's words about the plight of his countrymen to understand that most native Californians were undergoing worse trials than his. Everywhere he looked, he could see the sad condition of "our Spanish speaking people [who] are almost all of them uprooted from their own lands or impoverished and it is unbelievable that the majority of the time they have nothing to eat — so great is their poverty." In Monterey he saw Californians "in such misery that were it not for the fishing they would die of hunger."[66] He confided to Platon:

If the Californians could all gather together to breathe a lament,
it would reach Heaven as a moving sigh which would cause fear

and consternation to the Universe. What misery! And it is much
more intense than when everyone without exception lived in
abundance. The country was the true Eden, the land of promise
where hunger was never known, nor charity — if you can just
utter such an expression since no one had to exercise it.[67]

Nevertheless, the General was unable to resign himself to frugalities.
When he had ready cash, he made loans and did not ask for security, nor
did he require promissory notes. Members of the San Francisco business
community were aware that Vallejo was somewhat reckless in his dealings. Attorney Henry N. Clement of San Francisco said that Vallejo would
"sign anything his friends or those he regards as his friends ask him
to."[68] People who wanted to borrow money from him merely had to ask.
His generosity was proverbial. He felt that it was his obligation to give,
and he always subscribed to worthy causes. He seldom attempted to
dispel the illusion that he was still one of the state's richest men, but
suffered his losses with what he himself called "a certain studied calm
. . . [an] outward sang-froid with an austere philosophy, if you will, but
in reality burning in an abyssal inferno of griefs that have poisoned my
blood."[69]

After the Soscol disaster, Vallejo still hoped that, if he went East,
he could somehow reverse the Supreme Court's decision. He and John B.
Frisbie traveled together to the Atlantic seaboard, sailing January 4, 1865,
on the steamship *Constitution*, which was carrying substantial treasure
to the embattled U.S. government in Washington, D.C.[70] Vallejo had
always elevated the Founding Fathers to a plane above all other patriots — General Washington, of course, occupying the highest place of
honor. In the nation's capital, Don Mariano seemed to be restoring his
faith in American democracy as he handled objects the first president of
the United States had used, and "sat in the same seat where Washington
sat."[71] He visited more than seventy points of interest in Boston, including Bunker Hill, and saw the great elm tree where the Virginia leader
had first drawn his sword as commander-in-chief of the Continental Army.
Much of the eastern United States impressed Vallejo, but the only way he
could enjoy the cold weather of New York City was to take long walks, or
watch a vast "multitude of both sexes" skating in Central Park.[72]

Something about the East Coast's pulsating energy disturbed him.
This was especially true in New York City, where people did not seem to
have time to appreciate the beauty of the harbor at night, but rushed
around "without recognizing or talking to one another." Everyone

appeared to be "money mad . . . Friendship is for the sake of self interest alone and I have not regarded it so up to now and it makes me unhappy, just to think about it. The madness they have is desperate madness."[73] If Vallejo's fortunes had been following an upward curve, he might have been less distressed by the frantic commercialism. But the impersonal world he saw around him penetrated all the more deeply because of his own disintegrating affairs.

He experienced another financial tremor in 1866. One of the attorneys who had represented him in Washington, D.C. during the Soscol hearings, Thomas P. Madden, happened to be a business partner of John Frisbie's. Madden held a $15,000 note on the General's share of the Bolsa de San Cayetano Rancho near Watsonville. More alarming, he also held a $17,500 mortgage on Lachyrma Montis, Vallejo's Victorian-style home with interior adobe walls which sat on 228 acres about a half-mile west of the Sonoma plaza. In February of 1866, when Vallejo could not pay off the note, Madden assumed ownership of the costly property.[74] The only way Don Mariano and his family could continue to live there was to rent it back from Madden for $150 a month. The following year, the Casa Grande burned to the ground, taking with it the original manuscript of Vallejo's five-volume *History of California*, as well as other irreplaceable records. Lachyrma Montis was the General's only remaining link to the past.

The notion that John B. Frisbie was General Vallejo's economic champion is probably based on one undeniable fact: on December 9, 1871, Frisbie paid Thomas P. Madden $21,000 for Lachryma Montis. Four months later, the son-in-law deeded the property to Francisca Benicia Vallejo.[75]

Frisbie's generosity in this case can not be lightly dismissed. Another sort of man, instead of saving the Vallejo family estate, might have provided his aging in-laws with a small house in Sonoma at a fraction of the cost. But Frisbie was not the kind to do things halfway, which was one reason Vallejo always forgave him. In Vallejo's eyes, the American had a manner which was "fine and elegant." Moreover, he was "always good to our daughter. This makes up for what he has done to me sometimes." Frisbie had other positive traits. His graciousness enabled him "to capture the good will" of people, which led Vallejo to overlook his faults. "We ought to be proud of him," Don Mariano told his wife.[76] And because he had purchased Lachryma Montis, Frisbie deserved to be called Vallejo's financial savior. Amazingly, however, he also continued to be a cause of the General's economic grief.

In most instances, Frisbie had expedited Vallejo's disastrous policy of mortgaging land. As Vallejo's business manager, he could have used other methods or resigned. But he didn't. In fact, their relative fortunes had reversed. It was Frisbie who was now worth millions of dollars (in today's currency) and Vallejo whose asset sheet looked pitifully small. Frisbie's great fortune, of course, had branched out directly from Vallejo's, emerging from the same ground.

Luckily, Don Mariano had a philosophical turn of mind. "I think I will know how to be decently poor when the time comes," he said, "just as I have known how to be rich and support a family. . . ."[77] From the mid-1860s until his death in 1890, Vallejo became accustomed to the meaning of these words. After his land and cattle were gone, he derived most of his income from the rental of small plots of ground for truck gardening, and also from the operation of a water company that utilized the spring on his Lachryma Montis estate. To make ends meet, he did jobs that had previously been performed by his employees: mending fences, hauling wood, and fixing holes in the roof. To operate the Sonoma Water Works, he got up at five in the morning to turn on the machinery that piped water to Sonoma. His comments on the situation were typical of a spirit that had emerged earlier in his career. When he had returned from his imprisonment at Sutter's Fort, he had assessed his losses in herds and crops, remarking that he would have "to work and make it up again." Now he mused, "Everyone works to live, nevertheless I do not have the necessities at this age. Be it God's will and let more work come."[78] Doña Francisca's ability to appreciate this side of Vallejo's character was probably one of the things that held their marriage together. She did not hesitate to criticize his overindulgence of their children or his temperamental flare-ups, but she valued his "strength of will, rare at his age, a tremendous interest and furthermore, a strong spirit full of life. His philosophy seems to increase with his labors."[79]

Although it may seem difficult to believe — especially considering all the bad luck the Vallejo–Frisbie partnership had known — Frisbie, in the 1870s, was still managing most of the General's funds: a total of $30,000, which yielded a monthly income of $250. Then, in 1876, Vallejo witnessed the ruin of the son-in-law who had created such havoc in his own life. John B. Frisbie went broke. His banking institution, the Vallejo Savings and Commercial Bank, had invested heavily in Bonanza stocks, which were backed by William C. Ralston, president of the Bank of California. When Ralston died, these securities had spiraled downward. To satisfy his creditors, Frisbie began to sell off his assets, such as the Bernard Hotel in Vallejo, the White Sulphur Springs resort, and other property, including his private estate. He tried to reassure his depositors, telling them that his assets exceeded the liabilities. A recent student of Frisbie's affairs has said that after everything had been sold, no depositor lost money and the bank reopened.[80] Even if this is true, Frisbie himself lost everything.

General Vallejo's fortunes never rose again, but Frisbie seemed to have economic flotation devices in his hip pockets. In the late 1870s, he left California for Mexico, taking his wife and children. There, he worked for President Porfirio Díaz and became richer than he had been in California. Probably his greatest feat for the Díaz regime was the complete reversal of President Hayes' hostile trade policy toward Mexico. Using methods that included a personal address to the U.S. Congress, Frisbie fostered a commercial detente between the two countries. The grateful Díaz awarded him a handsome fee — plus a gold mine. Frisbie was also employed by the Huntington–Stanford railway, a position that helped him create a new empire for himself that included interests in railroads, banking, stock raising, sugar mills, gold mining, and an electric light and power company.[81]

Though Frisbie more than recouped his losses in Mexico, he never achieved the kind of status that Vallejo enjoyed in California. During the 1870s and 1880s, hardly a public event took place to which Vallejo was not invited — either as an honored guest or speaker. He turned down an opportunity to run for lieutenant governor, but in 1883 he did become a member of the state board of horticulture, on which he served for several years. When eighty years old, he supported one of the first resolutions to protect the redwoods.[82] In 1886, with Joaquin Miller and Adolph Sutro, Vallejo helped establish Arbor Day in California. He also devoted months of his time to visiting native Californians, collecting their journals, letters, and private reminiscences, which he turned over to Hubert Howe Bancroft. This thirty-six-volume collection, known as the *Documentos Para la Historia de California*, forms one of the cornerstones of the Bancroft Library and is the basis on which much research into California's past is done today. Vallejo also commissioned paintings by Oriana Day and other artists depicting California's history and the mission heritage.

Vallejo's detractors would one day portray him as a convenient Hispanic figurehead, someone whose presence at public events implied that past wrongs against the Spanish Californians had been made right. But Vallejo, whose frequent orations on Hispanic California were steeped in nostalgic glamour, was not on hand to soothe a bad Anglo conscience. He survived with immense dignity as a native Californian who insisted that the state's past was a rich legacy that deserved to be honored. It was a country that his father and other Hispanic pioneers had settled for themselves and for the future, and their achievements were by no means insignificant. Moreover, Vallejo himself was a ubiquitous public figure, an individual whose notoriety in his own day exceeded even Father Serra's. Nor was he entirely alone in his preeminence. Pablo de la Guerra, who had favored an English protectorate and had served in José Castro's army, became a California state senator, held the post of lieutenant governor, and was also a U.S. marshal and district judge. Even more prominent was Romualdo Pacheco, who, in addition to holding lesser state offices, served as California's governor, was elected U.S. congressman for two terms, and was the U.S. minister to Guatemala and Honduras. However, most Californians politely withdrew from a predominately Anglo society that discriminated against them, and for generations they remained out of the limelight.

Luckily, Vallejo never lost his hold on the Lachryma Montis estate, a refuge that provided him with the deepest satisfactions of his old age. In warm weather, the gold ridge of the Sonoma Mountains screened the afternoon sun, permitting Don Mariano to appreciate the different gradations of green in the valley. After dinner, in the evenings, Don Salvador would play guitar by the fountain. The General described one such event in detail, noting that the night was calm,

> but very dark; the driveway, the fountain playing, truly it seemed the place of a pastoral scene, a natural one to which was added enough of the artificial that Lachryma Montis possesses.[83]

Don Salvador's death was one of the most painful ordeals of Vallejo's later years. The captain's nature remained unchanged by old age. He was still Don Mariano's exact opposite: physically unappealing, where the graceful General had an open, friendly countenance; harsh with his children, a man of brutal habits, often hostile, where the General was engaging. Yet, for all that, the bond of love between the brothers survived. In the aftermath of Don Salvador's death, Vallejo delivered some of his most negative pronouncements concerning the U.S. conquest of California, more than once referring to the "American usurpation." Perhaps he was honoring the memory of a man who — if given a choice — would have opposed the U.S. takeover with all the grimness of his violent nature.

Vallejo, of course, was not immune to the peculiar indulgence of many nineteenth century gentlemen — self-pity — which represented the shadowy side of his prevailing optimism. As he recalled what had happened in the past, he condemned the ingratitude that had blinded his American friends. For instance, in regard to the city-building venture at Benicia, he said:

> After Semple, Larkin, Phelps and others assumed the management and direction of the city, they denied the debt to me; they took over everything as if something had possession of them.[84]

But during Vallejo's final years, resentful thoughts did not predominate. He wrote to his son-in-law (Ricardo Emparan, then Mexican consul in California), "Believe me, Ricardo, American Democracy is the Best Democracy in the world. . . ."[85] The major theme running through his correspondence with his son, Platon, was one of reconciliation. "Everything turned out for the best. Let be, as it is. . . .[W]e are in the United States, soon to be the foremost nation on earth. Love everybody. Be good. Obey just laws. Que mas? Harbor no rancor in your heart. Speak well of everybody. Remember De Mortuis nil nisi bono. We live." When Platon spoke of uncovering more past grievances, the father responded, "No, let it go. What good to keep open an old sore? Let the wound heal. I brought this upon myself. I did what I thought was best. It was best for the country and so far as I am concerned, I can stand it."[86]

Vallejo treasured California's Americanization, probably as much for the gift of education as for anything else. He often said that, in his day, a youngster had to leave the country to obtain intellectual training. Under American rule, the schoolhouse was open to everyone who wished to attend. His faith in reason, education, and progress led him to believe that the United States might one day prove to be the hope of the world. His resiliency probably saved him. It had been his fate, after all, not so much to go in search of the American Dream, as to experience the Dream's positive and negative effects after it had found him. True, he had endowed some of the first American settlers with a nimbus very few of them deserved. Perfection being impossible to find, these saints of material progress had fallen one by one. Yet, Vallejo remained a devoted American in the same way that he remained a Catholic (regardless of his many quarrels with the Church) — always insisting on his right to define his own credos within the establishment's religious and political framework.

Had Vallejo's remote ancestors never left Burgos, Spain, he might have lived the life of a Spanish nobleman — perhaps as a man of letters. But in California, his polished nature concealed an unconventional heart. He was an aesthete, dreamer, land speculator, politician, republican, and autocrat. The pragmatist was always at the elbow of the dreamer. This was obvious when, as a Mexican official, he had developed his habit of looking to the future. Even if that future under Mexican or American rule called for irreconcilable policies, he knew how to pave good roads to both eventualities, so that no matter what the outcome, his position would remain secure.

As mentioned earlier, he believed that "childhood has the right" to joy and, especially in Arcadian California, people should seek content-ment, for man "is perverted by reason of his unhappiness."[87] Any man who could leap out of bed during his last illness to do an Indian war dance, or who learned the language of the deaf so that he could converse with students from a school for the handicapped, had never quite lost touch with his own innocence.[88]

III

If Vallejo, Frémont, and Sutter, during the second half of their lives, somehow lost the knack of coping with change, they were nevertheless remembered with considerable honor. But of the three, only Vallejo died in California, in his home; and his was decidedly the showiest of the old guard funerals. Following his death on January 18, 1890, flags flew at half-mast, the state's newspapers gave long accounts of his career, and schools and businesses were closed in the pueblo he had founded. People in the North Bay grieved as though they had lost a member of their own family. General Nelson Miles sent a military band from the San Fran-cisco presidio, which played Chopin's "Funeral March" as Vallejo's body was carried past the old trees and roses of Castile lining the drive at Lachryma Montis. A procession of honored dignitaries circled the Sonoma Plaza, "stopping a few moments with bared heads at the site of the Casa Grande." The California State Legislature sent a silken flag, which was unfurled at his graveside, to help serve as a guard of honor for America's friend.[89]

By then, all that remained of Vallejo's extensive ranchos — once stretch-ing from Mendocino County to the Carquinez Straits — was 228 acres sur-rounding the Lachryma Montis homestead, one cow, and two aging horses. The funeral expenses were paid for by General John B. Frisbie.[90]

Mariano G. Vallejo's influence did not vanish immediately after his death, but extended well into the twentieth century. In 1921, more than 14,000 votes were cast in a Bay Area poll designed to select two repre-sentatives from the ranks of California's illustrious dead to have niches in the National Hall of Statuary in Washington, D.C. The four front-runners were General Vallejo, 4,417; Junipero Serra, 3,341; Thomas Starr King, 1,837; and Bret Harte, 1,174.[91] Somewhat incongruously, forty-five years later, at Mare Island Naval Station, the Polaris submarine *U.S.S. Mariano Vallejo* was christened near the place where Vallejo's favorite Arabian mare had saved herself from the waters of the straits by swimming to a wooded island.[92]

Notes

*Complete documentation for the references cited in
abbreviated format may be found in the Bibliography.*

Preface

1. William H. Thomes, *On Land and Sea*, 214, cited in McKittrick, *Vallejo*, 224–25. G. Simpson, vol. 1, 309.
2. DeVoto, 223; Dillon, *Great Expectations*, 87.
3. Hale, 194. This and other observations about the influence of the United States on Mexican liberalism are drawn from Hale's chapter 6, "Liberalism and the North American Model."
4. Emparan, 107.
5. Leon D. Adams, *Wines of America* (Boston: Houghton Mifflin, 1973), 164–185, 228.
6. The possible exception is *The Vallejos of California* by Madie Brown Emparan.

Chapter 1: The Gifts of Fortune

1. Beilharz, 81; Richard S. Whitehead, *Alta California's Four Fortresses* (Los Angeles: The Zamorano Club, 1985); Fr. Maynard Geiger, O.F.M., "A Description of California's Principal Presidio, Monterey in 1773," *Southern California Quarterly* 49 (September 1967): 327–336. Monterey's population between the years 1800 and 1820 is extremely difficult to pin down. Governor Pedro Fages estimated the capital's population to be 202 in the 1790s.
See *California in 1792* by Donald C. Cutter (Norman: University of Oklahoma Press, 1990), 28. But Bancroft put the number at 400 for the year 1796. (H.H. Bancroft, *History of California*, vol. 1, 677.) The number of military personnel was subsequently reduced, so I have suggested the approximate figure of 300.
2. Emparan, 2.
3. M. G. Vallejo, "Historical and Personal Memoirs," vol. 1, 225.
4. Coughlin, "Boston Smugglers," 100–103.
5. Ibid., 113. Father Caulas wrote Captain Eayrs, ". . . tomorrow (God willing) I come to your Fragata to dine, and we two will trade on our own account. I am now sending the corporal with a little vegetable stuff for you and the other two commandantes, and also some eggs. . . . There will be sent likewise the otterskins which on my coming we will examine. Also be pleased to receive

a small pig for yourself, and another for the two commandantes, —a present."

6. Morison, 46–53; Langum, 9–10. Monetary values are based on the United States government's statistical series, "Consumer Price Indexes —All items 1800 to 1970, Table E-135," published in U.S. Bureau of the Census, *Historical Statistics of the United States, Colonial Times to 1970, Bicentennial Edition, Part 1.* U.S. Government Printing Office, 1975, updated by monthly periodical, U.S. Department of Commerce, Bureau of Economic Analysis, *Survey of Current Business.* A comparison for the price levels for 1831–1846 with the levels of 1990 yields the ratio of approximately thirteen to one.

7. Hurtado, 22; McKittrick, *Vallejo*, 2.

8. M. G. Vallejo, "Historical and Personal Memoirs," vol. 1, 229.

9. Ibid., 253–55.

10. Emparan, 2–3.

11. M. G. Vallejo, "Historical and Personal Memoirs," vol. 1, 129.

12. Gordon, 32–39.

13. Ibid., 38; Rawls, 3, 4, 105. Also see Malcolm Margolin's Introduction to La Pérouse, 21–22. In his "Historical and Personal Memoirs," Vallejo remarked that the priests introduced the Indians to the crucifix at the same time the Spanish soldiers threatened them with their lances. "Succara, the great Indian Chieftain, was not far wrong when he said that the Christians gave him 'no room to choose between Christ and death.'" (vol. 1, 17)

14. H. H. Bancroft, *History of California*, vol. 2, 305–309; M. G. Vallejo, "Historical and Personal Memoirs," vol. 1, 117.

15. H. H. Bancroft, *History of California*, vol. 2, 225–26.

16. M. G. Vallejo, "Historical and Personal Memoirs," vol. 1, 182–204.

17. Fink, 53; H. H. Bancroft, *History of California*, vol. 2, 381.

18. M. G. Vallejo, "Historical and Personal Memoirs," vol. 1, 131, 255.

19. H. H. Bancroft, *History of California*, vol. 2, 141 n. 40; Fink, 53.

20. In fact, Sola was a splendid role model. See H. H. Bancroft, *History of California*, vol. 2, 471–73; M. G. Vallejo, "Historical and Personal Memoirs," vol. 1, 120–278.

21. Vallejo remembered that Sola tried to instill a respect for the monarchy in Monterey's youth (M. G. Vallejo, "Historical and Personal Memoirs," vol. 1, 274). Sola was also a great champion of learning. According to Don Mariano, the governor sent out "circulars to all presidio captains and pueblo commissioners to keep a vigilant watch to advance education of the young of both sexes and, should the fathers and mothers not send them to school, they were to be severely punished." (Ibid., vol. 1, 131).

22. Gibson, 189.

23. Ibid., 182–83.

24. M. G. Vallejo, "Historical and Personal Memoirs," vol. 2, 20.
25. The matter of flags seemed to be of relative indifference to the Californians. The Spanish insignia at the San Francisco presidio was allowed to remain above the *comandancia* during the entire span of Mexican rule, and most—if not all—of the soldiers' bullhide shields retained the Spanish emblem.
26. McKittrick, *Vallejo*, 11.
27. W. W. Robinson, 55–58.
28. Gibson, 191. Gibson notes that by 1826, the price the Russians had to pay for mission wheat had tripled. Largely because of competition from the rancheros, the price thereafter dropped down again from 14 to 7½ kopecks per pound.
29. Woolfenden, 76.
30. Ibid., 63.
31. After having experienced financial disappointments in North Carolina, Larkin arrived in California nearly penniless. From 1844 to 1848, he served as California's first American consul. (Hague and Langum, 13–36; Woolfenden, 12.)
32. Woolfenden, 27.
33. M. G. Vallejo, "Historical and Personal Memoirs," vol. 1, 341.
34. Woolfenden, 33–34.
35. Ibid., 51, 63; M. G. Vallejo, *Documentos*, vol. 1, 385.
36. The willowy, blue-eyed Smith had first entered California in November of 1826 on a beaver hunting expedition. California's Governor Echeandía had not liked the idea of Americans traveling overland to the province and had seen in Smith's arrival the disintegration of an historic barrier. In December of 1826, Smith was ordered out of the country. He left by way of the San Bernardino Valley, worked his way north, and crossed the Sierras, leaving some of his companions behind on the Stanislaus River in the Great Valley. They were not disturbed. Their activities in the valley led to the naming of the American River, near the future site of Sutter's Fort. In 1827 Smith reestablished contact with his companions, but Father Narciso Durán, fearing Indian troubles, had him arrested. (Morgan 204–53.)
37. For Piña's report and other documents relating to the battle see Sherburne F. Cook, ed. "Colonial Expeditions to the Interior of California: Central Valley, 1820–1840." *Anthropological Records* 20, no. 5 (February 1962), 169–180. Also see Holterman, 45–52; H. H. Bancroft, *History of California*, vol. 3, 111–14. On this occasion, as on many future ones, Vallejo found himself at odds with Padre Durán, a man he facetiously described as being "as fat as an Easter bull." (M. G. Vallejo, "Historical and Personal Memoirs," vol. 3, 405.) Only two years later Vallejo

was excommunicated by Durán for smuggling forbidden books
into California from the *Leanor* — volumes that included Voltaire
and Rousseau. The young officer was irked by the department's
clergymen who wanted to restrict his access to such books. As he
put it, the missionaries knew "that books were the most to be
feared emissaries of the goddess whom we call Liberty. . . ."
(Ibid., 109–17). Governor Echeandía ordered the investigation
of Vallejo's campaign against Estanislao, based on the accusation
that three women, not taken in battle, had been shot and then
hanged. H. H. Bancroft, *History of California*, vol. 3, 111–14.

38. The inflexible Governor Manuel Victoria probably deserved to
be ousted. Though his eyes could be jovial, his methods were
despotic. Some citizens were imprisoned without cause, harsh
executions were carried out, and Victoria refused to convene the
diputación. (Wrightington, 49; M. G. Vallejo, "Historical and
Personal Memoirs," vol. 2, 140–43.) In 1831 an outbreak occurred in southern California, backed by ex-governors Argüello
and Echeandía. In the skirmish that followed, the obstinate
Victoria was wounded; later, he was expelled to Mazatlán on
an American ship.

   Vallejo hurried to Los Angeles to celebrate the victory and participate in revolutionary events. Victoria's eviction was confirmed
when Pío Pico was elected governor. Inexplicably, ex-Governor
Echeandía refused to honor the election. When he failed to show
up to swear in Pico at Mission San Gabriel, Vallejo and his
nephew instated Pico themselves. The agile Alvarado let himself
into the mission through a skylight to obtain the necessary sacred
utensils, and Vallejo administered the oath in front of the church
door. (H. H. Bancroft, *History of California*, vol. 3, 16–21.)
Before long, three men were claiming the California governorship
and it seemed to Vallejo that the revolution had been betrayed.
He was still bitter about this betrayal when he wrote his cousin,
Domingo Carrillo, "May the day come when the devil may take
all of us Californians, after they have hanged those of us who have
even the slightest faith in ourselves! If this ever comes to pass,
even if I were the first one [to be hanged], I would be happy
provided that all suffered alike." (Quoted in Tays, vol. 16 [September
1937] , 231.) Written when he was twenty-five, the confession was a
painful lament acknowledging the extent of Vallejo's disillusionment
with California's political system.

39. H. H. Bancroft, *History of California*, vol. 3, 234, 296–97;
Monroy, 123.

40. A. Robinson, 39.

41. The Russians had been establishing farms farther and farther inland, which angered Governor Figueroa almost as much as the Russian fur-hunting expeditions had riled Governor Sola. The fort's manager, Peter Kostromitinov, was responsible for pushing the program of expansion to new limits. (Gibson, 117.)

42. The Sonoma mission was the youngest in the chain of twenty-one California missions, and like most of the other centers of conversion, it had experienced a mixture of ups and downs. In regard to the neophytes, the wording of the secularization laws showed a robust duplicity. If the Native Americans wanted to borrow money on their plots or sell them (or if they died without heirs), the property was to revert to the nation — not the Indian nation, of course, the Mexican nation. (Smilie, 48.)

43. Ibid., 51–53.

44. Figueroa's Orders to Vallejo, quoted in Emparan, 50–51.

45. Ibid.

46. Ibid.

47. Charles E. Brown, quoted in McKittrick, *Vallejo*, 124.

48. Alexander, 22.

49. M. G. Vallejo, "Historical and Personal Memoirs," vol. 3, 56.

50. H. H. Bancroft, *History of California*, vol. 3, 457–59; Pioneer Register, ibid., 762–63.

51. M. G. Vallejo, "Historical and Personal Memoirs," vol. 3, 221.

52. Ibid., 164–65; H. H. Bancroft, *History of California*, vol. 3, 459–67.

53. Alvarado to Vallejo, quoted in George Tays, "Surrender of Monterey by Governor Gutiérrez," *California Historical Society Quarterly*, 15 (December 1936): 341–42; McKittrick, *Vallejo*, 106. During Governor Chico's administration, it was agreed by prior arrangement between Vallejo and some of his associates that in case of a successful revolt, Alvarado would "take over the post of political executive, and *alférez* Vallejo the military command." (M. G. Vallejo, "Historical and Personal Memoirs, vol. 3, 92–93.)

54. He wound up his extemporaneous speech by saying he "was very grateful to them for the part they had taken in the revolution and that they could rest assured that lands and special privileges would be granted them, for the Territory of Alta California was of great extent and there was more than enough land to enrich them all." (M. G. Vallejo, "Historical and Personal Memoirs," vol. 3, 198–99.)

55. The new California leadership characterized themselves as "federalists" and declared California to be "independent of Mexico, until the federal system adopted in 1824 shall be reestablished." (M. G. Vallejo, "Historical and Personal Memoirs," vol. 3,

195–203.) Confirmation of Vallejo's commandant generalship and Alvarado's governorship arrived with Andrés Castillero on September 15, 1838. (Emparan, 12.)

56. Quoted in H. H. Bancroft, *History of California*, vol. 4, 3 n. 1.
57. Langum, 230; H.H. Bancroft, Pioneer Register, *History of California*, vol. 3, 763.
58. H. H. Bancroft, *History of California*, vol. 4, 5–6 n. 4.
59. Ibid., 8–9 n. 8.
60. Ibid., 17 n. 26.
61. M. G. Vallejo, *Documentos*, vol. 14, 52; H. H. Bancroft, *History of California*, vol. 4, 11–24. The General later tried to underplay his role in the Graham Affair (M. G. Vallejo, "Historical and Personal Memoirs," vol. 4, 126–30), but the record clearly indicates his support of Alvarado's policy.
62. Farnham, 90–96.
63. Quoted in H. H. Bancroft, *History of California*, vol. 4, 25 n. 42.
64. Ibid., 34.
65. Ibid., 32.
66. Ibid., 33.

Chapter 2: The Pivotal Year: 1841

1. M.G. Vallejo, *Documentos*, vol. 10, 3.
2. Ibid., 60, 62; Du Four, 250 – 52.
3. M. G. Vallejo, "Historical and Personal Memoirs," vol. 4, 243–45, 257.
4. Ibid., 253.
5. Dakin, 257–58.
6. Duflot de Mofras, vol. 2, 61–71.
7. Anderson, 9.
8. M.G. Vallejo, *Documentos*, vol. 10, 230.
9. Ibid., 229; Du Four, 255.
10. M.G. Vallejo, *Documentos*, vol. 10, 227; Du Four, 255.
11. Du Four, 252–53.
12. Fehrenbach, 57.
13. M.G. Vallejo, *Documentos*, vol. 10, 227.
14. Tays, vol. 17 (March 1938), 153.
15. M.G. Vallejo, *Documentos*, vol. 10, 236; Du Four, 260–61.
16. M.G. Vallejo, *Documentos*, vol. 10, 231; Du Four, 265.
17. Dillon, *Fool's Gold*, 22–25.
18. Ibid., 66–67.
19. Ibid., 76–77.
20. The contract was not actually witnessed by Alcalde Guerrero, however, until December 19, 1841. (See Ibid., 118.)
21. Ibid., 80–81.
22. M.G. Vallejo, *Documentos*, vol. 33, 251.

23. Reverend Walter Colton also applied, but as it turned out, neither man joined the cruise. (Tyler, 12.)
24. H. H. Bancroft, *History of California* vol. 4, 241.
25. M.G. Vallejo, "Historical and Personal Memoirs," vol. 4, 240.
26. Tyler, 304–305.
27. Wilkes, vol. 5, 171–72.
28. Ibid., 210–12.
29. Ibid., 163–64.
30. Dana, 202.
31. M.G. Vallejo, "Historical and Personal Memoirs," vol. 4, 241–42.

Chapter 3: The Advent of the Americans

1. Francis, 129, 133.
2. Ibid., 166.
3. Kern, vi, 61–67. Nearing the location of present-day Fremont, Don Mariano might have passed the mill his brother had erected that year. A congenial host and something of a libertine, Don José de Jesús Vallejo had earned his reputation for marksmanship against Hippolyte Bouchard's frigates in 1818, and was now serving as *administrador* of Mission San José. Since he was also military commandant of the pueblo some fifteen miles to the southwest, his position in the San Jose region was analogous to Don Mariano's in Sonoma.
4. Bidwell, 11.
5. H. H. Bancroft, *History of California*, vol. 4, 273–76; Giffen, 19–22; Tays, vol. 17 (March 1938), 56–59.
6. H. H. Bancroft, *History of California*, vol. 4, 272–73.
7. Fehrenbach, 151.
8. Ibid., 165–83.
9. H. H. Bancroft, *History of California*, vol. 4, 117.
10. Bidwell, 1–4.
11. Ibid., 7–8.
12. Ibid., 13.
13. H. H. Bancroft, *History of California*, vol. 4, 272–73.
14. Bidwell, 14–15.
15. Ibid., 21–22.
16. Ibid., 48–50.
17. Giffen, 17.
18. Ibid., 17–18; Bidwell, 53.
19. Ibid.
20. Giffen, 20; M. G. Vallejo, "Historical and Personal Memoirs," vol. 3, 384–85.
21. Wood, 69.

22. H. H. Bancroft, *History of California*, vol. 4, 274; Giffen, 21.
23. H. H. Bancroft, *History of California*, vol. 4, 274–75.
24. M.G. Vallejo, *Documentos*, vol. 10, 350; vol. 14, 28.
25. H. H. Bancroft, *History of California,* vol. 4, 275 n. 29.
26. Bidwell, 55–57.
27. Ibid.
28. Dana, 202.
29. M.G. Vallejo, "Historical and Personal Memoirs," vol. 3, 384.
30. In later years, when traveling through Mexico, Vallejo again noted the economic disadvantages attending the use (and abuse) of Indian workers. (Emparan, 142–43.)
31. M.G. Vallejo, *Documentos*, vol. 10, 384.
32. Ibid.
33. Ibid., 385.
34. H. H. Bancroft, *History of California*, vol. 4, 275.
35. M.G. Vallejo, "Historical and Personal Memoirs," vol. 4, 241–42.
36. H. H. Bancroft, *History of California*, vol. 4, 218.
37. Wood, 86.
38. Alexander, 19 – 21.
39. Albertson, 262 – 63. The doctor was married to Vallejo's niece, María Soberanes, and was one of the most belligerent men in the country. Before renting him the property, Larkin had warned Bale not to sell liquor on the premises, but the advice was ignored.
40. G. Simpson, vol. 1, 309.
41. Ibid., 311, 322.
42. M.G. Vallejo, "Historical and Personal Memoirs," vol. 4, 233, *passim*. Vallejo was probably little different from other Mexican liberals who pictured the United States as a "utilitarian dream world," a symbol of liberty, equality, and political stability. (See Hale, 188–203.)
43. G. Simpson, vol. 1, 324.
44. Ibid., 384–86.
45. Ibid., 41.
46. M.G. Vallejo, *Documentos*, vol. 4, 368; H. H. Bancroft, *History of California*, vol. 4, 112 n. 4.
47. G. Simpson, vol. 1, 327.
48. M.G. Vallejo, "Historical and Personal Memoirs," vol. 4, 175–76.
49. M.G. Vallejo, *Documentos*, vol. 10, 332; H. H. Bancroft, *History of California*, vol. 4, 239 n. 29.
50. H. H. Bancroft, Ibid.
51. M.G. Vallejo, *Documentos*, vol. 10, 349; vol. 11, 4.
52. M. G. Vallejo, *Documentos*, vol. 11, 22.
53. Ibid., 273.

Chapter 4: A New Governor Brings Crisis

1. H. H. Bancroft, *History of California*, vol. 4, 286.
2. A. Robinson, 144.
3. H. H. Bancroft, *History of California*, vol. 4, 290–91. Vallejo's role was now reduced to that of military commandant, with his authority extending from Sonoma to Santa Ines. (Ibid., 292 n. 32, 293.) A Monterey resident later recalled hearing Micheltorena complain "that General Vallejo had sent for him, had made him very good promises and when he arrived here, denied him his support. . . ." (Valdez, 11.) At first, this was not the case. Only by Vallejo's orders was General Micheltorena given official recognition at San Diego. Vallejo's other efforts to ensure a generous welcome for the new appointee were opposed by Governor Alvarado. Then, on September 20, Don Mariano asked the Monterey treasurer, José Abrego, to provide Micheltorena with all the financial assistance possible. (H. H. Bancroft, *History of California*, vol. 4, 292 – 93.) Handling the ongoing transition with bitterness, Alvarado left very little money in the treasury for Micheltorena to work with. He also claimed that Vallejo had exceeded his powers by ordering the immediate recognition of the Mexican leader; but, as he mused somewhat inappropriately later on, "The Mexicans always worship the rising sun." (Alvarado, vol. 5, 15–16; M. G. Vallejo, *Documentos*, vol. 11, 255–62).
4. Anderson, 3.
5. Ibid., 88.
6. H. H. Bancroft, *History of California*, vol. 4, 308 n. 17.
7. Quoted in Ibid., 310.
8. Hague and Langum, 49, 81; Larkin, *Chapters*, 12, 23, 49–50.
9. H. H. Bancroft, *History of California*, vol. 4, 311–12.
10. Anderson, 100.
11. M. G. Vallejo, "Historical and Personal Memoirs," vol. 2, 151; vol. 4, 322–23.
12. Ibid., vol. 4, 323–25.
13. Ibid., 341.
14. Coughlin, "California Ports," 26–27.
15. M.G. Vallejo, "Historical and Personal Memoirs," vol. 4, 330.
16. P. Vallejo, January 30, 1914.
17. "Autobiography of the Indian Princess Isidora Filomena, Widow of the Mighty Californian Indian Chief Solano," *Noticias Para Los Californianos*, 22 (April–June 1990).
18. P. Vallejo, February 4, 1914.
19. M. G. Vallejo, "Historical and Personal Memoirs," vol. 4, 339.
20. McKittrick, *Vallejo*, 222 – 23.

21. M. G. Vallejo, "Historical and Personal Memoirs," vol. 4, 334.
22. Sanchez, 367.
23. M. G. Vallejo, "Historical and Personal Memoirs,"
    vol. 4, 340–42.
24. William H. Thomes, quoted in McKittrick, *Vallejo*, 224–25.
25. Quoted in H. H. Bancroft, *History of California*, vol. 4, 347.
26. Hague and Langum, 108.
27. H. H. Bancroft, *History of California*, vol. 4, 390–91.
28. Ibid., 350.
29. Hague and Langum, 71–72.
30. For the text of the Deed, see chapter 19, note 50. Depending
    on whether a short- or long-term view of the bargain is taken,
    it's difficult to say who actually got the better end of the deal.
    The government was clearing up its outstanding debts to Vallejo
    for years of unpaid back wages—food, clothing, and ammunition
    he had supplied to his troops—and finally, the $9,000 the Gen-
    eral had spent on construction of the Sonoma barracks.
    (McKittrick, *Vallejo*, 228; Emparan, 20; Woodruff, 11–12; H. H.
    Bancroft, *History of California*, vol. 4, 352.)
31. H. H. Bancroft, Pioneer Register, *History of California*, vol. 4,
    697–98. Benjamin's wife Nancy was probably the first woman to
    enter the province from the United States via the direct overland
    route. But this honor has also been claimed for a member of Joel
    Walker's family.
32. McKittrick, "Salvador Vallejo," 318.
33. Albertson, 262–63; McKittrick, *Vallejo*, 226.
34. H. H. Bancroft, *History of California*, vol. 4, 444–45.
35. Tays, vol. 17 (June 1938), 155–56; Albertson, 264.
36. It should be pointed out that Sonoma, which was garrisoned by
    Vallejo's troops and Indian auxiliaries, was equal to this attack
    by fifteen armed men; the situation would be different two years
    later when Ezekiel Merritt invaded the pueblo with twice as many
    raiders.
37. Albertson, 265.
38. Ibid; M. G. Vallejo, *Documentos*, vol. 12, 88.
39. Albertson, 265–66.
40. Tays, vol. 17 (June 1938), 156.
41. McKittrick, *Vallejo*, 227.
42. H. H. Bancroft, *History of California*, vol. 4, 292 n. 32, 293.

Chapter 5: A Small War Heats Up

1. M. G. Vallejo, *Documentos*, vol. 12, 95; vol. 34, 112;
   H. H. Bancroft, *History of California*, vol. 4, 459–460.

2. H. H. Bancroft, *History of California*, vol. 4, 364 n. 32.

3. Ibid., 458–60.

4. Ibid., 461.

5. Larkin to Stearns, quoted in Larkin, *First and Last Consul*, 19.

6. Dillon, *Fool's Gold*, 150.

7. H. H. Bancroft, *History of California*, vol. 4, 463.

8. Ibid., 464 n. 12.

9. Ibid., n. 13.

10. Ibid., 465 n. 14.

11. M. G. Vallejo, *Documentos*, vol. 14, 30, 33; H. H. Bancroft, *History of California*, vol. 4, 466 n. 16.

12. M. G. Vallejo, "Historical and Personal Memoirs," vol. 4, 385; McKittrick, *Vallejo*, 229; Emparan, 21.

13. Davis, 105. Sir George Simpson gives a much lower figure, $10,000 annually—still a considerable sum for those times. (G. Simpson, vol. 1, 299.)

14. Emparan, 21.

15. Dillon, *Fool's Gold*, 157.

16. H. H. Bancroft, *History of California*, vol. 4, 470 n. 20.

17. Tays, vol. 17 (June 1938), 157.

18. Dillon, *Fool's Gold*, 159.

19. Quoted in H. H. Bancroft, *History of California*, vol. 4, 474 n. 29.

20. Quoted in Dillon, *Fool's Gold*, 156.

21. H. H. Bancroft, *History of California*, vol. 4, 478. Some of the damages he had sought had been disallowed, and he threw in his lot with Micheltorena, more to destabilize the government than to resolve the conflict. Rowland states that Graham eventually received $36,000 from Mexico as indemnity for his exile. See Leon Rowland, *Santa Cruz, The Early Years* (Santa Cruz: Paper Vision Press, 1980), 183.

22. M. G. Vallejo, *Documentos*, vol. 12, 122.

23. Ibid. This was the Stevens Company. Sutter also referred to another party of potential allies, some sixty wagons in all, which was on its way under Captain Hastings.

24. Tays, vol. 17 (June 1938), 159.

25. H. H. Bancroft, *History of California*, vol. 4, 483.

26. Tays, vol. 17 (June 1938), 159; McKittrick, *Vallejo*, 231.

27. Tays, Ibid.

28. M. G. Vallejo, "Historical and Personal Memoirs," vol. 4, 435–36.

29. Dillon, *Fool's Gold*, 159.

30. Ibid., 163.

31. H. H. Bancroft, *History of California*, vol. 4, 488–90.

32. Ibid., 501 n. 27.

33. Ibid., 501; Dillon, *Fool's Gold*, 178.
34. Dillon, *Fool's Gold*, 172–73, 182.
35. H. H. Bancroft, *History of California*, vol. 4, 516; Dillon, *Fool's Gold*, 173.
36. The battle bore more resemblance to an expensive day with shooting script in Studio City than to the bloody Alamo (which was the name some people wanted to give the battlefield). (H. H. Bancroft, *History of California*, vol. 4, 503.)
37. Dillon, *Fool's Gold*, 186.
38. H. H. Bancroft, *History of California*, vol. 4, 506–507.
39. Dillon, *Fool's Gold*, 187.
40. Larkin, *The Larkin Papers*, vol. 3, 37.

Chapter 6: *"Ojalá Que Lo Tomen Los Americanos"* ("I Hope the Americans Take It")

1. Abel Stearns to Larkin, June 12, 1846, quoted in Wright, 132.
2. Dillon, *Fool's Gold*, 205.
3. Ibid., 106.
4. Castro wrote Weber,
   . . . you may freely offer to all whom you may find useful and industrious all the guarantees they may desire for establishing themselves in this department, and for living securely in the exercise of their respective occupations. You will also inform them that the friendly feeling of this office toward them is already secured to them by the treaty of San Fernando. . . . (H. H. Bancroft, *History of California*, vol. 4, 605 n. 35.)
5. Larkin, *The Larkin Papers*, vol. 3, 266.
6. H. H. Bancroft, *History of California*, vol. 4, 534–35.
7. Larkin, *The Larkin Papers*, vol. 3, 267.
8. As Lord Ashburton put it, "We certainly do not want [more] colonies, and least of all such as will be unmanageable from this distance and only serve to embroil us with our neighbor." (Quoted in Couglin, "California Ports," 32.)
9. Larkin, *The Larkin Papers*, vol. 4, 46.
10. Ibid., 44.
11. Ibid., 44–46.
12. Baldridge, 39–40.
13. Ibid.
14. Giffen, 55; Baldridge, 42.
15. Baldridge, 39–40.
16. H. H. Bancroft, *History of California*, vol. 4, 608 n. 40.
17. Ibid., 576–81. The figures include the total number of people

who arrived in the McMahon–Clyman, Swasey–Todd, Sublette, and Grigsby–Ide parties.

18. Ibid., 607 n. 40.
19. Ibid., 606.
20. Ibid.
21. Dillon, *Fool's Gold*, 182.
22. McChristian, 2. McChristian recalled that the gathering took place in May of 1846 and that the interrogating officer was General Vallejo, not Castro. This seems unlikely, because in April of 1846 Vallejo gave his famous pro-American speeches in Monterey and was doing everything possible to prevent an outbreak of hostilities. So McChristian may have been thinking of the November 1845 interview. Vallejo later became aware of McChristian's statement and remarked that the American had probably "mistaken the date of the meeting in Sonoma." Ibid., 13.
23. H. H. Bancroft, *History of California*, vol. 4, 607 n. 40.
24. Ibid.
25. Dillon, *Fool's Gold*, 219.
26. Ibid., 220.
27. H. H. Bancroft, *History of California*, vol. 4, 607. Sutter was urged to inspire trust in Castro as commandant general and was asked to inform Vallejo of the skills, places of origin, and the numbers of newcomers as they arrived.
28. Dillon, *Fool's Gold*, 223.
29. Ibid., 221.
30. M. G. Vallejo, "Historical and Personal Memoirs," vol. 5, 29–30.
31. Ibid.
32. H. H. Bancroft, *History of California*, vol. 4, 610 n. 45.
33. Dillon, *Fool's Gold*, 223; Hague and Langum, 119.
34. M. G. Vallejo, *Documentos*, vol. 12, 157.
35. Quoted in H. H. Bancroft, *History of California*, vol. 4, 608 n. 41.
36. Quoted in Tays, vol. 17 (June 1938), 163.
37. Ibid.
38. Langum, 23. Estimates of the number of foreigners who entered the region in 1845 range from 250 to 420. (H. H. Bancroft, *History of California*, vol. 4, 571; Tays, vol. 17 (June 1938), 161.
39. H. H. Bancroft, *History of California*, vol. 4, 605 n. 38. The orders were issued on July 10, 1845.
40. Quoted in Coughlin, "California Ports," 28.
41. Ibid.
42. H. H. Bancroft, *History of California*, vol. 4, 583 n. 24.
43. Dillon, *Fool's Gold*, 213–14.
44. Ibid. Egan, 308–309. William Tecumseh Sherman described Carson as "a small stoop-shouldered man, with reddish hair,

freckled face, soft blue eyes, and nothing to indicate extraordinary courage or daring." (Sherman, vol. 1, 75.)

45. Egan, 308–309. In his *Memoirs*, Frémont said that "Captain Sutter received me with the same friendly hospitality which had been so delightful to us the year before"—a fair sampling of the inaccuracies found in his *Memoirs* and *Expeditions*. The published accounts of his life and travels are polished, fascinating, and humane. He and his wife were careful to delete all those unsavory elements that the nineteenth century audience would have found repugnant. For instance, in April of 1846, Frémont authorized Kit Carson to lead an attack on a Wintu village near Reading's Rancho, and 175 Indians were slain. (H. H. Bancroft, *History of California*, vol. 5, 22; Egan, 325–26.) This was one of the worst massacres in California's history, but Frémont usually characterizes himself as generous and tolerant toward the Indians.

46. Dillon, *Fool's Gold*, 214.

Chapter 7: Prelude to Revolt

1. Larkin, *Larkin Papers*, vol. 4, 10.
2. Ibid., 150.
3. E. B. Smith, 79–80; Chambers, 274–77.
4. Quoted in H. H. Bancroft, *History of California*, vol. 5, 21.
5. Ibid., 8.
6. Ibid., 5 n. 9; Hague and Langum, 121.
7. Egan, 318–19.
8. Fallon, 25.
9. Dakin, 270–71; Frémont, *Memoirs*, 458.
10. H. H. Bancroft, *History of California*, vol. 5, 9.
11. Ibid., 4.
12. Larkin, *Larkin Papers*, vol. 4, 161.
13. Ibid., 227.
14. Ibid., 228–29.
15. Egan, 319; H. H. Bancroft, *History of California*, vol. 5, 9–10.
16. Dakin, 271.
17. Larkin, *Larkin Papers*, vol. 4, 230.
18. Egan, 320.
19. Larkin, *Larkin Papers*, vol. 4, 239–40.
20. Ibid., 237.
21. Ibid., 245.
22. Ibid.
23. H. H. Bancroft, *History of California*, vol. 5, 14 n. 29.
24. Larkin, *Larkin Papers*, vol. 4, 341; H. H. Bancroft, *History of California*, vol. 5, 13.

25. H. H. Bancroft, *History of California*, vol. 5, 13; Egan, 321.
26. M. G. Vallejo, *Documentos*, vol. 12, 184, 185, 189; H. H. Bancroft, *History of California*, vol. 5, 17 n. 33; Tays, vol. 17 (June 1938), 163.
27. H. H. Bancroft, *History of California*, vol. 5, 21.
28. Quoted in Dillon, *Fool's Gold*, 231–32.
29. Ibid.
30. M. G. Vallejo, "Historical and Personal Memoirs," vol. 5, 31.
31. Dillon, *Fool's Gold*, 233–34.
32. Egan, 324.
33. W. B. Ide, vii.
34. M. G. Vallejo, "Historical and Personal Memoirs," vol. 5, 68.
35. Ibid.; H. H. Bancroft, *History of California*, vol. 5, 56 n. 3.
36. M. G. Vallejo, "Historical and Personal Memoirs," vol. 5, 73. Possibly, it was Manuel Castro, not José Castro who said this. (See Alvarado, vol. 2, 133–34.)
37. H. H. Bancroft, *History of California*, vol. 5, 64 n. 15.
38. Parkes, 209–210; H. H Bancroft, *History of California*, vol. 4, 528–29.
39. H. H. Bancroft, *History of California*, vol. 5, 42.
40. M. G. Vallejo, "Historical and Personal Memoirs," vol. 5, 73, 75–76.
41. Ibid., 64. Vallejo had long suspected that his nephew Pablo de la Guerra was trying to play off English Consul Forbes against American Consul Larkin in order to prevent either foreign nation from gaining control of the country.
42. Dakin, 262–70.
43. Revere, 28–30.
44. Alvarado, vol. 5, 133–46; McKittrick, *Vallejo*, 248–53; Davis, 141–42; Lancey, 164–71.
45. H. H. Bancroft, *History of California*, vol. 5, 59–63.
46. Ibid.; McKittrick, *Vallejo*, 248–53. Hague and Langum (256 n. 34) agree with McKittrick, citing, among others, the following references: John Sutter to John Marsh, April 3, 1846, Box 240, Marsh Collection, California State Library; Larkin to Leidesdorff, April 13, 1846, in Larkin, *Larkin Papers*, vol. 4, 284; Larkin to Abel Stearns, May 1, 1846, in Larkin, *First and Last Consul*, 61–62.
47. Written copies of the orders were on the way to California aboard the *Congress*. (Sellers, 334–36.) Hague and Langum (116, 130) note that the packet of Benton letters was sent with Gillespie as an afterthought.
48. H. H. Bancroft, *History of California*, vol. 5, 63.
49. Ibid., 64–65.

50. Alvarado, vol. 5, 122–28; M. G. Vallejo, "Historical and Personal Memoirs," vol. 5, 106–109; H. H. Bancroft, *History of California*, vol. 5, 28 n. 53. Alvarado remembered that Vallejo and Adelaida were dancing that night, and the ex-governor thought she might have dropped a hint to Vallejo about the disguised marine.
51. Hague and Langum, 127–28.
52. Larkin, *Larkin Papers*, vol. 4, 354.

Chapter 8: "Men With Nothing to Lose"

1. McKittrick, *Vallejo*, 310–11.
2. Carriger, "Autobiography;" Emparan, 51; P. Vallejo, January 27, 1914.
3. Dillon, *Fool's Gold*, 335–36.
4. H. H. Bancroft, *History of California*, vol. 5, 65. Sutter expected more wagon trains "about the middle of September."
5. Egan, 327.
6. Ibid., 329; H. H. Bancroft, *History of California*, vol. 5, 27.
7. Regarding the packet of Benton family letters, it is doubtful they urged Frémont to start trouble with Mexico. Even after two engagements had been won by American arms, Senator Benton still denied that a war with Mexico was either called for or justified. (Chambers, 306–307; Sellers, 418.) Earlier on, he had surprised many of his colleagues in the Senate by telling them that a conflict with Mexico over Texas would be "unjust in itself—upon a peaceable neighbor—in violation of treaties and of pledged neutrality—unconstitutionally made." (Chambers, 275). President Polk resented Benton's "decided aversion to a war with Mexico," but he pushed American troops past the Neuces River to the Rio Grande, where the battle of Resaca de la Palma took place on May 9 (at the very time Frémont and Gillespie were camped at Klamath Lake).
8. H. H. Bancroft, *History of California*, vol. 5, 26 n. 47.
9. Larkin, *Larkin Papers*, vol. 4, 354.
10. Egan, 337–38.
11. Ibid.
12. R. Simpson, 34.
13. M. G. Vallejo, "Historical and Personal Memoirs," vol. 5, 109.
14. Dillon, *Fool's Gold,* 234; H. H. Bancroft, *History of California*, vol. 5, 22.
15. Larkin, *Larkin Papers*, vol. 4, 283–84.
16. Ibid.; Underhill, 30, 32.
17. H. H. Bancroft, *History of California*, vol. 5, 71.

18. Quoted in H. H. Bancroft, *History of California*, vol. 5, 65 n. 16.
19. Ibid., 64–65.
20. Larkin, *Larkin Papers*, vol. 4, 331.
21. H. H. Bancroft, *History of California*, vol. 5, 43.
22. Ibid.
23. Ibid., 34.
24. Ibid., 46.
25. Ibid., 48. By 1845 the military in California was consuming two-thirds of the province's total budget—far more than in earlier years—which enraged Pico. (Francis, 311.)
26. Hargrave, 6.
27. Giffen, 58.
28. Baldridge, 32.
29. Ibid., 11.
30. Ibid., 28.
31. Ibid., 33.
32. Ibid., 53–54.
33. Quoted in DeVoto, 125–26.
34. Hargrave, 12.
35. Baldridge, 18.
36. W. B. Ide, 29–30; H. H. Bancroft, *History of California*, vol. 5, 105.
37. H. H. Bancroft, *History of California*, vol. 5, 105–106.
38. M. G. Vallejo, *Documentos*, vol. 12, 222; M. G. Vallejo, "Historical and Personal Memoirs," vol. 5, 110–11; Tays, vol. 17 (June 1938), 164; H. H. Bancroft, *History of California*, vol. 5, 105–106.
39. Warner, Porterfield file; H. H. Bancroft, Pioneer Register, *History of California*, vol. 4, 728.
40. H. H. Bancroft, *History of California*, vol. 5, 106; Ford 5–6.
41. Quoted in Rogers, *William Brown Ide*, 33; S. Ide, 33.
42. H. H. Bancroft, *History of California*, vol. 5, 106.
43. Ibid., 93, 107; Ford, 5–7.

Chapter 9: The Revolt Begins

1. H. H. Bancroft, *History of California*, vol. 4, 738–39; Emparan, 28; Bidwell, 107.
2. H. H. Bancroft, *History of California*, vol. 5, 108–109; Egan, 342–43.
3. Ibid.; W. B. Ide, 35; Larkin, *Larkin Papers*, vol. 5, 120.
4. Egan, 343; H. H. Bancroft, *History of California*, vol. 5, 108.
5. H. H. Bancroft, *History of California*, vol. 5, 93; W. B. Ide, 30–31.
6. M. G. Vallejo, *Documentos*, vol. 12, 321.
7. H. H. Bancroft, Pioneer Register, *History of California*, vol. 4, 688–89.

8. W. B. Ide, 31–33.

9. Ibid.

10. Baldridge, 22; Hargrave, 6; W. B. Ide, 34.

11. W. B. Ide, 35.

12. H. H. Bancroft, *History of California*, vol. 5, 109–110; Egan, 344.

13. Hargrave, 4; W. B. Ide, 38; Egan, 344; Rogers, *Bear Flag Lieutenant*, 11.

14. Dillon, *Fool's Gold*, 245.

15. Baldridge, 38; Bryant, 289; W. B. Ide, 40.

16. Baldridge, 38; Egan, 345.

17. R. Leese, 2; Emparan, 203; Tays, vol. 17 (September 1938), 219.

18. Tays, vol. 17 (September 1938), 219; H. H. Bancroft, *History of California*, vol. 5, 112.

19. Bryant, 336.

20. Tays, vol. 17 (September 1938), 219–20; H. H. Bancroft, *History of California*, vol. 5, 112; M. G. Vallejo, "Historical and Personal Memoirs," vol. 5, 112–13.

21. Emparan, 202.

22. Tays, vol. 17 (September 1938), 219–20; M. G. Vallejo, "Historical and Personal Memoirs," vol. 5, 112.

23. Tays, vol. 17 (September 1938), 219–20; M. G. Vallejo, "Historical and Personal Memoirs," vol. 5, 112.

24. Baldridge, 5.

25. Ibid., 30.

26. J. Leese, 1.

27. Ibid., 1–2.

28. H. H. Bancroft, *History of California*, vol. 5, 112–13.

29. M. G. Vallejo, "Historical and Personal Memoirs," vol. 5, 113.

30. Tays, vol. 17 (September 1938), 220; Egan, 346.

31. Dakin, 237.

32. J. Leese, 3.

33. Tays, vol. 17 (September 1938), 221; Baldridge, 39.

34. J. Leese, 3; H. H. Bancroft, *History of California*, vol. 5, 116 n. 27.

35. J. Leese, 3.

36. Tays, vol. 17 (September 1938), 221.

37. Baldridge, 45.

38. W. B. Ide, 42.

39. H. H. Bancroft, *History of California*, vol. 5, 113.

40. Ibid., 114 n. 24.

41. J. Leese, 4.

42. W. B. Ide, 43.

43. Tays, vol. 17 (September 1938), 222.

44. W. B. Ide, 44.

45. Ibid., 44–45.

46. Tays, vol. 17 (September 1938), 222.
47. W. B. Ide, 64–65.
48. J. Leese, 4–6.
49. Ibid., 6.
50. Ibid., 5–6; W. B. Ide, 45.
51. McKittrick, *Vallejo*, 263.
52. Lyman, "First Native Born California Physician," 286–87.
53. J. Leese, 6.
54. "Statement of the interview between El Señor Don José de la Rosa, and Commander Jno. B. Montgomery Comr. U.S. Ship Portsmouth by Lieut. W. A. Bartlett U.S.N. Interpreter, by order of Commander Montgomery," *California Historical Society Quarterly*, 1 (July 1922): 79–80.
55. Ibid.
56. Rogers, *Bear Flag Lieutenant*, 13.
57. H. H. Bancroft, *History of California*, vol. 5, 119.
58. Baldridge, 38.
59. J. Leese, 7.
60. Ibid., 8.
61. H. H. Bancroft, *History of California*, vol. 5, 120; J. Leese, 8–9; M. G. Vallejo, "Historical and Personal Memoirs," vol. 5, 126–27.
62. H. H. Bancroft, *History of California*, vol. 5; J. Leese, 8–9; M. G. Vallejo, "Historical and Personal Memoirs," vol. 5, 126–127.
63. H. H. Bancroft, Pioneer Register, *History of California*, vol. 3, 775.
64. J. Leese, 10.

Chapter 10: Ordeal on the Sacramento

1. M. G. Vallejo, "Historical and Personal Memoirs," vol. 5, 125.
2. Quoted in Devoto, 38.
3. Taylor, 53.
4. J. Leese, 10; M. G. Vallejo, "Historical and Personal Memoirs," vol. 5, 123–24.
5. M. G. Vallejo, "Historical and Personal Memoirs," vol. 5, 124.
6. Ibid.
7. J. Leese, 10.
8. Tays, vol. 17 (September, 1938), 224; M. G. Vallejo, "Historical and Personal Memoirs," vol. 5, 124–25.
9. M. G. Vallejo, "Historical and Personal Memoirs," vol. 5, 96.
10. Baldridge, 54.
11. Ibid., 45.
12. J. Leese, 10–11; H. H. Bancroft, *History of California*, vol. 5, 121 n. 33.

13. J. Leese, 10–11; H. H. Bancroft, *History of California*, vol. 5, 121 n. 33.
14. Bidwell, 100.
15. M. G. Vallejo, "Historical and Personal Memoirs," vol. 5, 126–29.
16. S. Vallejo, 61.
17. M. G. Vallejo, "Historical and Personal Memoirs," vol. 5, 126–27.
18. Ibid.
19. M. G. Vallejo, "Historical and Personal Memoirs," vol. 5, 100–101; Dillon, *Fool's Gold*, 244.
20. Quoted in Dillon, *Fool's Gold*, 247.
21. H. H. Bancroft, *History of California*, vol. 5, 125 n. 3.
22. J. Leese, 11.
23. Platon later said this was one of the few acts of his life that he regretted. (Lyman, "The First Native Born California Physician," 287.)
24. Bidwell, 102; H. H. Bancroft, *History of California*, vol. 5, 146–48.
25. G. Bancroft, vol. 1 (October 1922), 178.
26. Warner, *passim*. North Bay demographics tend to conflict with Warner's estimates.
27. W. B. Ide, 85.
28. "Report of Lt. Misroon," *California Historical Society Quarterly* 1 (July 1922): pp 87–89.
29. Emparan, 204.
30. "Report of Lt. Misroon, " *California Historical Society Quarterly* 1 (July 1922): pp. 89–90.
31. Quoted in Egan, 352.
32. Emparan, 204; H. H. Bancroft, *History of California*, vol. 5, 124.
33. Dillon, *Fool's Gold*, 245.
34. Bidwell, 57.
35. Ibid.; Dillon, *Fool's Gold*, 246.
36. H. H. Bancroft, *History of California*, vol. 5, 125 n. 3.
37. McKittrick, "Salvador Vallejo," 322.
38. The imprisonment occurred during Governor Echeandía's administration. One night while Vallejo was serving as acting commandant of the Monterey presidio, he was surprised by six rebellious soldiers who forced their way into his room. Despite the fact that Don José Castro was then a very popular officer, Vallejo, Castro, and Alvarado were all marched away to a lockup in the cavalry barracks. Other officers were rounded up, too; later they were moved to a reeking cell close to the embarcadero. As the prisoners were being led into the jail, the resident inmates were given a reprieve. Fearing that their liberators might have a change of heart, the convicts ran half-naked into the streets, carrying their clothes in their arms. Three weeks later, all the officers were freed, including Vallejo; but since his authority was still feared, he was banished to San

Diego. (Tays, vol. 17 [September 1938], 221–22; H. H. Bancroft, *History of California*, vol. 3, 69–74.)

Chapter 11: Murder and Misdirection

1. Davis, 22.
2. R. Leese, 2.
3. Ibid., 3–5.
4. Ibid.
5. Ibid.
6. Emparan, 200.
7. Larkin, *Larkin Papers*, vol. 5, 56.
8. Davis, 65.
9. Quoted in Regnery, 14.
10. Emparan, 203.
11. Russell, 7.
12. H. H. Bancroft, *History of California*, vol. 5, 152 n. 4.
13. W. B. Ide, 51.
14. Larkin, *First and Last Consul*, 81.
15. Larkin, *Larkin Papers*, vol. 5, 61.
16. Larkin, *First and Last Consul*, 81.
17. Larkin, *Larkin Papers*, vol. 5, 66.
18. M. G. Vallejo, "Historical and Personal Memoirs," vol. 5, 103.
19. Larkin, *Larkin Papers*, vol. 5, 40.
20. Knight, Statement, 7–11; H. H. Bancroft, *History of California*, vol. 5, 162 n. 10.
21. Davis, 59; H. H. Bancroft, *History of California*, vol. 5, 160–61.
22. Egan, 353; H. H. Bancroft, *History of California*, vol. 5, 163; Baldridge, 22.
23. Ramón Carrillo to Francisca Vallejo, in G. Bancroft, vol. 1 (Oct. 1922), 185.
24. M. G. Vallejo, "Historical and Personal Memoirs," vol. 5, 142–43.
25. Ibid., 122.
26. H. H. Bancroft, *History of California*, vol. 5, 160–61.
27. *The Californian*, September 12, 1846.
28. H. H. Bancroft, *History of California*, vol. 5, 161 n. 10.
29. Ibid., 162 n. 10.
30. Ibid.
31. M. G. Vallejo, "Historical and Personal Memoirs," vol. 5, 121–23.
32. H. H. Bancroft, Pioneer Register, *History of California*, vol. 3, 752.
33. Ibid.
34. Beard, 26; Baldridge, 70; Davis, 103.
35. Revere, 83.
36. Baldridge, 64; H. H. Bancroft, *History of California*, vol. 5, 166–67.
37. Baldridge, 64–70.

38. Ibid., 71.
39. Ibid., 19.
40. H. H. Bancroft, *History of California*, vol. 5, 171; Jasper O'Farrell letter to *Los Angeles Star*, September 27, 1856, in Davis, 293–94.
41. Egan, 356; H. H. Bancroft, *History of California*, vol. 5, 172 n. 2.
42. Robert A. Thompson, *Conquest of California* (Santa Rosa: Sonoma Democrat Pub. Co., 1896), 21.
43. Jasper O'Farrell letter to *Los Angeles Star*, in Davis, 293–94.
44. W. B. Ide, 104–6; H. H. Bancroft, *History of California*, vol. 5, 174–5.
45. H. H. Bancroft, *History of California*, vol. 5, 176.
46. R. Leese, 5.
47. Egan, 360–61.
48. Ibid., 361.

Chapter 12: What Friend Larkin Will Do

1. Russell, 9.
2. Revere, 74.
3. H. H. Bancroft, Pioneer Register, *History of California*, vol. 5, 695.
4. Emparan, 36.
5. Ibid.
6. H. H. Bancroft, *History of California*, vol. 5, 228 n. 6.
7. Larkin, *Larkin Papers*, vol. 5, 106; H. H. Bancroft, *History of California*, vol. 5, 230.
8. Emparan, 37.
9. M. G. Vallejo, "Historical and Personal Memoirs," vol. 5, 134.
10. Ibid., 160.
11. Emparan, 203.
12. Ibid., 206.
13. Bryant, 336.
14. Tays, vol. 17 (September 1938), 226–27.
15. Russell, 11.
16. Dillon, *Fool's Gold*, 250–51; Egan, 362.
17. Egan, 363–64.
18. On the southward march, each of Frémont's men had two horses, "the same that had been brought from Sonoma." (Russell, 12.)
19. Larkin, *Larkin Papers*, vol. 5, 242.
20. Ibid.
21. Emparan, 39.
22. Tays, vol. 17 (September 1938), 227.
23. Emparan, 39.
24. Egan, 364.

25. Baldridge, 29–30; H. H. Bancroft, *History of California*, vol. 5, 250. Considering that Frémont had strong motives at this point for revealing any "secret instructions" he might have received from his father-in-law or the war department, the interchange with Sloat indicates that his orders were either identical with, or very similar to, the ones received by Larkin and Gillespie.

26. Harlow, 138–39.

27. Larkin, *Larkin Papers*, vol. 5, 178.

28. Timothy Murphy, "The Liberation of Vallejo." *Morning Call*, July 10, 1886. The journey took William Tecumseh Sherman three leisurely days of travel the following year. (Sherman, vol. 1, 59–60.) Two days prior to Murphy's journey, Stockton had already sent orders to Sutter's Fort requesting the release of Vallejo and his brother-in-law.

29. Larkin, *Larkin Papers*, vol. 5, 179.

30. Ibid., 180.

31. Quoted in Harlow, 141.

Chapter 13: A Changed Man

1. See Secretary of War Marcy's orders to Kearny dated June 3, 1846, quoted in Clarke, 396.

2. Larkin, *Larkin Papers*, vol. 5, 124.

3. Revere, 25.

4. Larkin, *Larkin Papers*, vol. 5, 118; H. H. Bancroft, *History of California*, vol. 5, 232, 264–65.

5. The letter Stockton sent to Vallejo with Murphy is quoted in Tays, vol. 17 (September 1938), 228:

   Dear Sir:

   I have the honor to acknowledge the receipt of your letter of the 23d inst. addressed to my predecessor, Commodore Sloat.

   I hasten to inform you that one of the first acts of my administration was to order your immediate release from confinement and I hope before this reaches you, that you will be at liberty.

   I was not aware of the name and rank of others confined with you; I now send by courier (notwithstanding I have already sent one today) to Captain Montgomery for the release of your friends as well as yourself. . . .

   R. F. Stockton — Commander-in-Chief

6. M. G. Vallejo, Release from Fort Sutter, facsimile, Special Collections, Stanford University.

7. Tays, vol. 17 (September 1938), 229.

8. Emparan, 42. Another source, T. H. Chandler of San Francisco, stated that Vallejo was an inch under six feet in height. (Ibid., 397.)
9. H. H. Bancroft, *History of California*, vol. 5, 299 n. 11.
10. Parmelee, 40–41.
11. M. G. Vallejo, "Historical and Personal Memoirs," vol. 2, 31; vol. 3, 387–88.
12. Russell, 8.
13. *Morning Call*, July 10, 1886. Forty years later, in July of 1886, when Vallejo and Murphy embraced at a celebration commemorating the raising of the American flag by Commodore Sloat, Murphy made a humorous remark about the General's chin, noticing that after four decades, he was still clean-shaven. Vallejo reminded Murphy of the gift of 500 *vaquillas* (young cattle) he had offered the American in gratitude for his services.
14. Emparan, 43.
15. Ibid., 42.
16. Tays, vol. 17 (September 1938), 229.
17. Russell, 16; H. H. Bancroft, *History of California*, vol. 5, 160 n. 9.
18. S. Vallejo, 72, 78; McKittrick, *Vallejo*, 322.
19. H. H. Bancroft, *History of California*, vol. 5, 467.
20. Larkin, *Larkin Papers*, vol. 5, 236–37.
21. Egan, 367; Harlow, 145; H. H. Bancroft, *History of California*, vol. 5, 283 n. 35.
22. Davis, 209.
23. Quoted in Regnery, 31–32.
24. Colton, 28.
25. Ibid., 14.
26. Larkin, *Larkin Papers*, vol. 5, 133.
27. H. H. Bancroft, *History of California*, vol. 5, 268 n. 15.
28. Ibid., Pioneer Register, vol. 3, 741.
29. Harlow, 141.
30. H. H. Bancroft, *History of California*, vol. 5, 269 n. 16.
31. Ibid., 273.
32. Ibid.
33. Colton, 35.
34. Fallon, 28.
35. Russell, 20.
36. H. H. Bancroft, *History of California*, vol. 5, 286–87. Stockton asked Frémont to return to the north by land and raise more volunteers for the California Battalion. Then the commodore boarded the *Congress* and sailed north himself.
37. S. Vallejo, 80–81.
38. McKittrick, "Salvador Vallejo," 323; H. H. Bancroft, *History of California*, vol. 5, 301; Parmelee, 42.

39. H. H. Bancroft, *History of California*, vol. 5, 301.
40. Emparan, 44.
41. Larkin, *Larkin Papers*, vol. 5, 237.
42. Ibid.
43. Ibid., 243; vol. 6, 360–61.
44. Ibid., vol. 5, 243.
45. Ibid., 232.
46. Ibid., vol. 6, 173–74.
47. H. H. Bancroft, *History of California*, vol. 5, 295.
48. Davis, 28.
49. Harlow, 157; H. H. Bancroft, *History of California*, vol. 5, 296 n. 6.
50. Bryant, 330–31; Harlow, 158.
51. H. H. Bancroft, *History of California*, vol. 5, 298; Emparan, 126, 395.
52. Bryant, 334.

Chapter 14: The Californians Retake the South

1. Larkin, *Larkin Papers*, vol. 5, 262.
2. Russell, 31.
3. Ibid.
4. Harlow, 166–67.
5. Harlow, 167; L. Carrillo, 18.
6. Colton, 73.
7. Ibid., 82.
8. M. G. Vallejo, "Historical and Personal Memoirs," vol. 5, 167; Harlow, 195–96.
9. Harlow, 193–95.
10. Egan, 380–83; Harlow, 196.
11. Harlow, Ibid.; H. H. Bancroft, *History of California*, vol. 5, 369–72.
12. Larkin, *Larkin Papers*, vol. 5, 3.
13. Ibid., 3.
14. Harlow, 181.
15. Egan, 391.
16. Harlow, 187.
17. Larkin, *Larkin Papers*, vol. 5, 310.
18. Ibid., vol. 6, 3.
19. Harlow, 209–18; H. H. Bancroft, *History of California*, vol. 5, 391–97.
20. Clarke, 252; Larkin, *Larkin Papers*, vol. 6, 3–4.
21. H. H. Bancroft, *History of California*, vol. 5, 402.
22. Emparan, 206–207.
23. McKittrick, *Vallejo*, 169–70; 308.

24. Ibid., 181 n. 5; Northrop, vol. 2, 310.
25. P. Vallejo, February 4, 1914; Emparan, 93.
26. Larkin, *Larkin Papers*, vol. 5, 307.
27. Emparan, 93.
28. Ibid.; P. Vallejo, *passim*.
29. Emparan, 94-95.
30. Harlow, 174-75, 236; Sellers 422-26. Kearny's orders from Polk were more recent than Stockton's by approximately six months. Dated June 3 and June 18, 1846, Polk's instructions told the general to assume military control of the territory and to organize a new government. Stockton's authority was based on the naval command he had inherited from Commodore Sloat. Other instructions for General Kearny were on the way, conveying Polk's wishes that General Kearny assume both the military and "administrative functions" of California's government. (Clarke, 275, 277-78; Harlow, 250-51.)
31. Harlow, 231.
32. Ibid., 233.
33. Ibid., 232.
34. Ibid., 234.
35. Ibid., 235.
36. Ibid., 232.
37. The figures are compiled from H. H. Bancroft, Harlow, and Egan. The eight engagements referred to are Olómpali, Chino, Domínguez Hills, La Natividad, San Pasqual, Santa Clara, San Gabriel River, and the Battle of the Mesa. The figures do not include the deaths of Cowie and Fowler, the DeHaro Twins or José Berreyessa, which were the result of criminal acts committed apart from actual engagements. Omitted for the same reason are the eleven Californians killed by Luiseño Indians at Pauma, shortly after the Battle of San Pasqual. Eleven dead Californians General Kearny "thought he saw" on the battlefield after San Pasqual were not seen by anyone else, nor were they admitted as losses by Andrés Pico. Bancroft, Harlow, and Egan do not include them in their estimates.
38. Quoted in Egan, 410.
39. Harlow, 241.
40. Quoted in Emparan, 55. The invitation read:

    I have the honor to transmit to you the Commission of a member of a Council of State, intended to exercise the functions of a legislative body in the Territorial Government of California.

    Your great influence in the country, with the high respect and regard entertained for your person by the Californians will render your service of great value in tranquilizing the people and effecting the restoration of order and civil government.

I shall feel great pleasure in being associated with you in the accomplishment of these objects and trust that it will not be incompatible with your private engagements to accept the post offered you.

J. C. Frémont
Governor, Commander-in-Chief of California

41. Larkin, *Larkin Papers*, vol. 6, 16.
42. Emparan, 55.
43. Harlow, 242; H. H. Bancroft, *History of California*, vol. 5, 571. In Los Angeles, the enigmatic Frémont was attending balls, befriending the local population, and wearing a big sombrero; but he was also running up a stupendous debt (estimated to be about $600,000), funded at high rates of interest. In the meantime, duties collected in California for 1847–1848 totaled only $120,000.
44. Quoted in Emparan, 57.
45. Quoted in Ibid., 56.
46. Ibid., 57.
47. Clarke, 276–77; Harlow, 250–51.
48. Harlow, 262.

Chapter 15: The Slip and Slide Transition

1. Wood, 106.
2. H. H. Bancroft, *History of California*, vol. 5, 539.
3. Clarke, 297; H. H. Bancroft, *History of California*, vol. 5, 568; Hurtado, 93; Rawls, 84–85.
4. Dillon, *Fool's Gold*, 256.
5. Parmelee, 55; see Joseph A. King's "Lewis Keseberg 'An Unfortunate Victim,'" in *The Californians* 10 (July/August 1992): 22–27.
6. Conmy, "Benicia," 7–8; H. H. Bancroft, *History of California*, vol. 5, 670–71 n. 3.
7. Colton, 228.
8. H. H. Bancroft, Pioneer Register, *History of California*, vol. 5, 758; McKittrick, *Vallejo*, 282–83.
9. M. G. Vallejo, *Documentos*, vol. 12, 304.
10. Emparan, 47.
11. Larkin, *Larkin Papers*, vol. 6, 150.
12. H. H. Bancroft, *History of California*, vol. 5, 450; Egan, 426–27. At the conclusion of Frémont's court martial, he was found guilty of the three charges brought against him (mutiny, disobedience to

a superior officer, and "conduct to the prejudice of good order and military discipline"). The court recommended that he be "dismissed from the service." Based on evidence presented during the trial, President Polk agreed with the court's opinion on the last two counts but did not approve the charge of mutiny. The chief executive ordered that the "penalty of dismissal from the service be remitted." Frémont, in a characteristic gesture, refused the executive pardon and resigned. Within less than two years, he returned to California. (Egan, 441, 461–62.)

13. H. H. Bancroft, *History of California*, vol. 5, 467 n. 57.
14. M. G. Vallejo, *Documentos*, vol. 12, 332.
15. Fox, 60; H. H. Bancroft, *History of California*, vol. 6, 65–66.
16. *Sonoma Democrat*, July 8, 1876.
17. H. H. Bancroft, *History of California*, vol. 6, 50–58.
18. Ibid.
19. Ibid., 62 n. 20.
20. Emparan, 255.
21. Atherton, 112.
22. Emparan, 290.
23. Ibid., 257.
24. *Treaty of Guadalupe Hidalgo 1848*, Article VIII, 12.
25. Ibid., Article XXI, 26.
26. Ibid., 16. It needs to be pointed out that opinion in Mexico was by no means unanimous. Some people still thought of the surrendered territory as arid and worthless, but others were far better informed about California's potential value. The ratifying vote in the Mexican Chamber of Deputies was 51 to 35, and in the Senate was more lopsided in favor of ratification, 33 to 4. Protests against the treaty were lodged by the state governments of Coahuila, Oaxaca, Tamaulipas, Jalisco, Veracruz, Zacatecas, Chihuahua, and Mexico. But the majority of leaders believed that the treaty would not only prevent a worse military disaster from occurring, but would promote a spirit of unity in the country by concentrating Mexico's social order within a defensible region. (Griswold del Castillo, 46–54, 118–122.)
27. Sierra, 243.
28. Merrill, 72.
29. Marryat, 55; Emparan, 259.
30. Menefee, 47–49; Emparan, 258.
31. Roske, 249. The Indian population decreased from about 150,000 in 1848 to approximately 30,000 in 1860. (Hurtado, 1.)
32. M. G. Vallejo, "What the Gold Rush Brought to California," 55–56.
33. Rogers, *William Brown Ide*, 66.

34. Taylor, 153–59; Harlow, 328; Royce, 257. President Taylor later sanctioned the act.
35. Taylor, 107.
36. Emparan, 60.
37. Royce, 263.
38. Browne, 11. Gwin's figures were inaccurate (see text below).
39. Hargis, "Native Californians," 7.
40. Ibid., 3; H. H. Bancroft, *History of California*, vol. 6, 305.
41. Browne, *passim*; Hargis, "Native Californians," 5–6.
42. Quoted in Emparan, 70.
43. Hargis, "Native Californians," 5.
44. Egan, 441, 461–62.
45. Taylor, 119.
46. Emparan, 258.
47. Taylor, 119.
48. Browne, 63–68.
49. Ibid., 259–60, 267; Hargis, "Women's Rights," 325–28.
50. Browne, 29, 257; H. H. Bancroft, *History of California*, vol. 6, 290 n. 76.
51. Browne, 323.
52. Ibid., 303.
53. Ibid.; Emparan, 70–71.
54. Oxford, 32.
55. Fink, 120; Emparan, 72.
56. Quoted in Taylor, 189.
57. Emparan, 74; H. H. Bancroft, Pioneer Register, *History of California*, vol. 5, 730.

Chapter 16: Consequences

1. Emparan, 125.
2. Larkin to Abel Stearns, in Larkin, *First and Last Consul*, 104.
3. Atherton, 124–29. In a reminiscence of old California, novelist Gertrude Atherton described the career of a venerable ranchero whom she called Don Diego Vibora. This "Vibora" was lucky enough to have an American son-in-law to pay off all the debts on his quarter-of-a-million-acre estate. Rather than see the property jeopardized again, Vibora's son-in-law gave the old man a handsome allowance, but title to the property was always reserved for his grandchildren. Atherton implied that the arrangement was not uncommon after the American takeover, and she may have been thinking of the relationship between Juan Bandini and Abel Stearns. There is no doubt, however, that she placed the

fictionalized Vibora in the same category with General Vallejo.
She referred to Don Mariano by name, saying that after his
fortunes had declined, he was well cared for by his in-laws.

4. Ibid., 28.
5. Ibid., 119.
6. Ibid.
7. Oxford, 40; McKittrick, *Vallejo*, 298.
8. San Jose received 1,292. (Oxford, 41.) Emparan gives a margin of
   nearly seven to one, stating that Vallejo received 8,949 votes to
   San Jose's 1,371. (Emparan, 80.)
9. Emparan, 78–79.
10. Ibid.
11. Oxford, 33, 46.
12. *San Francisco Alta California,* January 16, 1852.
13. Quoted in Oxford, 50.
14. Graham received $2,500 to shift his block of friends into the
    Benicia camp. (Oxford, 56; Hague and Langum, 205.)
15. Gates, "California's Embattled Settlers," 336.
16. Emparan, 261.
17. Quoted in Oxford, 57.
18. Emparan, 75 – 76.
19. Ibid., 211.
20. California Legislature, *Statutes of California*, 1st sess., Chap.
    133 (1850), 408–410; Rawls, 85–91, 104–108, 132, 163–66;
    Hurtado, 1, 3, 128–31. In a very real sense, the statute backfired
    on its creators. The gold miners and the majority of Anglo new-
    comers saw the Indians as obstacles to be removed, not as impor-
    tant parts of the economy. In the 1850s and 1860s, many Indians
    were actually enslaved, mainly in the more isolated parts of the
    state. Sheriffs seemed to go blind or lose their hearing when mas-
    sacres of the Indians took place. Between 1848 and 1860, the
    Native American population fell from 150,000 to 30,000. Far
    from guaranteeing a supply of workers (as Vallejo and Bidwell
    had hoped), the labor pool all but vanished because of this law.
    Probably the law's worst provision was that a child could be
    brought before a Justice of the Peace by his or her parents or by
    "friends of the child" and could be handed over to an employer
    until the youngster had reached his or her majority. Here again,
    the practice was not far different from what had gone on in
    Mexican times. But because of abuses of the law, what the
    Indians suffered between 1848 and 1870 was far worse than
    anything they had experienced under Hispanic rule.
21. Emparan, 84 – 85.

22. Ibid., 263.

23. Ibid., 262, 265. Frisbie sometimes handled money matters for Platon Vallejo, as well as for other Vallejo family members. While Platon was attending college on the East Coast, Frisbie sold a farm for him. The young man later wrote Frisbie, "You have been a brother more than kind to me. . . ." (Ibid., 319 – 20.) Besides being likeable, possessing refinement, and knowing "the right way" to do things, Frisbie was also something of a scrapper. In New York, he had been elected captain of the Van Rensselaer Guard, reputed to be one of the best-drilled units in the state. In later years, he formed the Vallejo Rifles and Frisbie Guards, and during the Civil War was given the rank of adjutant-general by Governor Leland Stanford.

24. Ibid., 330.

25. Ibid., 87.

26. M. G. Vallejo, "Historical and Personal Memoirs," vol. 4, 199.

27. Emparan, 384.

28. H. H. Bancroft, Pioneer Register, *History of California*, vol. 5, 741; Emparan, 304. Granville Swift resented Vallejo's prominence in the Sonoma Valley and got even by building a palatial house called Temelec Hall. It was much grander than Lachyrma Montis and boasted four swan fountains to the Vallejo estate's one.

29. Emparan, 290.

30. Ibid., 434.

31. G. Simpson, vol. 1, 383–84.

32. Davis, 139.

33. Emparan, 293.

34. Ibid., 290–91.

35. Ibid.

36. Ibid., 210. Some of Vallejo's letters to Ruiz de Burton are in the Huntington Library.

37. Ibid., 109.

38. Ibid., 292.

39. Ibid., 293.

40. Ibid., 380.

41. Ibid., 381–82.

42. Ibid., 104, 294.

43. *Guadalupe Hidalgo Treaty of Peace*, 12–18.

44. W. W. Robinson, 106.

45. Davis, 105.

46. Emparan, 265–66.

47. Ibid., 106.

48. W. W. Robinson, 237; H. H. Bancroft, Pioneer Register, *History of California*, vol. 4, 714.

49. Gates, "Suscol Principle," 454.

50. Quoted in Underhill, 263. The complete document runs as follows:

> Whereas the citizen Mariano Guadaloupe Vallejo, Colonel of Cavalry and Military Commandant of the frontiers of Sonoma has solicited from this Government the purchase of the land known by name of SOSCOL in the jurisdiction of said Frontiers, bounded on North by lands called Tulcay and Suisun, and on the East and South by the Straits of Carquinez, Mare Island and Napa Creek; the necessary and investigations having previously been taken: I have in virtue of the faculties with which I am invested by the Supreme Government of the Mexican Nations, sold him the said land, Soscol, for the sum of Five Thousand Dollars, which this Government has received to its satisfaction; declaring him the ownership thereof by these present letters, in virtue whereof, he may occupy and possess it freely and exclusively, destining it to the use and cultivation which may best suit him, without any restriction.
>
> Therefore I command that these presents serve him for a Title, to be recorded in the corresponding book and acknowledged by all the authorities of the Departments of the Republic, and be delivered to the party interested as private property, bought from the Government of the Department in due and legal form.
> Given in Monterey on the nineteenth of June, One Thousand, eight hundred and forty four.
>
> Manuel Micheltorena
> Francisco Arce, *Secretary, ad interem.*
> I the undersigned do hereby certify that the foregoing is a true and faithful translation of the original title.
>
> Monterey, February 18, 1848
> W.E.P. Hartnell
> Gov't. Translator

51. *The United States v. M. G. Vallejo* (1 Black 541), in *United States Supreme Court Reports*, vols. 66–69 (Newark, New York: The Lawyers' Co-Operative Publishing Co., 1884), 232–40.

52. Lucy, 2.

53. Emparan, 107–108.

54. Ibid., 296.

55. Ibid., 320.

56. Ibid., 213–14.

57. Ibid., 215–16.

58. Ibid., 119, 232, 431.

59. Ibid., 316–17.
60. Ruiz de Burton, 8–14, 77. Also see the correspondence between Vallejo and Amparo Ruiz de Burton in the Huntington Library.
61. Emparan, 68–69.
62. Ibid., 358–59.
63. Ibid., 368–74.
64. Ibid., 362–64.
65. Ibid., 247–48.
66. Ibid., 216, 226.
67. Ibid., 139–40.
68. Ibid., 187, 210.
69. Ibid., 122.
70. Ibid., 112.
71. Ibid.
72. Ibid., 112–14.
73. Ibid.
74. Ibid., 115.
75. Holding title in the wife's name was a legal precaution used by Spaniards both in Europe and in California.
76. Ibid., 223.
77. Ibid., 214.
78. Ibid., 435.
79. Ibid., 226.
80. Lucy, 2.
81. Ibid., 3; Emparan, 273.
82. Emparan, 160, 177.
83. Ibid., 119.
84. Ibid., 64.
85. Ibid., 413.
86. Ibid., 345.
87. M. G. Vallejo, "Historical and Personal Memoirs," vol. 4, 199.
88. Emparan, 183, 342.
89. Ibid., 193–94.
90. Ibid., 236, 282.
91. McKittrick, *Vallejo*, 353.
92. W. B. Ide, ix.

Bibliography

Manuscript Primary Sources

Alvarado, Juan B. *Historia de California,* 5 vols. Bancroft Library, University of California, Berkeley.

Baldridge, William. "Days of '46." Bancroft Library, University of California, Berkeley.

John Bidwell Collection. California State Library, Sacramento.

Boggs, William. "Statement." Bancroft Library, University of California, Berkeley.

Brown, Charles E. "Statement." Bancroft Library, University of California, Berkeley.

Carriger, Nicolas. "Autobiography." Bancroft Library, University of California, Berkeley.

Carrillo, Julio. "Statement." Bancroft Library, University of California, Berkeley.

Ford, Henry L. "The Bear Flag Revolution in California, 1846." Bancroft Library, University of California, Berkeley.

Hargrave, William H. "California in 1846." Bancroft Library, University of California, Berkeley.

Knight, William. "Statement." Bancroft Library, University of California, Berkeley.

Lancey, Thomas C. "U.S. Sloop-of-War Dale, its Cruise, together with gleanings by the Wayside, including the Conquest of California." Bancroft Library, University of California, Berkeley.

Leese, Jacob. "Bear Flag Statement." Bancroft Library, University of California, Berkeley.

Leese, Rosalia. "History of Bear Flag Party." Bancroft Library, University of California, Berkeley.

Marsh, John. Manuscript Collection. California State Library, Sacramento.

McChristian, Pat. "Statement." Bancroft Library, University of California, Berkeley.

Valdez, Doroteo. "Reminiscences." Bancroft Library, University of California, Berkeley.

Vallejo, Mariano G. *Documentos para La Historia de California.* 36 vols. Bancroft Library, University of California, Berkeley.

————. "Historical and Personal Memoirs Relating to Alta California." Translated by Earl E. Hewitt. 5 vols. Bancroft Library, University of California, Berkeley.

————. Vallejo Collection. Huntington Library, San Marino, California.

Vallejo, Salvador. "Notas Historicas." Bancroft Library, University of California, Berkeley.

Published Primary Sources

Anderson, Charles R., ed. *Journal of A Cruise to the Pacific Ocean, 1842–1844, in the Frigate United States.* Durham, N.C.: Duke University Press, 1937.

Bancroft, George. "Documentary." Edited by Robert E. Cowan. *California Historical Society Quarterly* 1 (July 1922), 78–95; (October 1922), 178–85; (January 1923), 290–95.

Bandini, José. *A Description of California in 1828.* Berkeley: Friends of the Bancroft Library, 1951.

Bidwell, John. *In California Before the Gold Rush.* Los Angeles: Ward Ritchie Press, 1948.

Browne, J. Ross. *Report of the Debates in the Convention of California.* Washington, D.C.: John T. Towers, 1850.

Bryant, Edwin. *What I Saw in California.* Reprint, Minneapolis: Ross & Haines, 1967.

California Star. [Yerba Buena and San Francisco]

The Californian. [Monterey and San Francisco]

Cerruti, Henry. *Ramblings in California.* Edited by Margaret Mollins and Virginia E. Thickens. Berkeley: Friends of the Bancroft Library, 1954.

Clyman, James. *Journal of a Mountain Man.* Edited by Linda M. Hasselstrom. Missoula: Mountain Press Publishing Company, 1984.

Colton, Rev. Walter. *Three Years in California.* New York: A. S. Barnes & Co., 1850.

Dana, Richard Henry, Jr. *Two Years Before the Mast.* Illustrated by Alexander Mueller. New York: The Heritage Press, 1947.

Davis, William Heath. *Seventy-Five Years in California.* Edited by Harold A. Small. San Francisco: John Howell Books, 1967.

Duflot de Mofras, Eugene. *Exploration du territoire de l'Oregon, des Californies et de la Mer Vermeille.* 2 vols. Paris: Arthus Bertrand, 1844.

Du Four, Clarence John, ed. "The Russian Withdrawal from California." *California Historical Society Quarterly* 12 (September 1933): 249–76.

Fallon, Thomas. *California Cavalier, the Journals of Captain Thomas Fallon.* Edited by Thomas McEnery. San Jose, Calif.: Inishfallen Enterprises, 1978.

Farnham, Thomas Jefferson. *Travels in California.* Oakland: Biobooks, 1947.

Figueroa, José. *The Manifesto to the Mexican Republic.* Foreword by Jos. A. Sullivan. Oakland: Biobooks, 1952.

Frémont, John Charles. *The Expeditions of John Charles Frémont.* Edited by Donald Jackson and Mary Lee Spence. 3 vols. Urbana: University of Illinois Press, 1970–84.

———. *Memoirs of My Life.* Chicago: Belford, Clarke & Company, 1887.

Ide, William B. *An Authentic History of the Conquest of California.* In *Who Conquered California? The Conquest of California by the Bear Flag Party* (Glorieta, N.M.: Rio Grande Press, 1967).

Journal of the Senate. 1st sess., 1850. San Jose: J. Winchester, 1850.

La Perouse, Jean Francois de. *Monterey in 1786, The Journals of Jean Francois de la Perouse.* Introduction and Commentary by Malcolm Margolin. Berkeley: Heyday Books, 1989.

Larkin, Thomas O. *Chapters in the Early Life of Thomas Oliver Larkin, Including His Experiences in the Carolinas and the Building of the Larkin House in Monterey.* Edited by Robert J. Parker. San Francisco: California Historical Society, 1939.

———. *First and Last Consul: Thomas Oliver Larkin and the Americanization of California.* 2d ed. Edited by John A. Hawgood. Palo Alto: Pacific Books Publishers, 1970.

———. *The Larkin Papers: Personal, Business, and Official Correspondence of Thomas Oliver Larkin, Merchant and United States Consul in California.* Edited by George P. Hammond. 10 vols. Berkeley: University of California Press, 1951–1968.

Marryat, Frank. *Mountains and Molehills*. Stanford: Stanford University Press, 1952.

Morning Call. [San Francisco]

New Helvetia Diary: A Record of Events Kept by John A. Sutter and his Clerks at New Helvetia, California from September 9, 1845 to May 25, 1848. San Francisco: Grabhorn Press, 1939.

Ord, Augustias de la Guerra. *Occurrences in Hispanic California*. Translated and edited by Francis Price and William H. Ellison. Washington, D.C.: Academy of American Franciscan History, 1956.

Pico, Pío. *Don Pío Pico's Historical Narrative*. Translated by Arthur P. Botello, edited by Martin Cole and Henry Welcome. Glendale, Calif.: Arthur H. Clark Co., 1973.

Revere, Joseph Warren. *A Tour of Duty in California*. New York and Boston: C. S. Francis & Co., 1849.

Robinson, Alfred. *Life in California Before the Conquest*. Reprint, Santa Barbara and Salt Lake City: Peregrine Smith, 1970.

Ruiz de Burton, María Amparo. *The Squatter and the Don*. Edited by Rosaura Sánchez and Beatrice Pita. Houston: Arte Publico Press, 1992.

Russell, William. "Reminiscences of Old Times, A Private-Eye View of the Mexican War in California." Edited by Fred B. Rogers. *The Historical Society of Southern California Quarterly* 33 (March 1951): 5–36.

San Francisco Alta Calfornia.

Sherman, William T. *Memoirs of General William T. Sherman Written by Himself*. Appendix by James G. Blaine. 2 vols. New York: C. L. Webster & Co., 1891.

Simpson, Sir George. *Narrative of a Journey around the World, During the Years 1841 and 1842*. 2 vols. London: Henry Colburn, 1847.

Statutes of California. 1st sess., 1850. San Jose: J. Winchester, 1850.

Taylor, Bayard. *Eldorado, or, Adventures in the Path of Empire*. Reprint, Lincoln: University of Nebraska Press, 1988.

United States Supreme Court Report. Vols. 66—99. Newark, New York: The Lawyers' Co-Operative Publishing Company, 1884.

Vallejo, Guadalupe. "Ranch and Mission Days in Alta California." *The Century* 19 (New Series, December 1890): 183–192.

Vallejo, Mariano G. "What the Gold Rush Brought to California." In *The Course of Empire, First Hand Accounts of California in the*

Days of the Gold Rush of '49. Edited by Valeska Bari. New York: Coward–McCann, 1931.

Vallejo, Platon. "Memoirs of the Vallejos." Arranged for publication by James H. Wilkins. *San Francisco Bulletin.* January 26–February 14, 1914.

Wilkes, Charles. *Narrative of the United States Exploring Expedition, During the Years 1838, 1839, 1840, 1841, 1842.* 5 vols. Philadelphia: Lea and Blanchard, 1845.

Wrightington, Doña Juana Machado Alipaz. "Times Gone by in Alta California: The Recollections of Sonora Doña Juana Machado Alipaz de Wrightington." *The Californians* 8 (November–December 1990): 43–51.

Secondary Sources

Albertson, Dean. "Dr. Edward Turner Bale, *Incorrigible Californio.*" *California Historical Society Quarterly* 28 (September 1949): 259–69.

Alexander, James B. *Sonoma Valley Legacy.* Sonoma, Calif.: Sonoma Valley Historical Society, 1986.

Ames, George Walcott, Jr. "Gillespie and the Conquest of California." *California Historical Society Quarterly* 17 (June 1938): 123–40; (September 1938): 271–350.

Atherton, Gertrude. *Golden Gate Country.* New York: Duell, Sloane, & Pearce, 1945.

Bancroft, Hubert Howe. *California Inter Pocula.* San Francisco: The History Company, 1888.

———. *California Pastoral.* San Francisco: The History Company, 1888.

———. *History of California.* 7 vols. San Francisco: The History Company, 1884–1890.

———. *History of the Northwest Coast.* 2 vols. San Francisco: The History Company, 1890.

Beck, Warren A. *New Mexico: A History of Four Centuries.* Norman: University of Oklahoma Press, 1962.

Beard, Yolanda S. *The Wappo, A Report.* St. Helena, Calif.: Privately printed, 1977.

Beilharz, Edwin A. *Felipe de Neve, First Governor of California.* San Francisco: California Historical Society, 1971.

Benicia's Early Glory. Ed. [Anonymous]. Vallejo, Calif.: Solano County Historical Society, 1958.

Brown, Madie D. "Gen. M. G. Vallejo and H. H. Bancroft."
California Historical Society Quarterly 29 (June 1950): 149–159.

Carrillo, Leo. *The California I Love.* Englewood Cliffs, N.J.:
Prentice–Hall, 1961.

Chambers, William Nisbet. *Old Bullion Benton.* Boston: Little Brown, 1956.

Chapman, Charles E. *History of California, the Spanish Period.*
New York: Macmillan, 1925.

Clarke, Dwight L. *Stephen Watts Kearny, Soldier of the West.*
Norman: University of Oklahoma Press, 1961.

Cleland, Robert Glass. *The Cattle on a Thousand Hills.* San Marino,
Calif.: Huntington Library, 1941.

———. *A History of California: the American Period.* Reprint.
Westport, Conn.: Greenwood Press, 1975.

Conmy, Peter Thomas. "Benicia, Intended Metropolis." Privately
printed, 1958.

———. *A Centennial Evaluation of the Treaty of Guadelupe Hidalgo.*
Oakland, Calif.: Oakland Public Library, 1948.

Cook, Sherburne. *The Conflict Between the California Indian and
White Civilization.* Berkeley: University of California Press, 1976.

Coughlin, Sister Magdalen, C.S.J. "Boston Smugglers on the Coast
(1797–1821): An Insight into the American Acquisition of California."
California Historical Society Quarterly 46 (June 1967): 99–120.

———. "California Ports: A Key to West Coast Diplomacy,
1820–1845." *Journal of the West* 5 (April 1966): 153–72. Reprinted in
The Mexican War, Changing Interpretations. Edited by Odie B. Frank
and Joseph A. Stout, Jr. Chicago: Swallow Press, 1973.

———. "The Entrance of the Massachusetts Merchant into the
Pacific." *Historical Society of Southern California Quarterly* 48
(December 1966): 327–35.

Dakin, Susanna Bryant. *The Lives of William Hartnell.* Stanford:
Stanford University Press, 1949.

DeVoto, Bernard. *The Year of Decision: 1846.* Boston: Little Brown
and Company, 1943.

Dillon, Richard. *Fool's Gold. The Decline and Fall of Captain John
Sutter of California.* New York: Coward–McCann, 1967.

———. *Great Expectations: the Story of Benicia, California.*
Fresno: Thomas Lithograph and Printing Company, 1980.

Egan, Ferol. *Frémont, Explorer for a Restless Nation.* New York: Doubleday, 1977.

Emparan, Madie Brown. *The Vallejos of California.* San Francisco: The Gleeson Library Associates, 1968.

Essig, E. O. "The Russian Settlement at Ross." *California Historical Society Quarterly* 12 (September 1933): 191–209.

Fehrenbach, T. R. *Lone Star; A History of Texas and Texans.* New York: Macmillan, 1968.

Fink, Augusta. *Monterey, The Presence of the Past.* San Francisco: Chronicle Books, 1971.

Foote, Shelby. *The Civil War, A Narrative.* 3 vols. New York: Random House, 1958–1974.

Fox, Frances L. *Luis María Peralta and His Adobe.* San Jose: Smith McKay, 1975.

Francis, Jessie Davies. *An Economic and Social History of Mexican California, 1822–1846.* New York: Arno Press, 1976.

Gates, Paul W. "California's Embattled Settlers." *California Historical Society Quarterly* 41 (June 1962): 99–130.

————. "The California Land Act of 1851." *California Historical Society Quarterly* 50 (December 1971): 395–430.

————. "The Land Business of Thomas O. Larkin." *California Historical Society Quarterly* 54 (Winter 1975): 323–44.

————. "The Suscol Principle, Preemption, and California Latifundia." *Pacific Historical Review* 39 (December 1970): 453–71.

Geiger, Maynard. *Franciscan Missionaries in Hispanic California, 1769–1848.* San Marino, Calif.: The Huntington Library, 1969.

Gibson, James R. *Imperial Russia In Frontier America.* New York: Oxford University Press, 1976.

Giffen, Helen S. *Trail-Blazing Pioneer, Colonel Joseph Ballinger Chiles.* San Francisco: John Howell Books, 1969.

Gonzales, Manuel G. *The Hispanic Elite of the Southwest.* El Paso: Texas Western Press, 1989.

Gordon, Burton L. *Monterey Bay Area: Natural History and Cultural Imprints.* Pacific Grove, Calif.: Boxwood Press, 1974.

Griswold del Castillo, Richard. *The Treaty of Guadalupe Hidalgo: A Legacy of Conflict.* Norman: University of Oklahoma Press, 1990.

Guadalupe Hidalgo Treaty of Peace, 1848, and the Gadsen Treaty with Mexico, 1853. Truchas, N.M.: Tate Gallery, 1967.

Hague, Harlan, and David J. Langum. *Thomas O. Larkin, A Life of Patriotism and Profit in Old California*. Norman: University of Oklahoma Press, 1990.

Hale, Charles A. *Mexican Liberalism in the Age of Mora, 1821–1853*. New Haven: Yale University Press, 1968.

Hargis, Donald E. "Native Californians in the Constitutional Convention of 1849." *Historical Society of Southern California Quarterly* 36 (March 1954): 3–13.

————. "Women's Rights: California 1849." *Historical Society of Southern California Quarterly* 37 (December 1955): 320–34.

Harlow, Neal. *California Conquered: The Annexation of a Mexican Province,1846–1850*. Berkeley: University of California Press, 1982.

Herr, Pamela. *Jessie Benton Frémont: a Biography*. New York: Franklin Watts, 1987.

Holterman, Jack. "The Revolt of Estanislao." *The Indian Historian* 3 (Winter 1970): 43–54.

Hubbard, Harry D. *Vallejo*. Boston: Meador Publishing Co., 1941.

Hurtado, Albert L. *Indian Survival on the California Frontier*. New Haven and London: Yale University Press, 1988.

Ide, Simeon. *A Biographical Sketch of the Life of William Brown Ide*. In *Who Conquered California? The Conquest of California by the Bear Flag Party* (Glorieta, New Mexico: Rio Grande Press, 1967).

Jones, Oakah L., Jr. *Los Paisanos: Spanish Settlers on the Northern Frontier of New Spain*. Norman: University of Oklahoma Press, 1979.

Kern, Ruy E. *The Vallejos of Mission San José*. Fremont, Calif.: Mission Peak Heritage Foundation, 1983.

Langum, David J. *Law and Community on the Mexican California Frontier*. Norman: University of Oklahoma Press, 1987.

Lavender, David. *California: Land of New Beginnings*. New York: Harper & Row, 1972.

Long, Jeff. *Duel of Eagles: The Mexican and U.S. Fight for the Alamo*. New York: William Morrow and Company, 1990.

Lothrop, Marian Lydia. "The Indian Campaigns of General M. G. Vallejo." *Quarterly of the Society of California Pioneers* 9 (September 1932): 161–205.

————. "Mariano Guadalupe Vallejo, Defender of the Northern Frontier of California." Ph.D. diss., University of California, Berkeley, 1926.

Lucy, Thomas. "General John Frisbie, Solano Entrepreneur." *Solano Historian* 1 (December 1985): 1–3.

Lyman, George D. "The First Native Born California Physician." *The California Historical Society Quarterly* 4 (September 1926): 284–89.

————. *John Marsh, Pioneer: The Life Story of a Trail-blazer on Six Frontiers*. New York: Charles Scribner's Sons, 1931.

McKittrick, Myrtle M. "Salvador Vallejo." *California Historical Society Quarterly* 29 (December 1950): 309–331.

————. *Vallejo, Son of California*. Portland, Oregon: Binford & Mort, 1944.

Menefee, C. A. *Historical and Descriptive Sketch Book of Napa, Sonoma, Lake, and Mendocino*. Napa City: Reporter Publishing House, 1879.

Merrill, James M. *William Tecumseh Sherman*. Chicago and New York: Rand McNally & Co., 1971.

Miranda, Gloria E. "Hispano–Mexican Childrearing Practices in Pre-American Santa Barbara." *Southern California Quarterly* 65 (Winter 1983): 307–320.

Monroy, Douglas. *Thrown Among Strangers*. Berkeley and Los Angeles: The University of California Press, 1990.

Morgan, Dale L. *Jedediah Smith and the Opening of the West*. Lincoln: University of Nebraska Press, 1953.

Morison, Samuel E. *The Maritime History of Massachusetts, 1783–1860*. Boston: Houghton Mifflin, 1941.

Murphy, Celeste G. *The People of the Pueblo: The Story of Sonoma*. Sonoma, Calif.: Privately printed, 1935.

Northrop, Marie E. *Spanish–Mexican Families of Early California, 1769–1850*. Vol. 1 (New Orleans: Polyanthos, 1976); vol. 2 (Burbank: Southern California Genealogical Society, 1984).

O'Brien, Bickford, editor. *Fort Ross: Indians, Russians, Americans*. Jenner, Calif.: Fort Ross Interpretive Association, 1980.

Oxford, June. *The Capital That Couldn't Stay Put, The Complete Book of California's Capitols*. San Jose: Smith McKay Printing Co., 1983.

Parkes, Henry Bamford. *A History of Mexico*. Boston: Houghton Mifflin, 1966.

Parmelee, Robert D. *Pioneer Sonoma*. Sonoma, Calif.: Sonoma Valley Historical Society, 1972.

Pitt, Leonard. *The Decline of the Californios: A Social History of the Spanish-Speaking Californians, 1846–1890*. Berkeley and Los Angeles: University of California Press, 1970.

Rawls, James J. *Indians of California: the Changing Image*. Norman and London: University of Oklahoma Press, 1984.

Regnery, Dorothy F. *The Battle of Santa Clara*. San Jose: Smith and McKay Printing Company, 1978.

Robinson, W. W. *Land in California*. Berkeley and Los Angeles: University of California Press, 1948.

Rogers, Fred B. *Bear Flag Lieutenant*. San Francisco: California Historical Society, 1951.

————. *William Brown Ide, Bear Flagger*. San Francisco: John Howell, 1962.

Rolle, Andrew. *John Charles Frémont, Character as Destiny*. Norman: University of Oklahoma Press, 1991.

Roske, Ralph J. *Everyman's Eden, A History of California*. New York: Macmillan, 1968.

Royce, Josiah. *California, From the Conquest in 1846 to the Second Vigilance Committee in San Francisco, A Study of American Character*. Boston and New York: Houghton, Mifflin, 1886.

Sanchez, Nellie V. *Spanish Arcadia*. Los Angeles: Powell Publishing Co., 1929.

Sellers, Charles Grier. *James K. Polk*. Princeton, N.J.: Princeton University Press, 1957–1966.

Sierra, Justo. *The Political Evolution of the Mexican People*. Austin: University of Texas Press, 1969.

Simpson, Richard. *Ooti: A Maidu Legacy*. Milbrae: Celestial Arts, 1977.

Smilie, Robert S. *The Sonoma Mission*. Fresno: Valley Publishers, 1975.

Smith, Elbert B. *Magnificent Missourian: The Life of Thomas Hart Benton*. Philadelphia: Lippincott, 1958.

Smith, Henry Nash. *Virgin Land, the American West as Symbol and Myth*. Cambridge: Harvard University Press, 1950.

Starr, Kevin. *Inventing the Dream: California Through the Progressive Era*. New York: Oxford University Press, 1985.

Stellman, Louis J. *Sam Brannan: Builder of San Francisco*. New York: Exposition Press, 1953.

Tays, George. "Mariano Guadalupe Vallejo and Sonoma." *California Historical Society Quarterly* 16 (June, September, December 1937), 99–121, 216–255, 348–372; and 17 (March, June, September 1938), 50–73, 141–167, 219–242.

Treaty of Guadalupe Hidalgo 1848, a Facsimile Reproduction of the Mexican Instrument of Ratification and Related Documents. Sacramento: Telefact Foundation and The California State Department of Education, 1968.

Tyler, David B. *The Wilkes Expedition*. Philadelphia: The American Philosophical Society, 1968.

Underhill, Reuben C. *From Cowhides to Golden Fleece*. Stanford: Stanford University Press, 1939.

Warner, Barbara. "Report on the Bear Flag Party and Sonoma." Unpublished Manuscript, Sonoma Depot Museum.

Weber, David J. *The Mexican Frontier, 1821–1846: The American Southwest Under Mexico*. Albuquerque: University of New Mexico Press, 1982.

Williams, Mary Floyd. "Mission, Presidio and Pueblo." *California Historical Society Quarterly* 1 (July 1922): 23–35.

Wood, Ellen Lamont. *George Yount*. San Francisco: Grabhorn Press, 1941.

Woodruff, Jacqueline McCart. *Benicia, The Promise of California*. Vallejo, Calif.: Privately printed, 1947.

Woolfenden, John, and Amelie Elkinton. *Cooper: John Bautista Rogers Cooper*. Pacific Grove, Calif.: Boxwood Press, 1983.

Wright, Doris M. *A Yankee in Mexican California: Abel Stearns, 1798–1848*. Santa Barbara: Wallace Hebberd, 1977.

Young, Wood. *Vaca–Peña Los Putos Rancho and the Peña Adobe*. Vallejo, Calif.: Wheeler Printing and Publishing Co., 1965.

Index

N.B.: Subentries for Bear Flag Revolt and Mariano G. Vallejo are in chronological order; all other subentries are in alphabetical order; the abbreviation V refers to Mariano G. Vallejo